Praise for
A New Map for Relationships: Creating True Love at Home & Peace on the Planet

"This is the most impressive book I've ever read. I've never seen anything as personally touching and thought provoking. I will embrace the journey."

—Axel Merk, President of Merk Investments,
Manager of the Merk Mutual Funds

"Marty and Dorothie Hellman have written a truly unique book that tells an engaging and persuasive story relating domestic peace to world peace. This book should be read by married couples seeking peace at home, as well as by diplomats seeking peace in the world. This is an especially important work considering the enormously destructive power of nuclear weapons. The struggle for interpersonal dominance can lead to the end of a marriage, but the struggle for geopolitical dominance can lead to the end of civilization."

—William J. Perry, Secretary of Defense 1994–1997

"Your personal story is both charming and very valuable. It has helped me to improve my relationship with my wife, even though she has not yet read the book. I'm looking forward to her doing so, so that we can discuss it together. I really loved the way you integrated resolving interpersonal and international conflicts. Your journey of discovery and transformation is one of hope for couples and for the planet. Thank you so much for sharing it."

—David Krieger,
President of the Nuclear Age Peace Foundation

"This is the most thoughtful, unique, and fascinating book I have ever read on personal and international diplomacy. Drawing from their own poignant experiences in managing spousal relations—candid stories that will resonate with all readers—Dorothie and Marty Hellman persuasively apply their life lessons to the domain of foreign affairs. We are often puzzled when peoples of two nations seem to get along, while their governments are at loggerheads. The Hellmans have much to say about why this does not have to be so."
—*Ambassador and Lt. Gen. Karl W. Eikenberry (U.S. Army, Ret),*
Commander of Coalition Forces in Afghanistan (2005–2007)
and US Ambassador to Afghanistan (2009–2011)

"*A New Map for Relationships* is an ambitious and bold study that thoughtfully combines the personal and the political-historical to relate helpful insights to the improvement of both personal and international relations. Its analysis of international conflicts is probing and heavily historically-oriented. It urges honesty, truth, and understanding, and stresses the value of empathy, tolerance, and forbearance with both wisdom and compassion."
—*Barton J. Bernstein, Professor of History,*
Emeritus, Stanford University

"Marty and Dorothie Hellman offer a 'unified field theory' for successful relationships at all levels of the human family. The Hellmans use compelling personal and historical examples to illustrate how compassionate, holistic solutions will provide personal security, national security, and international security. Every spouse, partner, citizen, and world leader should read this book!"
—*Daniel U. Smith, Appellate Attorney and*
Board Member of The Ploughshares Fund

"Thank you for sharing your story. It is indeed true that each of us carries the fuse of the nuclear threat in her individual heart. It is also true that we generally do not know that simple fact. Some of us go out of our way on a mission to solve the nuclear threat 'out there,' without recognizing that the only way to solve it is 'in here.' When a person finally discovers the hatred that harbors in his heart, he crosses the threshold that leads to wisdom. Your book can greatly accelerate that process."

—*Dr. Federico Faggin,*
Designer of the world's first microprocessor

Critical acclaim for Marty's 1988 book *Breakthrough: Emerging New Thinking* co-edited with Prof. Anatoly Gromyko.

"An impressive and immensely valuable product of Soviets and Americans trying to surmount the mountains which separate our cultures in a search for a common way of thinking about the central threat to us all ... the ultimate obscenity of nuclear war. Our differences are real, but this book and the collaboration which produced it, are the only way to thread through them to produce a world in which all our children can live in safety."

—*William Colby, Former CIA Director*

"I have examined your book with interest. This collective work of Soviet and American scientists ... represents a valuable experience in the promotion of new thinking. I wish you a fruitful cooperation."

—*Mikhail Gorbachev,*
President of the Soviet Union

"This book is a fascinating first of its kind. Since the greatest task of our time is that of avoiding a Soviet-American nuclear war that might end the human species, what can be more important than a collection of essays by both American and Soviet scholars who tackle the problem and, meeting on common ground, enlighten us all and give us hope."

—*Isaac Asimov, Author*

"Listen to what some wise people in various countries say… in *Breakthrough: Emerging New Thinking*."

—*Dr. Karl Menninger,*
The Menninger Foundation

"*Breakthrough* is the story of an extraordinary and exciting adventure in cooperation and collaboration by scholars and authors of the United States and the Soviet Union as they examine together the thesis that war simply does not work anymore. … Your children and grandchildren and great-grandchildren will thank you for seriously exploring this idea."

—*Mary Louise Smith,*
former Republican National Chairman

"The publication of this book is in itself a remarkable event. The views expressed in it make it even more remarkable. It gives American readers an opportunity to acquaint themselves with some of the best and freshest thinking in the Soviet Union. It gives Russian readers an array of facts and arguments they have not usually encountered in Soviet works. A surprising milestone!"

—*Professor Alexander Dallin, Director,*
Center for Russian and East European Studies,
Stanford University

A New Map
for Relationships

A New Map
for Relationships
Creating True Love At Home
& Peace On The Planet

DOROTHIE AND MARTIN HELLMAN

Printed in the United States of America

Paperback ISBN: 978-0-9974923-0-9
Hardcover ISBN: 978-0-9974923-1-6
eBook ISBN: 978-0-9974923-2-3

Cover and Interior Design: Ghislain Viau

Grateful acknowledgment is made for permission to reprint excerpt #61: "A great nation is like a great man:/ ... as the shadow that he himself casts." from TAO TE CHING BY LAO TZU. A NEW ENGLISH VERSION, WITH FOREWORD AND NOTES, by STEPHEN MITCHELL. Translation copyright © 1988 by Stephen Mitchell. Reprinted by permission of HarperCollins Publishers.

To our daughters, Sonja and Gretchen, our grandchildren Zoe, Celeste, and Max, and all the other young people of the Earth. May we leave you a better and safer world in which to live.

A great nation is like a great man:
When he makes a mistake, he realizes it.
Having realized it, he admits it.
Having admitted it, he corrects it.
He considers those who point out his faults
as his most benevolent teachers.
He thinks of his enemy
as the shadow that he himself casts.

—*Tao Te Ching*
by Stephen Mitchell

Table of Contents

Part 2: Healing International Relationships in a Personal Setting

Conclusion

A Note to the Reader

When we started on this journey thirty-five years ago, we weren't trying to make the world a better place. Rather, our goal was to save our relationship and get out of the unbearable pain in which we found ourselves after thirteen years of marriage, two kids, and a house we couldn't afford. But, as we did that, we not only built a relationship in which we haven't been angry with one another in well over ten years (honestly!), but we came to see an intimate interplay between our personal struggle and that of the nations of the world as they grapple with global challenges and survival in the nuclear age.

There are many books on how to improve your marriage or other relationship. There are also many on how to solve global challenges. What makes this book unique is its premise—backed by our experience—that working on interpersonal and international problems at the same time accelerates progress on both.

Working on global issues was essential to bringing magic back into our marriage, and that success allows us to advocate a more peaceful, sustainable world with a conviction we otherwise would not have. The experiments we carried out in our marriage allowed us to see how adversaries could eventually achieve a level of harmony that would seem impossible from their starting point. At the personal level, we reclaimed the true love that we felt when we first fell for one another. Extending what we learned in our marriage to the global level would result in something that, from today's perspective, would look like world peace, and we are closer to that than the media would have you believe.

We should also explain several other unusual aspects of this book. First, while it is about constructing a new map for relationships, that is not a linear process in which you go from Point A to Point B and so on. Rather, constructing that map is more like the first story in the book in which Dorothie gets so mad that she rips a map to shreds and then, to get to our destination, we have to piece it back together out of the jigsaw puzzle it has become. That's not a linear process. Hence, parts of the book are more like a series of interconnected short stories than a purely logical flow for how to fix the problems we face.

Second, much of the text is in a conversational style with one of us saying something, followed by the other's response. As husband and wife co-authors, our process of writing this book was based on many conversations over the past several years. Give-and-take dialogue is fundamental to our relationship, and this conversational style invites you to eavesdrop as we learn from one another.

Third, while this book is concerned with global challenges in general, we emphasize the issues of war, peace, and nuclear weapons because those are the ones we have studied most deeply. They are also less discussed within society than environmental degradation, making it important to highlight them. Fortunately, both of those global challenges require the same shift in mindset, so the solutions advocated here will solve both, as well as other global challenges that are on the horizon.

While each person's journey is unique, we hope that revealing our mistakes through these conversations, and how we overcame them, might help others do the same more quickly and with less pain. And, if enough of us do that, the world's problems will also be resolved, since societal behavior derives from our individual beliefs and behaviors. We invite you to join us on this voyage of discovery and healing.

—Dorothie and Martin Hellman,
Stanford, California, 2016

Part 1

Healing Personal Relationships in a Global Setting

Chapter 1

A New Map for Relationships

Tearing Up the Map

One sparkling fall day in 1989, we drove up to San Francisco for an afternoon event. We went early so we could enjoy some time together taking in the panoramic bird's-eye view of the city from Twin Peaks. But that's not how it worked out.

MARTY: When we were ready to leave Twin Peaks, Dorothie unfolded the map to figure out how to get to the event. This was 1989, before GPS and smartphone navigation.

I must have thought Dorothie needed help, because I reached over and took the map out of her hands without asking. Not a smart move, as this was not only impolite, it was also one of

3

Dorothie's pet peeves. She was an adult, and she could ask for help if she needed it. Being shouldered aside this way felt like a major insult.

Dorothie exploded. She stormed out of the car, slammed the door, and stomped off like she was never coming back, leaving me wounded and wondering what to do. It felt stupid to just sit there hoping she would calm down and return—like she was the princess and I was her attendant-in-waiting (literally). But driving off seemed even more stupid. Sometimes the smart thing feels stupid.

DOROTHIE: I wasn't as totally out of my mind as it appeared to Marty. I left the car not just because I had to get away from an intolerable situation, but also because I was afraid I would say something hurtful to Marty. We had made enough progress by this time that I didn't want to do that, even as hurt as I was.

After a few minutes, I calmed down enough to return to the car. But I was deeply hurt, and Marty was extremely tense, fearing that he might step on another emotional land mine. He was trying to calmly read the map, as if nothing had happened. That charade brought my fury back with a vengeance. It felt like Marty cared more about the map than he did about me.

I reclaimed the map by ripping it out of his hands, and I tore it to pieces. For a few seconds, we both held our breath, waiting for Marty to react. Would he escalate the fight? That was a real possibility—but instead, miraculously, he laughed.

How would I respond? Would I take his laughter in the right spirit, or would I feel that he was laughing at me? I, too, broke out laughing. What a relief!

MARTY: But now we had to put the jigsaw puzzle that had been our map back together so we could find our way to the event.

This led to yet more laughter—as much from relief as from the comedy of the situation.

Personal Relationship Maps

Our "tearing up the map" had a deep symbolism to it. Back in 1967, each of us came into our marriage with unconscious maps for how to navigate our relationship. We were madly in love, so what more was needed? We assumed our marriage would evolve naturally, without conscious effort. It did evolve, but far from the way we wanted. In spite of constantly losing our way, we stuck to those old, unconscious maps, and we kept getting lost. Only when we were willing to admit that we needed a totally new map could we find the courage to try new approaches and achieve what we both wanted. To piece together our new map, we had to reexamine our deeply-held beliefs and correct those that were found wanting.

DOROTHIE: Part of the problem was that our initial "relationship maps" were different—something we didn't realize at first. We married as polar opposites. Marty was an intellectual who relied heavily on logic. I was interested in relationships and put more stock in feelings. While both of those are valid points of view, each by itself is limiting, so we were fortunate to choose one other and have the opportunity to learn about the other's perspective.

MARTY: Opportunity? It was a necessity! At least if we were going to stay married. For the first ten to fifteen years of our marriage, we repeatedly butted heads because we failed to understand the value in the other person's perspective.

Dorothie's right that our initial relationship maps were very different. And her ultimate destination was more than I ever thought possible. We needed to get there, and were able to, because she is like the princess who was so refined that even a tiny pea buried under twenty mattresses disturbed her sleep. But, in her case, she's "the Princess and the Pea of relationship conflict." Dorothie is so sensitive that she picks up on my smallest frustration, my tiniest shred of anger. So imagine how my full-blown rage devastated her. And imagine how often I got angry when she demanded that I deal with issues that most people wouldn't even notice. It was a vicious circle that came close to ending our marriage.

A handwritten letter that Dorothie wrote to me before we had learned how to really love one another reminded me of how far we've come. After asking me to work collaboratively with her to get more of what we both needed and wanted, she ended the letter by saying that, if we didn't do that, she was afraid that we would move on to new partners and have to start all over again.

When I remembered that, tears welled up in my eyes. The thought that I might have lost the love of my life through ignorance and stupidity was more than I could bear. Given what we now have, that would have been the crime of the century—and it was a disaster we came dangerously close to creating by following our old relationship maps.

Given how reasonable Dorothie's cry for help now seems—and especially the last sentence in her letter: "I do love you"—why was I so resistant to the changes she wanted? The stories in this book will give a fuller picture, but here I'll mention two sources of the problem.

First, because Dorothie was in such pain over our broken relationship, her pleas were often made in anger, and I confused her reasonable requests with having to surrender to her onslaughts. Second, there was a mismatch in our levels of sensitivity. The little boy who cries is ridiculed as a "cry baby." If he shows fear, he becomes a target for bullies. So my sensitivity was beaten out of me as I grew up. Dorothie, on the other hand, is a highly sensitive person who cannot ignore conflict in our relationship.

Her being "the Princess and the Pea of relationship conflict" used to drive me crazy. Now I treasure it, much as a scientist will spend large sums and countless hours to keep a sensitive instrument working as part of an important experiment to delve more deeply into the secrets of the universe. My "experiment" (which is also Dorothie's) is to come as close as I can to the ideal human state, to be the most honest and loving person I can be. So what better partner could I ask for on that journey than a woman sensitive to my smallest frustration or my tiniest shred of anger? And now that we have learned how to truly love one another, she can point out those small failings in much more tender ways.

My current over-arching goal—to be the most honest and loving person I can be—wasn't even a point of interest on the map I brought to our marriage. I knew that acquiring fame, wealth, and prestige would be an uphill journey, but never thought that becoming an honest and loving person required hard work. Yet in the new relationship map that we've pieced together, it is the ultimate destination from which all good things flow.

DOROTHIE: And, of course, both of us had to make that kind of profound change. Marty's right that, earlier in our relationship, he didn't know how to love me. But neither did I know how to love him. The key to achieving the kind of love we have today was a profound shift in each of us: from demanding to be loved, to working at being both loved *and* loving—as well as recognizing that being loving takes work.

I still need love from Marty, but now that need is part of a larger goal to do what is best for the relationship and best for the world. He's made the same shift, so now we are on the same side of the table. Instead of fighting each other, we each work really hard to do what is needed. Somewhat paradoxically, and as you'll see throughout this book, life ends up being far better for each of us that way than if we'd gotten exactly what we thought we wanted going into our disagreements.

MARTY: Life is better not only in our marriage, but in every way. The new map isn't just about our relationship. It's about how we live every moment of our lives and about our relationship to the whole world. That holistic approach is key.

Of course, holistic thinking includes how we behave toward each other. But the changes that eventually made our fights a thing of the past could not have been achieved without the larger goal.

My deep gratitude to Dorothie isn't just about building a relationship that surpasses what I thought was possible. I'm also grateful she helped me become a better person than I ever imagined I could be. And that deepens my love for her. She helped me find my true self—a part of me that I didn't even know existed.

Before we got here, I kept telling Dorothie that what she wanted was impossible. Fortunately for me, she wouldn't settle for less than unconditional love. Those of you reading this don't have to settle either.

DOROTHIE: It's interesting that, earlier in my life, even I couldn't picture what we now have. I knew that where we were was intolerable, and I knew that where we needed to go involved a much deeper love on both our parts. But, never having experienced unconditional love, it's not surprising that I couldn't fully picture it or know how to get there.

I'm unbelievably grateful to Marty for helping us arrive at this place, and for having the courage to join me on this voyage of discovery to a destination I couldn't fully envision, much less describe. If you and your partner are willing to do what's required, we can tell you from personal experience that it is possible to build a truly loving relationship, even if the foundation from which you're starting seems shaky and prone to earthquakes. Differences of opinion, which used to become fights over who was right, can be transformed into opportunities to expand your horizons and learn from one another.

The essence of this book can be summarized as this: "You have to believe in the seemingly impossible gift of unconditional love, and then dedicate yourself to discovering how to achieve it."

International Relationship Maps

In the same way that we brought unconscious, outdated maps to our marriage, the nations of the world are using a dangerously outmoded guide to ensure their security and well-being. The old map says that they shouldn't sacrifice to solve global environmental problems until other nations are willing to do the same. It says that the stronger they are, the safer they are, and that strength comes from having more destructive weapons than anyone else.

But if society were to look around, it would see that we've made a wrong turn and are going down a dead-end street. If every nation waits until the others are willing to make the changes needed to put the planet on a sustainable path, global environmental collapse is a real possibility.

On the national security front, we have invested trillions of dollars since 1945 trying to ensure our safety. We have put many of our best minds to work developing weapons and strategies in an effort to maximize the value of that investment. Yet in that same period, the United States has gone from a nation that was inviolate to one that can be destroyed in under an hour. The other nations of the world are no better off. The old map is not working, and it is leading us toward disaster.

The new map we had to piece together in our marriage bears a strong similarity to the new one needed by the nations of the world. Only when we gave up trying to get what we thought we wanted—and shifted to doing what was best for both of us—did we get what we really needed. Nations must make a similar holistic shift to prevent a global environmental disaster that would devastate every one of them.

Just as we used to continually stumble into arguments, nations seem to fall into one war after another. Aside from the cost in blood and treasure, unless nations learn how to stop that cycle of violence, it's only a matter of time before one of those wars escalates out of control, leading to nuclear threats. And if we teeter on the nuclear abyss repeatedly, it's only a matter of time before we fall in.

DOROTHIE: People have always yearned for a more just and peaceful world, but most dismiss that vision as naive and unattainable. We can achieve that goal if we will open our minds to new possibilities, tear up the old map for international relations, and piece together a new one that is consistent with the current reality.

In an age in which global environmental collapse is a real possibility, developing a sustainable economic model is not a luxury—it's essential to national well-being. In the nuclear age, a more peaceful world is not just desirable—it's essential for long-term human survival. In the same way that Marty and I had to move away from thinking that fighting would win the argument, nations need to give up the outmoded notion that having the most weapons, being the most aggressive, and taking the most risk will get them what they want.

MARTY: One of the key changes from the old map to the new, both personally and internationally, is to move from blame to responsibility and to re-examine the nature of power.

DOROTHIE: When we used to fight, each of us felt like the innocent victim, and that the other was solely to blame. Nations do that, too, and it doesn't work any better for them than it did for us. When Marty and I focused on each other's faults, it robbed us of the power we needed to change the dynamic. Only I can change myself, and only Marty can change himself.

MARTY: I remember having an epiphany about that. Dorothie and I had just had a huge argument and, when I cooled down a bit, an idea suddenly hit me. If my perception was right that Dorothie was solely to blame for the argument and I was the innocent victim, then I was powerless to get out of the pain I was in. I would have to wait for Dorothie to come to her senses. But if my perception was wrong, then I would have power to get out of the awful pain I was in. With that motivation, I was able to see the role I had played in the argument. I went and apologized to

Dorothie for my misbehavior, which led to her apologizing for hers. Argument ended.

In the old map, admitting error is a sign of weakness at both the individual and the national levels. In the new map, it's a sign of maturity and responsibility that conveys great power: not *power over* the other, but *power to fix* an intolerable situation.

The same approach would work miracles at the international level, with the conflict between the United States and Iran being a good example. Americans tend to start the narrative with Iran's taking our embassy staff hostage in 1979, in violation of all international norms. In that view, we are the innocent victim, and the conflict is entirely their fault.

In contrast, Iranians focus on the 1953 CIA-sponsored coup that overthrew a popular, democratically elected government and ushered in a police state under the Shah. They see themselves as the innocent victims and the conflict as being entirely *our* fault.

Both perspectives have validity, but each is, at best, only half of the picture. Worse, each of our nations focuses on the other's mistakes, where it has no power to bring about positive change. If either the United States or Iran were to move from blame to responsibility and see the power inherent in admitting its own mistakes, who knows what would follow?

DOROTHIE: In the new map, at both the interpersonal and international levels, instead of trying to force the other party in the conflict to see things your way and do what you want, you are committed to doing what's right. In fact, trying to force someone to change usually has the opposite of its intended effect. When they feel pushed around, they dig in their heels. Marty and I certainly did that earlier in our marriage. In the same way, the nations of the world exacerbate their conflicts by focusing on each other's mistakes, rather than their own.

MARTY: That point can be seen in a June 2014 article by Dimitri Simes about the current low-level war in the eastern part of Ukraine. Simes, who advised President Nixon on the Soviet Union, warned that, "the bellicose stances that Obama's critics espouse are unlikely to deter Moscow and might even do the opposite."[1]

But none of the mainstream American media reports that kind of news. Instead, they put all of the blame on Russia. A July 2014 *New York Times* editorial stated: "The Ukrainian conflict has gone on far too long, and it has become far too dangerous. There is one man who can stop it—President Vladimir Putin of Russia."[2]

Putin is far from blameless, but pretending that we have made no mistakes robs us of whatever power we have to stop the human suffering in Ukraine. Just as in my epiphany, if our nation were to put its energy into searching out its own mistakes—instead of wasting our energy on hating Putin—we just might find a way to stop the carnage in Ukraine.

DOROTHIE: Our old relationship map said that when one of us wasn't feeling heard, we needed to yell louder. Now when we feel unheard, we see that as a sign that we need to listen better. We have shifted from demanding what we think we want to being committed to finding a solution that gives both of us what we need—no matter how impossible that might seem at first.

At a personal level and at the international level, it's time to tear up the old maps and put the pieces back together in a new, holistic way. That's how to save both personal relationships and the world.

Navigating With Our New Map

An incident that occurred recently is a good example of how the new relationship map works for us now. It also illustrates what we mean when we say we haven't been angry with one another in years. As you'll see, we started down a path that previously would have led to both of us becoming angry. But this time, we were rescued by the new pathways we committed to follow. As we continue on our journey, we hope that even incidents like this will become a relic of the past.

MARTY: We were driving to Oakland to visit friends. Rush hour was approaching and traffic was building up, so we were anxious to get moving. I should have seen the need to behave differently as soon as I felt anxious. In my old map, anxiety seemed unavoidable in a time-sensitive situation like this. Now I see it as a sign that I need to slow down, since anxiety often leads to mistakes that reduce my effectiveness and add unnecessary stress to my relationships. I've found that getting anxious because there doesn't seem to be enough time often ends up taking longer, rather than saving time.

DOROTHIE: To make things worse, the GPS navigation in the car got into a strange state and wasn't working. Marty tried turning the car off and then on again, so the GPS would reboot. It still didn't work. He tried a third time. Still no luck. Finally, on the fourth try, it worked.

During the two failed attempts to reboot the system, I started to press a button in response to a prompt on the touch screen—but each time Marty put his hand up, between me and the screen, to stop me from doing that.

MARTY: This behavior on my part may sound familiar. Remember my grabbing the map out of Dorothie's hands in the first section, that story that ended with her tearing the map to shreds?

DOROTHIE: Marty's stopping me from helping made me feel like a small child whose hand had been slapped for no good reason. While my reaction is a sign of unresolved childhood traumas I still need to work on, that's not how I saw it in the moment. Our relationship is supposed to be one of equals, not parent and child, so I curtly told him to cut it out.

MARTY: I recognized that Dorothie had a valid complaint, but I was hurt by what I felt was her snapping at me. Years ago, my response would have focused on how she had mistreated me. That would have made her feel unheard and resulted in an ever-escalating argument. But now I responded differently. First, I told her I was sorry for not treating her more respectfully. Only after she had acknowledged my apology did I ask if it had been necessary to snap at me.

DOROTHIE: This threw me into turmoil. I immediately recognized that Marty was right and I had not treated him compassionately, but I was still in the throes of feeling hurt. His asking if it had been necessary to snap at him didn't help.

MARTY: You're right. Sorry about that. I should have put it less judgmentally.

DOROTHIE: My being in turmoil over mistreating Marty added to the problem. That made me upset with myself for not being able to just leave the whole thing behind us. Earlier in our relationship, I would have kept such an embarrassing admission to myself, probably causing Marty to think my turmoil was over his mistreating me, rather than the other way around. But now I am committed to being honest, so I told Marty what was bothering me.

MARTY: When Dorothie told me of her turmoil, I replied that, rather than being upset with her for still being hurt, I was proud of both of us for how we had handled a difficult situation.

DOROTHIE: Marty's saying that gave me the time I needed to move from being hurt to appreciating him for how he had handled the resolution of this conflict. It really helped to know that he wasn't mad at me for my behavior. Within a couple of minutes, Marty's inappropriate behavior was no longer an issue for me. Instead of feeling hurt, I appreciated him for helping me grow even more.

MARTY: And that feeling was mutual.

DOROTHIE: I also realized that this was an opportunity to renew my dedication to being compassionate in all circumstances, even when I've felt mistreated. If I had remembered that when the incident started, there wouldn't have been any problem at all.

This conflict was particularly ironic because, before it erupted, I had planned on using our time in the car to tell Marty how much I appreciated him for really seeing me. My whole life, I've been somewhat of an odd duck, seeing things differently from most other people, and I often got flack for that.

MARTY: Although, early in our relationship, I often failed to see value in Dorothie's different perspective, now it's one of the aspects of her personality that I treasure the most. It's what got us to where we are today.

DOROTHIE: I had almost despaired of anyone ever seeing me that way. In fact, I think Marty sees me more clearly in that sense than I do myself.

MARTY: This incident also makes an important point. While we haven't been angry with one another in years, that doesn't mean that we don't sometimes disagree or get our feelings hurt. But now we have a different approach for dealing with disagreements and hurt feelings.

DOROTHIE: That different approach is what we've called "the new map." As we follow the new map further, I believe that we can get to a place where even hurt feelings become a thing of the past. We're already at a point where my feelings rarely get hurt, whereas I used to feel raw much of the time.

MARTY: Each of us is learning. Soon after this flaky GPS incident, we were working on a section of this book and I needed the laptop Dorothie was using. Since I had to type something on it, I reached over to take it from her—but I caught myself and asked, "Is it okay for me to use the computer?" Dorothie beamed and said, "Of course."

Our Quest

DOROTHIE: Once, during a week of practicing silence, I was out walking on the San Francisco Baylands. White pelicans were floating on the water and herons were padding their feet on the bottom of the slough to kick up some delicious morsel. The weather was perfect for a walk, with a sweet breeze whispering across the water.

I had been contemplating what my purpose was on this planet. Somehow, all of a sudden, I knew that expressing love was my destiny here. That made perfect sense on one level, but it was surprising on another.

We yearn for a perfect love that we seldom, if ever, experience. How could a quest for something we almost never encounter be burned so indelibly into our souls? We must have known it somewhere prior to our current existence.

At that moment, I knew that learning how to love was my life's mission. As with all great quests, it was mine to either fail or succeed at during my time on Earth. Since somewhere, somehow, I had been programmed to love, I was determined to succeed.

This was one of the most intense emotional experiences of my life, my "Aha!" moment. I had spent years trying to discern my path, and there it was: so simple, so obvious, and so right. How had I missed it until now? This was the spiritual awakening for which I had been searching. With that realization, I made a decision to devote my life to learning to love. While that was a one-time decision, learning how to love turned out to be a lifelong quest.

MARTY: Almost everyone has a passionate desire to be loved. If fulfilled, it is one of the greatest gifts we can receive. If it is thwarted, that same passion tends to create frustration, and then we behave in ways that make it unlikely we will receive the love we crave. It can become a downward spiral. That's certainly how it worked in the early years of our marriage. The trick, as Dorothie realized in her Baylands epiphany, is to see love in a whole new way. An immature, egotistical drive to be loved has to be transformed into a mature, holistic quest for a loving relationship.

DOROTHIE: I also realized that my quest was much larger than learning how to love Marty. I felt an intense desire to be at one with all of creation. I needed to learn to love everything—of

18

course, and especially Marty. With all the horrible things going on in the world, trying to love everything is an ideal I may never fully realize. But because it is so difficult to achieve—and maybe even unattainable—it gives me a lifelong goal.

This longing for oneness is a powerful vehicle for climbing the steep hills we encounter on the road that leads to loving relationships. If we can tap into the deep desire for connection with one another and know that it is our true purpose, then we can overcome primitive urges and feelings that otherwise would create impassable roadblocks.

Embracing Our Shadow Side

DOROTHIE: Many times when Marty and I seemed stuck in an argument, I would come back to my Baylands realization. We are all interconnected. We cannot live in hate, anger, or fear and stay loving—or expect true love—at the same time.

All of those are normal human emotions, and as we try to overcome them, we cannot hate them in others. That would be one of the very emotions we are working to move beyond. What's even harder, but also more important, is to learn not to hate these emotions in ourselves. It's easy to love our socially acceptable sides. They're happy, sunny, and optimistic. It's really hard to love our hateful, angry, fearful sides. But, somewhat paradoxically, embracing them can transform them into love, compassion, and courage.

MARTY: It's so hard to love those socially unacceptable sides of ourselves that most people do not even see them at a conscious level. Instead, those aspects of ourselves are pushed down into our unconscious, where they can wreak havoc. When they are in that unseen state, psychology calls them our *shadow side* or *dark side*.[3]

Until I recognized my shadow side, seeing those same faults in others would disgust me, almost as if hating them would prove that I was immune from those human failings. Psychology calls that *projection of my dark side on an enemy*, a phenomenon that will be vividly illustrated later. In that incident, I was tied up in psychic knots by another Jewish professor from New York who impressed me as being arrogant. Arrogance was so unacceptable to me at the time that I couldn't see when my courage—a desirable trait—crossed the line into arrogance. That meant that I crossed that line far too often, with devastating effects on our marriage and my personal life in general.

There's tremendous power in our shadow sides that needs to be harnessed for good, instead of creating chaos. We can accomplish that by not only recognizing our shadows, but also making friends with them. As that later story will show, once I embraced my "arrogant, Jewish professor from New York" shadow side, I was able to utilize his courage without being run around by his arrogance.

Nations also have shadow sides that they project onto enemies. During the Cold War, the Soviet Union continually chastised our nation for its racial injustice while overlooking its own human rights abuses. We reciprocated in kind, focusing on their sins instead of our own. By ignoring their shadow sides, both nations lost most of the power they had to produce positive change in the world. Only the Soviets could change their nation, and only we could change our own.

Embracing our shadows, rather than having them run us around, is one of the most exciting points of interest on the new map, both personally and internationally.

Where the Personal and Global Meet

It's unusual to combine improving personal relationships with concern for global issues. But the approach that transformed our marriage dealt with both the personal and the global in a way where the two complemented one another. Many readers will come to this process, as we did, with global issues being of secondary, if any, concern. So we will first examine why including them can contribute to your marriage or other relationship. Then we will look at why readers more concerned with global issues will accelerate progress on that front by improving their personal relationships.

DOROTHIE: To solve the problems in our marriage, we had to make a holistic shift, putting our relationship above our *perceived* individual needs. Of course, when our relationship got better, we each got more of what we needed.

Making that holistic shift worked wonders for us, whereas nothing else had dented our cycle of endless conflict. Instead of each of us fighting to get what we thought we wanted, we had to figure out—and then do—what was best for our relationship while also keeping our individual needs in mind. We had to look beyond our normal ego boundaries and take in the bigger picture.

By definition, holistic thinking required us to look at more than just our marriage. We couldn't think holistically about a piece of the whole. *Holistic thinking is global thinking.*

MARTY: While it sounds simple, developing a compassionate, holistic perspective is a huge challenge. If we had practiced it only in our marriage, we would have been missing out on a large number of opportunities to speed up our learning process. The times when we most needed to make the shift in our marriage were times of great personal turmoil. Applying holistic thinking to global problems was easier because we weren't as emotionally invested in those issues, and doing that gave us practice for resolving our personal conflicts.

One of the things I had to learn in our marriage was to value the opposing point of view—Dorothie's perspective, when it conflicted with mine—rather than automatically rejecting it. Often her alternative perspective contained a piece of the puzzle that I didn't realize I had been missing, and that gave me a valuable new insight. From the point of view of learning, the greatest value is in the opposing point of view because only that view might contain useful new information.

Again, it was easier to take this approach with global issues than with interpersonal ones, and for the same reason: I was less emotionally involved with global conflicts. Today, nations seek *national* security—but in the nuclear age, national security has become an oxymoron. Given that the United States and Russia each possess thousands of nuclear weapons, the more insecure one of them makes the other feel, the less secure they both become. Even though it is rarely recognized, and even more rarely acted upon, national security is becoming synonymous with international security. That truth was much easier for me to see than that my well-being was synonymous with our marriage's well-being.

DOROTHIE: There's another reason that including the global dimension was crucial to success in our marriage. When I felt like I couldn't go further in that process—and that happened more often than I like to remember—I'd often go into our bedroom, fall down on the bed, spread my arms wide, and plead to the heavens for help. Now, it's hard to understand why I kept begging for help because, after just a few times, I had learned the answer. I couldn't do what was needed for my own sake or Marty's. But I always found the strength to persevere when I remembered that it literally would be the end of the world if I failed. If I couldn't figure out how to solve problems with those I love, how could I expect world leaders to resolve their differences and find a way out of the nuclear dilemma or the environmental challenges we face?

To make our marriage work, we had to become concerned with the good of something bigger than our individual selves, namely our relationship. Making that bigger thing greater than even our marriage—making it something close to "peace on earth"—stretched us and helped us gain the broader perspective needed in our marriage.

If you're able to piece together a new map from the shreds of the old, it takes you to a place where you are a more loving, compassionate human being. And you can't be loving in your personal relationships while being hateful in other areas of your life, such as how you view other nations or ethnic groups. Being loving and inquisitive instead of hateful and judgmental is a mode of being. You can't separate out different parts of your life for one or the other.

There's yet another way that your personal life will benefit from also working on global challenges while you tackle your personal problems. Because you love your family, you want them to grow up in a more just and peaceful world, where the risks to their well-being from global challenges such as environmental damage and nuclear war are as small as possible.

Nobody's truly safe in the world in which we now live. Personal well-being and security require global well-being and security. The personal really does meet the global.

DOROTHIE: Having just seen why people who want to improve their personal relationships will benefit by expanding that concern to include global issues, we now explore the reverse: why people working to solve global challenges will accelerate their progress by also building more peaceful personal relationships.

At the most fundamental level, how can anyone be at war with their spouse and say, with a straight face, that a more peaceful world is possible? "Do as I say, not as I do," is not only hypocritical. It provides ammunition to those who discount a more peaceful world as naive, wishful thinking. It's much easier to espouse world peace than it is to produce personal peace. For anyone who wants to improve the world, their personal relationships are a testing ground for their larger vision.

MARTY: Conversely, because our marriage has evolved from frequent fights to arguments being a nightmare of the past, we can say with conviction that a more peaceful world is possible. Our marriage was a laboratory in which we carried out repeated experiments for learning how adversaries might solve their seemingly insoluble conflicts. Having achieved true peace in what had been a turbulent marriage, we now know with certainty that the same is possible at the international level. Just as in our marriage, it will take hard work. We'll need the courage to try experiments that the old map says will go nowhere. But the results will more than justify the effort.

DOROTHIE: There's another important advantage in solving global problems by also working on your personal relationships. When people are confronted with the urgent need for radical change in international relations, they often ask, "What difference can I make on such a big issue?" But if the first step is for them to radically improve their personal relationships, who else can bring that about?

MARTY: As we just saw, holistic thinking—which clearly is the solution to the global challenges we face—is a state of being that affects everything you do. Bringing holistic thinking into your personal relationships, by becoming more inquisitive and loving, will help you do the same when trying to understand international conflicts.

DOROTHIE: In my more right-brained, intuitive approach to life, it seems like everybody has their own little piece of energy. I'm in charge of mine, and the sum of everyone's little pieces adds up to the energy of the nation and the world. What we do affects everyone around us, and what they do affects everyone around them. How I interact with others ripples out. This means that making my personal interactions as compassionate as possible is what I can do to make the world a better place.

No individual can heal the planet. But if enough of us work hard enough to succeed in healing our personal relationships, we will plant the seed for global change. It's somewhat mysterious, maybe even mystical. But it is true.

Chapter 2

Practicing Compassion and Holistic Thinking

A friend asked us how our book approached solving the many personal and global challenges we face. Marty told him the solution is holistic thinking, while Dorothie said it was compassion. Our friend said that difference in our perspectives was not surprising, since Marty operates more from his logical left brain, while Dorothie tends to be more intuitive and right-brained. Marty thinks more. Dorothie feels more. The first section of this chapter explores the connection between those two perspectives.

Compassion and Holistic Thinking

MARTY: While Dorothie sees compassion as the solution to the challenges we face, initially, only holistic thinking made sense to me. Compassion didn't seem big enough.

Finding solutions that felt right to both of us—rather than each of us fighting for what we thought we wanted—seemed to call for holistic thinking: thinking about what's right for the whole. The same was true at an international level, since national security and well-being are becoming increasingly inseparable from global security and well-being. It was harder for me to see our goal, and the goal of this book, as compassion. But having talked it through, I now fully agree.

DOROTHIE: I'm drawn to the spiritual, even the mystical side of life, so it's not surprising that I had trouble explaining why holistic thinking and compassion were two sides of the same coin. Spiritual truths often don't fit neatly into the logical framework required for words, but I finally came up with an explanation that both of us like.

The kind of compassion I'm talking about is a profound sense of interconnectedness, which is clearly a holistic perspective. But it feels deeper to me than thinking about something, no matter how holistic that thinking might be.

For holistic thinking to work, you need to do more than just have the thought. Your actions need to be congruent with the thought. Living life compassionately demands both thinking and acting from a holistic perspective.

MARTY: Thinking back to our early steps in this process helped me to see what Dorothie was saying. Back then, each of us *thought* we were committed to doing what was right for our marriage, but we were not *doing it*, as evidenced by our frequent fights over what was right.

We thought we were practicing holistic thinking—yet the fact that we fought over finding the holistic solution proved that neither of us was acting holistically. And that means we were not really thinking holistically, either. We just fooled ourselves into believing we were. Given that potential pitfall, I can see why Dorothie prefers compassion to holistic thinking. It's harder to fool yourself into believing you are acting compassionately when, in fact, you are not.

DOROTHIE: Holistic thinking is not the same as compromise. Rather, the goal is to find a solution that meets both parties' needs completely, while still respecting their individuality.

MARTY: Initially, I thought that was impossible. I was proved wrong as Dorothie kept following her heart and we progressed on this path. After years of hard work, we are now able to do that every time a disagreement comes up, and each of us gets far more than we initially were asking for. You'll see examples throughout this book.

DOROTHIE: The best thing that we get from these holistic solutions to seemingly insoluble problems is an overwhelming feeling of love and appreciation for each other. That's far more precious than anything else we might desire.

MARTY: This book also provides a number of examples in which nations also would have been far better off if they had taken a more holistic view and asked more questions. The US intervention in Vietnam in the 1960s is a good example. Our claimed reason and the legal basis for the Vietnam War was unprovoked aggression by North Vietnam when their PT boats attacked an American destroyer, the USS *Maddox*, in the Tonkin Gulf on August 2, 1964. But as you'll see in the Vietnam case study, President Johnson knew that the North's attack had been provoked by our covert operations, which involved "blowing up some bridges and things of that kind, roads, and so forth," to use Johnson's own words.[4]

If we had taken a more holistic view—if we'd tried to understand North Vietnam's perspective and questioned the lies Johnson told the public and Congress—we would have ended up with the same situation we have now, a unified Vietnam under a nominally Communist government. But we would have gotten there without the humiliation of an American defeat at the cost of 58,000 American lives and somewhere between one and three million Vietnamese lives.

DOROTHIE: Bringing holistic thinking and compassion into our marriage healed our rocky relationship in astonishing ways that most people would have discounted as impossible. Bringing those same principles into international relations will work similar miracles at the global level.

Living Life More Consciously

While we focus primarily on holistic thinking and compassion as solutions to both the personal and global challenges we face, there are other, equivalent perspectives that are covered in this section. These other ways of looking at the solution all fit under the concept of living life more consciously. That should not be surprising, since holistic thinking and compassion require increased consciousness.

As we dedicated ourselves to living our lives more consciously, we became aware of inner motivations that previously had run us around at an unconscious level and had left chaos in their wake. When we developed more conscious, more honest pictures of ourselves, that knowledge gave us power over our conflicts, rather than the other way around. And of course, that's the same shift that is needed at the national level to solve the global challenges we face.

DOROTHIE: Years ago, on a beautiful sunny day, I was walking on a crowded sidewalk when a young woman came into view and shocked me. She was wearing a black bra under her see-through, white blouse. Didn't she understand that this was unacceptable? Couldn't she see how offensive it was to other people? It was like she was walking on the street in her underwear.

You may laugh at my reaction to this trivial incident, as I now can, but it was a transformative experience for me at the time. I realized that my sitting in judgment of her black bra caused everything else to totally stop for me. I was unable to enjoy the sunshine on my shoulders or the beauty of the woman herself. I was so wrapped up in judging her attire that nothing else existed for me.

After my initial feeling of shock, I woke up—I became more conscious—and realized that her brassiere proclaiming its existence didn't seem to bother her. Even if it bothered other people, that was none of my business. So why was it bothering me? Why was I letting it rob my positive energy? Was it my job to sit in judgment on the world? Was that a job I wanted?

As I thought about this more broadly, I realized I wasted far too much time judging my world and didn't spend enough time enjoying it. With that realization, I was able to drop my resistance to the woman's black bra and move on. But because most of my judgmentalism went on at an unconscious level, it took hard work to overcome. The good news: I can report that only rarely do I now experience such judgmental intrusions on my enjoyment of life, and when they do crop up, I recognize them almost immediately

("There it goes again!") and I'm able to return to a place of joy and gratitude.

There is also a humorous side to this story about the woman wearing a black bra under a see-through blouse. I later learned that, while visible underwear was considered very poor taste during my formative years in the 1950s, at this point in time, it was considered very stylish.

Living consciously has many other benefits. When I am conscious, I am in a state of compassion from which forgiveness and love flow automatically. When I'm conscious, my feelings can't get hurt and there's no point in getting angry. It's like stepping into another world.

Living consciously requires me to accept things the way they are, rather than resisting reality. I had far more resistance to reality than I realized when we started this process. Every time I fought with Marty, I was resisting the reality that only he could change himself and that a loving environment would speed that process.

MARTY: The need to accept reality was summarized well in one of the main teachings of Creative Initiative, the group we worked with in the 1980s: "Resist not evil."

"Resist not evil" comes from the Gospel according to Matthew, 5:39, which produced some real resistance in me. My 1950s Jewish upbringing saw studying the teachings of Jesus as traitorous, so I had an understandable, unconscious resistance to "Resist not evil." But then, as I studied it, that Scripture became a key part of my life. Since it has a Zen-like quality, I'll mention four ways I found to better understand Jesus' admonition.

The first was by seeing that, in resisting evil, we have a tendency to become evil ourselves. In resisting the evils of Communism, the

United States built tens of thousands of nuclear weapons and was ready to commit genocide on a scale that would make Hitler look like a schoolboy. In resisting the evils of capitalism, the Soviet Union did likewise. Much the same is true today between Russia and the United States. And the chaos following our invasion of Iraq shows the danger of resisting evil even through conventional military force.

The second way I came to see value in "Resist not evil" was to think of it as "Resist not reality." That's because reality sometimes appears evil, even though it cannot be. Reality just is. Resisting reality is an ineffective way to deal with situations as they are. Yet that's what I did whenever I said, "This can't be happening," while something was, in fact, happening.

The third way was to think of it as "Resist not *perceived* evil." Of course, we can only resist what we perceive as evil, but that important distinction usually is lost. We unconsciously confuse our perception with reality. In doing so, we can make big mistakes.

In the fights I used to have with Dorothie, I perceived her as being flat out wrong—"evil" is too strong a word, but it's close. I didn't realize that, often, my perception was clouded. The first story in this book, "Tearing Up the Map," is a good example. When Dorothie initially stormed out of the car and my feelings were hurt, I was focused solely on how her actions had impacted me. I had no conscious awareness of how my taking the map out of her hands had affected her.

The fourth way I came to understand "Resist not evil" was by learning that Gandhi's non-violent resistance owes a large debt to that saying of Jesus. Gandhi regarded Leo Tolstoy as his spiritual teacher; he even named his South African commune "Tolstoy

Farm." While I had known Tolstoy was a great writer, as I looked more deeply into his life, I discovered that he was also a profound philosopher and theologian. After a long, painful search, Tolstoy concluded that "Resist not evil" was the key to understanding the Gospels and living a worthwhile life. And it's a relatively small step from Tolstoy's "Resist not evil" to Gandhi's non-violent resistance.[5]

DOROTHIE: For me, "Resist not evil" is simpler. No matter what happens to me, I've learned to say, "I accept the gift"—especially if, at first, what happened doesn't feel like a gift.

Marty told me that, while he wouldn't want to again live through all the painful things that had happened to him, if he had a magic wand and could reverse them, he wouldn't. That's because he could see how all of his experiences, including those painful ones, had helped bring him to this state of being in which we have recaptured true love and brought peace into our lives.

"But," he continued, "what about your migraines? I can't see that there were any positive aspects to that life-limiting illness. Were there?"

At first I couldn't say "I accept the gift" for that. I hate having migraines. But after thinking about it, I realized that I had done much deeper personal work than I would have otherwise, in the hope that some childhood trauma had produced the migraines. While I found no migraine-inducing trauma, I benefited tremendously from that effort. My migraines also slowed me down and forced me to spend interminable hours in bed, being able to do nothing except contemplate life. Many of my insights came from that period.

I do everything I can to minimize my migraines and make them go away. I wish I didn't have them—but given that I do, I try to find whatever positive impact they have had on my life. So I guess I have "accepted the gift" that came with my migraines, even though they themselves are far from a gift.

Leaving "Resist not evil," and turning to other aspects of living life more consciously, I had another realization: Whenever I felt hurt or angry, I was mistaken about how the universe works.

MARTY: We "turned off the keyboard" for a while after that last statement of Dorothie's. At first, I didn't understand how being hurt or angry was the same as being mistaken about how the universe works. I'll let her explain. In fact, I have to let her explain, since I'm still chewing on what she said.

DOROTHIE: I like it when a statement forces people to think. How could something as common as hurt feelings or anger be a mistake about how the universe works?

As a child, everyone around me got hurt and angry when things didn't go their way, so it's not surprising that I grew up believing that was the right way to interact with the world. With that model, if Marty said something that hurt me, I thought what he said was about me, and I got hurt. But what he said wasn't about me. No matter how much it was directed at me (and often that was much less than I thought), his words only reflected something about him and where he was at that moment. Once I understood that, I didn't get hurt.

How is that being mistaken about how the universe works? When I mistakenly took what Marty said as being about me instead of about him, I made myself the center of the universe. Everything was about me. I needed to take in the bigger, holistic picture to see how Marty's state of being figured into what he'd said. Sometimes it turned out that I just misunderstood him. But I'd never see that when I mistakenly thought everything was about me.

MARTY: That explanation helped a great deal, though I have to admit it's still something I'll have to think about. I also have to remember that Dorothie sometimes uses hyperbole to emphasize a point.

As she was talking, I saw another way that getting hurt or angry means I'm mistaken about how the universe works. When I was in those states, I must have believed that they made me more effective at getting what I wanted; otherwise, I wouldn't have stayed there. Of course, being hurt or angry made me *less* effective. That means I was mistaken about how the universe works.

Nations do the same thing. When an adversary does something they don't like, they get angry. They must believe that anger makes them more effective at getting what they want, although it usually has the opposite effect. Nations are also mistaken about how the universe works.

Another way of living more consciously is through critical thinking: carefully re-examining the assumptions that underlie our worldview and discarding any that turn out to be false. Even one wrong assumption underlying a line of reasoning can make its conclusion not only wrong, but even absurd.

Just above, I gave an example of an incorrect, implicit assumption at the personal level that I failed to question for far too long: expecting to get what I wanted by acting hurt or angry. As I now recognize, those states of being made me less effective at realizing my desires. Critically re-examining my assumption has improved my life immeasurably.

There also is significant evidence that some wrong assumptions underlie our current approach to national security. Why else would our investment of trillions of dollars since 1945 have given us a nation that can be destroyed in under an hour? Here are just a few of the questions that critical thinking would have us ask: Are we really the world's sole remaining superpower, and what would that even mean? Do nuclear weapons form a protective "nuclear umbrella"? President Obama, among others, has assured us that our nuclear weapons are "safe, secure, and effective" and most people seem to accept him at his word—but what does that mean? How safe is it to put a nuclear doomsday machine into the hands of fallible human beings?

DOROTHIE: Another way to live more consciously is for us to grow up, both individually and societally. When Marty and I used to fight, we regressed to childlike behavior, sometimes reminiscent of the "terrible twos." That's not surprising, since many of those fights had their roots in childhood traumas of which we were unaware at a conscious level. If we had demanded more mature behavior—in ourselves, not in each other—that would have gone a long way toward defusing those fights.

The same is true at the international level, with all nations (including our own) often behaving in childlike ways that would embarrass them if they were to see themselves clearly.

MARTY: But there's an even deeper problem with our lack of maturity as a species. Science and engineering have given us physical powers that were historically thought of as belonging only to God: We can cause floods, create new life forms, and potentially destroy the world. But in contrast to our godlike physical power, humanity's social progress is, at best, in the irresponsible adolescent phase.

This chasm between our technological power on the one hand and our social development on the other has created a recipe for disaster that demands our urgent attention if the human race is to survive. Humanity is like a sixteen-year-old with a new driver's license who somehow got his hands on a 500-horsepower Ferrari. We will either grow up really fast or kill ourselves.

DOROTHIE: There are yet other ways to view the solution to our challenges. For example, we've not specifically cited the spiritual dimension, even though it played a significant role in our own growth process. We wrestled over whether or not to highlight it, but we decided not to, out of deference to different readers' religious beliefs or lack thereof. We hope that the universal message underlying all religions and philosophies will come through to those who practice one discipline or another.

Why It's a Process

We'd love it if we could tell you how we reclaimed true love in our marriage, you could implement that immediately in your own relationship, and never fight again. But that's not how it works. Learning to resolve conflict is a process, both interpersonally and internationally. Understanding that it is a process turns what otherwise would seem like an impossible leap into a reasonable sequence of steps: holistic thinking in time.

We both made a decision and commitment to become the best people and the most loving partners we could be, but that goal is an ideal that can only be approached, not realized. Getting ever closer to the ideal is a learning process. We have to continually unlearn old habits and acquire new ones. Learning is a process that takes time.

MARTY: Remember the first story in this book, when I grabbed the map out of Dorothie's hands, leading her to storm out of the car and then tear up the map when she returned? That occurred eight years after we dedicated ourselves to behaving differently. While that behavior, by itself, makes it look as if we had learned nothing in those years, the positive outcome shows that there was a process at work. The incident ended with both of us laughing at how ridiculously we'd behaved. That would not have happened eight years earlier.

DOROTHIE: It's important to remember that you're involved in a learning process. Otherwise, you will be too hard on your partner when he or she fails to meet the ideal. Equally important, you'll be too hard on yourself when you fail. An incident that occurred a few years after I tore up the map on Twin Peaks is a good example, and also shows how our process continued to evolve.

We were seeing a family therapist, Dr. Sheldon Starr, who was immensely helpful to us. In one of our sessions, Marty was complaining about my saying, "I want a divorce," whenever I couldn't handle an argument. He knew I didn't mean it, but it hurt him. I promised repeatedly that I wouldn't say that again, but I couldn't stop. Every time I failed, it devastated me.

During that session, Marty said something that struck a deep nerve. I felt white-hot pain so intense that I had to run out of Sheldon's office without saying a word. From Marty's perspective, I had stormed out yet again. He felt abandoned one more time.

I sat down in the waiting room and tried to cool down, but I had trouble getting myself under control. After my pain over what Marty had said subsided, a new hurt set in. I felt horrible about running out of the room. Had I learned nothing in all these years? Was my commitment to resolving conflict just hot air?

When I finally found the courage to venture back in, Sheldon surprised me with what he said: "I see that we were going too fast for you." What a relief! I hadn't been the bad person—I'd been the person who couldn't handle that pace.

As we discussed the session, we realized that my habit of walking out on Marty or saying "I want a divorce" was just my way of ending an argument that was too painful for me to continue. Marty has a higher tolerance for conflict than I do, so we needed to find a better way for me to say I needed a breather.

Once we understood this, we found a much better solution: We agreed that, if we were having a fight and either of us was afraid we might lose control or say something hurtful, that person had not just the right, but the obligation, to leave the room without saying anything. Not saying anything is important because, at such volatile moments, even saying, "I need to leave," is likely to come out wrong or be taken wrong.

Unlike the fights we had early in our relationship, in which one of us stormed off, leaving the other feeling abandoned, we now had an agreement: whichever of us had to leave would bridge back to make things right when they'd calmed down. At first, it was hard to trust that the other one really would come back. But after a few successes, it became much easier. Still later, we no longer needed this agreement, because fights became a relic of our past.

Once we found this way to hit the pause button on arguments, I never again stormed out of a car or room, leaving Marty feeling abandoned. We had taken another important step in our process. Finally, I had the new tool I needed to stop hurting Marty while still taking care of myself when I needed to slow things down.

This story makes an important point about this process. Each "mistake" needs to be seen as a new learning opportunity. A friend of ours joked that we were following NASA's definition of success: longer and longer times between failures. In both cases, it is clearly a process.

MARTY: Another reason our journey is a process is that every relationship has a "bank account" of goodwill that needs to be built up over time. As we learned to treat each other better, the balance went from negative to positive, and small annoyances that previously would have snowballed into huge arguments could be dealt with in short order. Now, we feel so grateful for one another—and we tell each other that in so many ways—that our "account balance" allows us to "buy" almost anything we want.

DOROTHIE: There are many ways we've added to that balance. Some are big, like learning to really listen to one another. But we also take advantage of the much more frequent opportunities, like giving each other a hug or kiss, or just a gentle touch, or a quick phone call to say "I love you."

Whoops. I'm showing my age. Younger people will probably text.

MARTY: I also may be showing my age, but I had difficulty at first telling Dorothie those frequent "sweet nothings." In the culture I grew up in, men didn't do things like that. We were supposed to be independent to the point of not needing anyone.

A friend once told me that, as a young man, his ideal had been the cowboy who rode into town, sauntered into a bar, sat at a table by himself, downed a bottle of whiskey, and was fine with that. Contrary to John Donne's admonition that no man is an island unto himself, my friend's ideal man had been exactly that.

It's also important to check in and learn what makes your partner feel loved. Early on, I assumed I knew how to love Dorothie. It was only after we started this process that I learned that some of the things I saw as loving didn't feel that way to her. For example, when I used to find her reading in the dark, I'd turn on a light and ask her if that was better. This drove her up the wall. She was quite happy reading in the dark and resented being interrupted.

DOROTHIE: We've overcome that old conflict in several ways. After I committed to this process, if Marty mistakenly thought it was helpful to play with the lights, I could ask him to handle it differently without getting frustrated. Also, I've reframed what used to be an annoyance into his playing "silly light games." Early in the process, I'd tell him, "I'm not playing silly light games." As we've gone deeper into this new territory, later in our process, I came to realize that, even though it wasn't what I'd asked for, varying my lighting was an attempt on Marty's part to love me and take care of me. With that larger, holistic perspective, what used to annoy me, became a sweet reminder of how much I am loved.

MARTY: Technology also helped. A few years ago, Dorothie got a Kindle, so I don't worry that reading in the dark will strain her eyes.

DOROTHIE: We've described the main tool we used to develop holistic thinking and compassion—both of us committing to giving up fighting for what we thought we wanted and instead putting all that energy into figuring out what's right for the relationship, and then doing what was right. All of this culminates in compassion and holistic thinking, of course.

But in the early years of this process—meaning around the first ten years for us—we often disagreed on "the right thing to do," and we could get into fights over that. How circular!

When we seemed hopelessly deadlocked over those different perspectives on what was right, we needed outside help to unravel the knot.

MARTY: In our case, that outside help initially came from a retired Stanford professor, Harry Rathbun,[6] and his wife Emilia,[7] now both deceased. The Rathbuns had founded Creative Initiative, a group that got us started on this process and later morphed into another group called Beyond War. Both Harry and Emilia had spent many years helping other couples. They brought a great deal of wisdom to the table when we vehemently disagreed on "the right thing to do."

But Harry and Emilia and Creative Initiative could take us only so far. At that point, Sheldon Starr, the therapist whose office Dorothie stormed out of, became an invaluable resource for our going further. Needing a sequence of "relationship wizards" is another example of why this is a process.

DOROTHIE: It's important to remember that the goal of this process is not just to learn to "fight fair." Rather, the ultimate goal is to honor and love each other so deeply that fighting would be a sacrilege.

MARTY: Solving global challenges, such as climate change and the nuclear threat, also involve processes. In one sense, skeptics are right when they say those problems can't be solved: They cannot be solved in the current environment. We can't jump to the required solutions, but we can get there in a sequence of smaller steps that change the environment and create new possibilities that did not exist before.

All the major societal changes that have occurred have involved such processes. In the election of 1840, anti-slavery candidate James Birney received just 0.3 percent of the vote. Twenty years later, after enough people had challenged the conventional wisdom that slavery was an immutable part of human nature, the process had reached the point that Abraham Lincoln could be elected president.

In author Malcolm Gladwell's parlance, society first has to reach a tipping point, meaning that enough individuals have to embrace a new idea before it can be transformed into societal change. Prior to the tipping point, the idea seems too radical for most people to consider seriously. After the tipping point, the radical concept can become the societal norm. Ironically, once that happens, going back to the previously accepted conventional wisdom becomes outrageous. Anyone who proposed reinstituting slavery today would be as much of a social outcast as those who proposed ending it in 1840.

That's what happened to rancher Cliven Bundy in 2014. When he refused to pay grazing fees to the federal government, he became the darling of the far right—until he offered this opinion about African-Americans: "I've often wondered, are they better off as slaves, picking cotton and having a family life and doing things, or are they better off under government subsidy? They didn't get no more freedom. They got less freedom."

Fox News dropped him like a hot potato, with former supporter Sean Hannity calling Bundy's remarks "beyond repugnant."

Women's suffrage also involved a process, and we appear to be in the middle of another shift in societal thinking, this time about gay marriage.

It's encouraging that the fraction of the population required to reach such a tipping point is much smaller than might first appear. When only a very small percentage of the population has adopted the new idea, few people give it serious consideration. After 5 to 10 percent embrace the idea, it begins to gain serious consideration within the larger society. Then it has reached a tipping point.

Most people won't respond the first time they hear someone support the new idea, whether it's ending slavery in 1850, women voting in 1900, or applying holistic thinking to our foreign policy today. But as with advertising, hearing that message a second or third time begins to have an impact. That happens when somewhere around 5 to 10 percent adopt the new thought because, while few people want to be the first to embrace what is initially seen as a radical idea, an equally small number want to be the last to get on board with the new societal norm.

Only by our taking responsibility for our own individual process will the required changes be realized throughout the society. Global change depends on personal change.

When we keep in mind that personal and societal change occur as processes, we have a more realistic, optimistic perspective at both the personal and global levels. Don't get discouraged if you haven't reached your goal yet. Just be patient and keep working the process.

Viewing existential global issues through that lens significantly changes how they look. The media makes it look as if war is as big a scourge as ever, yet as we will see later, statistics show that the number of people killed annually by war has fallen by roughly a factor of four over the last thirty years. In that same period, the number of nuclear weapons in the world has fallen by a similar amount.

Far too many people are still dying in wars, and the current arsenal's 16,000 nuclear weapons still can destroy civilization. But we are making progress. We would like to see the process accelerated, so that fewer people die horrible deaths and the risk of civilization being destroyed fades into history.

When we look at the solutions to those problems as processes in which we've already made significant progress, we see a much more hopeful picture than the usual doom and gloom perspective that ignores the gains we've made already.

Implementing the Process

A friend who read an early draft of this book asked how we managed to implement our decision to live our lives more holistically and compassionately. He said, "If it were as easy as making the decision to do that, it would be done much more frequently." The last section gave part of the answer to his question: While our decision was a one-time affair, implementing it has been a never-ending process of learning and coming ever closer to the ideal.

It was critically important that our decision was a real decision, not "I'll try this new map and see if I like it." To truly be a decision, our attitude had to be, "We are going to make this work, no matter what!" This section provides a personal example that illustrates how hard it was for Marty to ensure that he really was committed to change—and not just fooling himself.

MARTY: While in some ways we started our process in the summer of 1980 when Dorothie dragged me to our first Creative Initiative meeting, my one-time decision came a year later, when we attended a weeklong seminar run by the group. By that time, I had dropped much of my resistance and was beginning to see that, "these people know something I need to learn if my marriage is going to survive." With that realization, I committed to tear up my old map and piece together a new one that was holistic and compassionate.

One of my most impactful experiences that week occurred when we watched a video documentary, *The Day After Trinity*, about the making of the world's first atom bomb. "Trinity" was the code name for the detonation of the first such weapon in the New Mexico desert in July 1945.

During the video, an interviewer asked several of the Manhattan Project scientists what their motivation had been for working on this weapon of mass destruction. To a man—and they were all men—they answered the same. Fission had been discovered in Germany, and we had to get the bomb before the Nazis did. When responding to this question, the men being interviewed became animated, reliving the exhilaration they felt when they joined the project and the fight against Nazism. The physicist Robert Wilson enthusiastically declared that, if Hitler got the bomb first, it could have led to "a thousand years of dark ages, and everything that we meant by civilization could have come to an end."

Later in the documentary, the interviewer asks the scientists another question. When Germany surrendered in May 1945 and their stated motivation of beating the Nazis to the bomb was gone, why did they continue working on the project? In answering this question, their demeanors change markedly. They become quiet, even defensive. Wilson was deeply disturbed by his lack of introspection and said:

> *I would like to think now that at the time of the German defeat that I would have … walked away from Los Alamos … I cannot understand why I did not take that [action]. On the other hand, it simply was not in the air. … Our life was directed to do one thing. It was as though we had been programmed to do that, and we as automatons were doing it.*[8]

When Wilson heard that the bomb had been dropped on Hiroshima, the horror of what he had done hit him so hard that he vomited.

Watching the video, I thought I knew why the Manhattan Project scientists continued working on the bomb after Germany was defeated. In addition to their stated, socially acceptable motivation of defeating Hitler, I believe they had "shadow motivations"—unstated, socially unacceptable goals that were hidden even from their own conscious minds. If I had been one of them, mine might have been: "Could I, the nerd who got picked on by the other boys, become a war hero? Is my brain powerful enough to destroy a city?"

That's why I believe they were so puzzled. Given the consequences of their actions—well over 100,000 men, women, and children killed at Hiroshima and Nagasaki, and many suffering horribly before being blessed with death—such unstated motivations would seem so deplorable that they would not be allowed to see the light of day. I believed this because the video got me to see how I had deceived myself in just that fashion five years earlier, as you'll see in this next story.

MARTY: I had started doing research in cryptography in the early 1970s and, in the summer of 1975, along with my colleague Whit Diffie, discovered that a proposed data encryption standard was breakable. For about six months, we tried working through channels to improve the standard, but we hit roadblock after roadblock. We eventually realized that NSA (the National Security Agency) was behind the weakness and we would have to go public with our discovery if we wanted to make the standard more secure. We would have to fight NSA. As we prepared to do that, the Agency got wind of our intentions and tried to stop us. Two high-level employees flew to California and warned us that going public would cause "grave harm to national security."

After their visit, I sat down to figure out the right thing to do. I had NSA telling me that going public would be a disaster for my country, but I could also foresee the coming computer-communications revolution, which is now apparent in the Internet affecting almost every facet of our lives. Keeping quiet would expose people's confidential information to prying eyes, including the eyes of our own government. Government spying was a particularly scary prospect at that point in time since it was less than two years after the Watergate revelations of such activity had forced President Nixon to resign.

As I was trying to decide the right thing to do, an idea popped into my head: "Forget about what's right and wrong. You have a tiger by the tail and will never have as much chance to influence events. Run with it!"

Somehow, what would normally be an unconscious shadow motivation had managed to bubble to the surface and became a "devil on my shoulder," just like in the movies. At the time, I thought I brushed the devil off my shoulder and made a rational decision to go public with our analysis of the standard's weakness. But five years later, as I watched *The Day After Trinity*, I realized that, like the scientists on the Manhattan Project, I had fooled myself. Instead of doing what was right, I had figured out what I wanted to do, and then had come up with the rationalization for doing it.

I was fortunate that my decision to go public was the right one, even though I'd fooled myself about my motivation. But that was sheer luck. If I had been working on the Manhattan Project, I would have done the same thing as those scientists. I vowed never to fool myself again, although implementing that one-time decision proved tricky.

Around the same time that I started fighting to make the standard more secure, two of my students and I invented a new kind of encryption system—public key cryptography—that revolutionized the field. Today, that technology secures your electronic banking and your Internet credit card purchases. It also secures $5 trillion a day in foreign exchange transactions, so even a tiny royalty would make me a millionaire many times over.[9]

Unfortunately, our patents didn't make me and my students wealthy. There were several reasons, and one of them was a patent fight with a company called RSA Data Security. RSA had been founded by three of my colleagues at MIT who had come up with another way of doing what we had proposed.

In the paper describing their approach, they credited us with inventing public key cryptography, but when they were asked to pay royalties, they claimed that our patents were invalid and told us to sue them. This was probably a bluff since, at the time, RSA didn't have the kind of money needed for a patent fight. But neither did we.

Stanford University owned our patents, with each of the three inventors getting roughly 10 percent of whatever royalties Stanford took in. Stanford would be the one to sue RSA and foot the legal bill. I'll never forget the meeting with Stanford's patent counsel. He warned the university not to start litigation unless it could give him a budget of at least a quarter of a million dollars—the equivalent of well over a million dollars today. Stanford did not want to risk that kind of money on an unproven technology, so RSA's bluff won and created a dangerous legal precedent for the patent fight that eventually took place.

Several years later, the CEO of a Silicon Valley startup, Cylink, approached me trying to get an exclusive license to Stanford's patents. Lew Morris was a scrappy little Jewish guy from Philadelphia who reminded me of the kids I'd grown up with in the Bronx. His language did, too: "Help me get an exclusive license from Stanford, and I promise you, we'll get those RSA bastards by the balls."

This was after Dorothie and I had committed to doing what was right instead of what we thought we wanted. I should work with Cylink only if it made good business sense—not out of a desire for revenge.

As I thought it through, it seemed clear to me that working with Cylink did make good business sense. But I was so mad at RSA that I couldn't be sure I wasn't fooling myself again—something I'd vowed never to do. When you're that emotionally involved in a fight, it's impossible to be sure you're being objective.

I went to Dorothie, told her my conundrum, and asked if she saw a way out. She asked if Niels Reimers, Stanford's Director of Technology Licensing, had the same kind of emotional involvement in this fight that I did. He did not. She asked if Niels and I had the same business interests, which we clearly did. Dorothie then suggested that I let Nils make the decision. Clouded by my emotions, that simple, brilliant solution had eluded me.

I set up a meeting with Niels, explained my dilemma, and asked what he thought. He said it was clearly a good business decision for

Stanford to go with Cylink, and we did. It was the same decision I would have made on my own, but this way I was able to rest assured that I hadn't fooled myself again.

Nations also need to guard against "shadow motivations" that can cause them to fool themselves in ways that can be very dangerous. Our nation's claim that NATO's expansion into Eastern Europe does not threaten Russia is a good example. A 1997 OpEd by then Deputy Secretary of State Strobe Talbott is even titled "Russia Has Nothing to Fear." Talbott asserted that, "the new NATO is not a threat to Russia."[10] Many subsequent actions have violated that assertion, with the most recent occurring early in 2016, when the United States announced plans to deploy heavy weapons in NATO countries bordering Russia.[11]

Some insight into Talbott's thinking can be found in his memoirs, which were published six years after that OpEd. He describes a 1993 meeting in which the Russian Foreign Minister told him, "You know, it's bad enough having you people tell us what you're going to do whether we like it or not. Don't add insult to injury by also telling us that it's in our interests to obey your orders." Talbott describes his assistant complaining soon afterward, "That's what happens when you try to get the Russians to eat their spinach. The more you tell them it's good for them, the more they gag." He then concludes, "Among those of us working on Russia policy, 'administering the spinach treatment' became shorthand for one of our principal activities in the years that followed."[12]

MARTY: There's an interesting postscript to the story about Stanford's patent fight with RSA. Even though Stanford partnered with Cylink, we still didn't make much money from our patents, while RSA was sold a few years later for $250 million. But far from still being mad at my three MIT colleagues who had founded RSA, I am now friends with them. I'm also friends with Jim Bidzos, who was CEO of the company and directed its legal battle. How did that happen?

After the patent fight ended, and as Dorothie and I progressed on our journey, I realized that being mad at my colleagues was inconsistent with my new relationship map. I tried re-thinking the legal battle through from their point of view, much as I had learned to see our marital conflicts partly through Dorothie's eyes. That holistic, compassionate perspective helped me realize how RSA could see me as having started the fight—the opposite of how I'd seen things up until then. I approached Jim Bidzos, who responded very positively. He helped me reconnect with my three colleagues. In a short time, we were able to turn animosity into friendship.[13]

A similar thing happened with NSA, with the credit for resolving that conflict going to Admiral Bobby Inman, who served as Director of the Agency in the late 1970s. He approached me during the heat of our battle and told me that he was meeting with me against the advice of all the other senior people at NSA. Inman said he understood their concerns but didn't see any harm in talking. He hoped it might lead someplace good—a much more holistic approach.

The others at NSA must have depicted me as a devil, because one of the first things Inman told me was, "It's nice to see you don't have horns." I returned the compliment, since I had seen myself as Luke Skywalker to NSA's Darth Vader. I was in my early thirties at the time, so the young hero model was more appropriate than it would be now, when I am seventy years old.

My relationship with Inman was cautious at first, but it grew into friendship as we came to appreciate one another's concerns. In a recent interview, when asked if he now would make the same decision as he did forty years ago to try to quash our work, he replied, "Rather than being careful to make sure they [weren't] going to damage [NSA's intelligence operations] ... I would have been interested in how quickly they were going to be able to make [encryption widely] available." He cited the theft of portions of the F-35 jet fighter design as proof that strong commercial encryption was in the nation's broader national security interests.[14]

Not surprisingly, it's far better to have friends than enemies. As just one example, both Admiral Inman and Jim Bidzos signed a statement of support for my effort to bring a more objective, risk-informed approach to our nuclear strategy.[15] They wouldn't have done that if they hadn't agreed with the statement, but they also wouldn't have done it if they hadn't trusted me.

The fact that two formerly bitter foes are now friends willing to take an action like that proves that even entrenched enmities can be healed. But those approaches will not become evident until we tear up our old maps and start following the new map to holistic thinking and compassion.

Developing Compassion

The dictionary defines compassion as "sympathetic pity and concern for the sufferings or misfortunes of others," but we see it as something much bigger than that. To us, compassion is acceptance of all creation and our place in it. It is a state of being. When we fall out of it, life becomes disjointed and we are reminded to rededicate ourselves to the ideal of always being compassionate. Because it's impossible to always be compassionate, what we do is *practice* compassion. Developing compassion was essential to piecing together a new map for relationships.

DOROTHIE: Learning how to love and be loved is such an important part of my life, and compassion is so integral to that goal, that I've spent more than twenty-five years studying it. In our experience, acting judgmentally or out of fear, anger, or hate is a sure-fire way to destroy love. Doing so makes it impossible to be compassionate and see the larger, holistic picture that is essential to creating true peace in our marriage and in the world.

Exploring compassion has been largely a self-guided tour. I've read a lot, talked to many people and, most importantly, explored my own inner struggle to be compassionate. That last part is key because, especially in the early phases of the process, I often found myself in circumstances in which it seemed impossible to be compassionate.

How could I not be judgmental, fearful, or angry when I felt mistreated by Marty in some painful way that had happened time and again? Of course, as I now know, his perspective was often the mirror image in which I was the offender and he was the victim. Until we developed compassion, each of us was vainly trying to change the other, and neither of us was focused where we needed to be: on changing ourselves.

Compassion has become the answer to almost every problem I face. If I can ground myself in the world of compassion—as I am now able to do almost all of the time—then it's impossible for me to be thrown off balance.

MARTY: As you can see from what Dorothie said, this "journey to the land of compassion" hasn't always been smooth sailing. And, to our surprise, the hardest and most important part was learning to have compassion for ourselves. You'll see examples of that in several stories yet to come.

DOROTHIE: Five tools proved invaluable in learning to have compassion for myself and others. The first was, rather than getting discouraged or frustrated when I failed, gently and compassionately bringing myself back to the goal. In a kind of Zen perspective, I had to have compassion for myself when I failed to have compassion. That did not mean letting myself off the hook. Rather, every failure became an opportunity to rededicate myself to the goal and learn from the experience.

The second critical tool in achieving compassion was having faith that I really could do it, even after repeated failures. I now can see that they weren't failures, just steps in the process leading to the ultimate goal.

A third critical tool is just plain practice. When I feel hurt, angry, or treated unfairly—and therefore cannot have compassion for others—I remember who I want to become and practice coming from that place, rather than from a place of pain. I also do that when I feel judgmental or blaming. Only by practicing compassion have I been able to become ever more proficient at accessing it when needed.

Based on the difficulty I've experienced in trying to communicate this to interested friends, I'd say the importance of practice is as difficult to understand as it is critical to success. At first, I tended to get stuck in my feelings of pain. But at some point, I realized I needed to leave the pain of the past behind and tune into the joy that was all around me, which was just waiting for me to be still enough to receive it. I had done enough to heal my wounds, and I needed to move on. Joy is much more fun than suffering. A Buddhist saying puts it beautifully: Pain is inevitable, suffering is optional.

The fourth tool I have found invaluable in learning compassion is to remember that I am doing this not only for myself, but also to save the world. If I can't learn to do it, how can I ask the nations of the world to behave more reasonably and live in peace? Conversely, if enough of us make this shift, I am convinced that amazing things will happen in the larger world. That's been a great motivator for me when confronted by seemingly insurmountable barriers to having compassion. I often have found superhuman strength by remembering that how we live our individual lives will help determine whether or not humanity survives.

My fifth and last critical tool for developing compassion is gratitude: gratitude for life, for this beautiful world, and for finding this path. When I am in a deep state of gratitude, compassion flows spontaneously.

When we first wrote this section, I listed forgiveness as a sixth tool, but then I realized it was a consequence of compassion, not a tool for achieving it. Once I have compassion for someone who I think has hurt me, forgiveness is automatic. In fact, compassion goes beyond forgiveness. It's a higher level of making peace with that person, at least within myself. Making my own, internal peace with him frees me from holding a grudge and being a prisoner of my painful memories.

MARTY: Dorothie's exploring compassion at such a deep and total level was a good thing for me in many ways. It opened the door to her loving me in the way I'd always yearned for, but previously had only experienced in the first blush of our infatuation. It also blessed me in another way. Being intimately associated with a person who had dedicated her life to the ideal of always responding compassionately gave me a role model to emulate, and a "proof of concept" for a state of being I otherwise never would have thought possible. Dante had his Beatrice. I have my Dorothie. She truly lived up to the meaning of her name, a gift from God.

DOROTHIE: Stop! I love what you're saying, but it's making me blush.

MARTY: Okay, but as I followed you on this path to compassion, I found another helpful tool for achieving it. Whenever someone had hurt me and I'd wonder, "How could he be so cruel?" or "stupid" or some other negative trait, I would search in my own history to see if I had done something similar. And usually, I had.

With minor events, like someone cutting in front of me in heavy traffic, it wasn't very hard. With more personal insults, it took longer and more "unpeeling the layers of the onion" for me to find similar incidents in which I had behaved badly. But in time, I was able to find them. In addition to bringing greater inner peace to my life, this was helpful in sanding off many of my rough edges, making me a more loving, more lovable person.

DOROTHIE: It's strange that, even though becoming compassionate made both our lives infinitely better, when people hear that compassion plays such a large role in my life, they often raise objections. Their objections usually fall into one of two categories.

The first consistent objection is that my studying compassion does nothing for the state of the world. One of Marty's colleagues, another Stanford professor, put it this way: "How does that help people starving in India?" The other consistent objection is to ask why I would want to feel compassion for Hitler. It's curious to me why people jump to such extreme cases, rather than thinking about those closer to home, but it's a very common reaction.

MARTY: I think I have the answer—or at least *an* answer—to that question. Almost everyone would say they want to be compassionate, and many probably think they already are. When you talk about your struggle to be as compassionate as possible, it's confrontational. At some level, people know that they ought to be interested, but they're so busy with other things that they don't want to be bothered. So they come up with an objection that lets them off the hook.

DOROTHIE: Whoa! Aren't you being judgmental?

MARTY: I can see how it sounds that way now, but it won't when I'm finished—because I've been guilty of that myself.

At our very first Creative Initiative meeting in 1980—which was Day 1 of our process—they showed us a video about the need to be better stewards of the Earth. There was a great deal of talk about recycling and the need to take a long-term view, to not just worry about our needs today.

At the end of the video, I objected—much as people object to your working on compassion. I said, "I agree that we need to be concerned about the long-term survival of civilization. But if you're going to talk long-term, what are we going to do when the sun burns out in five billion years?"

I was looking for an excuse, however flimsy, not to participate. So I'm not judging people who raise Hitler as an objection to your studying compassion. But given how common that defense mechanism is, I think it's important to highlight it—and to have compassion for people suffering from it, including ourselves. As ridiculous as my "five billion year" comment was, I'm not embarrassed by it. In fact, there's a positive side to my having said something so ridiculous all those years ago, since it helps me to have compassion for people who make similar objections today.

DOROTHIE: Now that you've explained, I see value in what I originally thought was judgmental. If you can go from where you were in 1980 to where you are today—where even "the Princess and the Pea of relationship conflict" feels blessed to be married to you—then people reading this who have a seemingly impossible partner can still harbor hope of fundamental change.

Returning to "the objectors," of course my studying compassion, all by itself, won't solve world hunger. However, if more people worked at being compassionate, then we'd be much more likely to find a solution. I only have control over my own life, but I'd love it if more people on this planet would join in this compassion quest. Maybe writing this book will help.

As far as having compassion for Hitler, I am horrified at the human misery he caused and I can't imagine living his life or what happened to make him do such monstrous things. What a hell on earth that must have been. I wouldn't wish his life on anyone. And if my wish came true, none of the horrible things he did to other people would have happened.

MARTY: This objection about having compassion for Hitler reminds me of how I had to wrestle with a portion of the Sermon on the Mount that we studied in Creative Initiative: "pray for those who persecute you." How could that be?

But now it makes perfect sense. It's not that I'd pray for them to be more successful in persecuting me. Rather, my prayer is for them to be blessed with insight, compassion, and peace, in which case their bad behavior would cease. Our goal is to have compassion for the whole world and everyone in it.

DOROTHIE: I wish that people who challenge the value of our quest by jumping to extreme cases would focus more on feeling compassion for their partner who annoyed them, their next-door neighbor who committed some seemingly unpardonable sin, or the person who cut them off in traffic. What do people have to lose by trying that experiment?

MARTY: The same is true for citizens of one nation experimenting with trying to understand the perspective of an adversary and having compassion for that nation, instead of hating it. What do they have to lose? Just as I found it invaluable when someone angered me to search for similar misdeeds that I had done, nations—our own included—would benefit immensely from that exercise.

DOROTHIE: I have found that compassion will solve most interpersonal problems, and I am convinced that the same is true internationally. It's impossible to remain angry at or be hurt by people when you think of all they've been through or the miracles of creation that they are. But it's easy to forget in the early stages of the process.

When I'm dealing with an interpersonal problem and I move to a place of compassion, the problem itself may not go away, but its negative impact on me abates, and that is usually enough. Of course, there are times when change on the other person's part is needed, but that change is much more likely to happen if I can bring compassion out to play instead of angrily and judgmentally demanding that the other person change.

Dedication and integrity are essential to becoming compassionate. Compassion's inner peace only came to me after I made an irrevocable decision to follow its path. I had to have faith that compassion was all around me, just waiting for me to let it in. I really can't say it any other way. Compassion was there just for the asking. As my anger and judgmentalism dissipated, compassion and joy rushed in to fill the void.

Chapter 3

Get Curious, Not Furious

One of the most important changes we had to make as we moved from our old maps to our new one was to ask questions instead of getting mad—to "get curious, not furious." But first we had to stop letting anger take us over by moving from blame to responsibility. This critically important idea was briefly discussed earlier, but it warrants deeper exploration in the next section.

Moving From Blame
To Responsibility

DOROTHIE: Earlier in our marriage, if Marty did something that made me mad and I reacted by mistreating him, I saw it as his fault: *He* had made me mad. In our new map, no one else can make me mad. Each of us is totally responsible for how we treat one other, no matter how justified our anger might seem.

In the early phases of this healing process, I still got mad at things that Marty did, but now there was a crucial difference. If I lost it and mistreated Marty, I couldn't blame my bad behavior on him. I had a responsibility, once I had calmed down, to apologize for hurting him, whether or not he apologized to me for what I thought he had done—and sometimes what I thought he had done was very different from what he actually had done.

MARTY: Of course, that worked both ways. I couldn't blame my bad behavior on Dorothie. I needed to recognize that I might see an insult when none was intended, and I had exactly the same responsibility to apologize unconditionally when I had mistreated her, no matter what I thought she had done. I couldn't say, "I'm sorry, but …" That "but" would totally cancel my apology. And I couldn't just be saying the words. I really had to be sorry that I'd mistreated the woman I cherished.

Not surprisingly, at first, there were times that neither of us was able to rise to that level of maturity. When that happened, we'd have to pick ourselves up and recommit to the ideal we had set as the goal for our relationship. And I couldn't hold a grudge against Dorothie for falling down, because I had done the same.

DOROTHIE: For me, too, recognizing that I had blown it was a real problem at first. When arguments erupted, I felt like I was doing all the work and Marty was just letting his anger run rampant.

MARTY: I had the mirror image problem, which raises an important question. How can someone tell the difference between our situation—in which not focusing on the other's mistakes was critical to our eventual success—and situations in which a person's partner is not willing to pull his or her weight? Telling the difference is really hard, and while we don't have a complete answer, we can offer some suggestions.

If your partner is addicted—to alcohol, drugs, anger, physical abuse, gambling, lying, irresponsible spending, sex, or anything else—then the addiction has to be dealt with before this process has any hope of success. An addicted person can't develop a holistic perspective because he's too focused on the object of the addiction. The same applies to compulsions that are less than addictions, if they are strong enough to interfere with a holistic perspective.

We also found it helpful to get impartial, professional input. Dorothie was seeing a therapist, and I felt like he was getting a distorted picture of our situation. He was only hearing Dorothie's side of the story and didn't know all that I had to put up with. So, with Dorothie's permission, I went to see him. After painting my side of the story—in which I was working hard to improve our relationship, but she was not—he smiled and told me that Dorothie was presenting the same picture, but with our roles reversed. That made a big difference in my focusing where I needed to—correcting my own mistakes—rather than on trying to change Dorothie.

DOROTHIE: This brings us to a related, equally crucial question. What's the point of working on holistic, compassionate solutions if, as may be the case, your partner is not willing to do the hard work needed for that process? There are four answers to that question, depending on your situation.

First, it may only seem that your partner isn't pulling his or her weight. That's how it felt to each of us, early on. By continuing to work the process anyway, we eventually reached the point that we could see how wrong our initial perceptions had been.

Second, your initial perception may be right, but as you work to become the best person you can be, a truly worthwhile partner will be blown away by—and will want to follow—your example.

Third, even if your partner isn't committed to this process and you decide to stay in the relationship, your life will still be much better. It's an old adage, but true, that it takes two to fight. Life won't be nearly as good as if both of you had worked the process, but it will be far better than if neither of you did.

Fourth, if you have to leave the relationship at some point, you will be in a much better place for your next one. If you've moved from blame to responsibility, your next relationship has a much higher chance of success. And no matter what happens to your relationship, you are doing your part to increase critically needed global consciousness.

MARTY: It's really true that you have nothing to lose, other than false pride, by working on holistic, compassionate solutions—no matter what your partner does. You have much to gain. Based on my experience, I'd say you have *everything* to gain.

You're Not Listening

DOROTHIE: My not feeling heard was at the root of many of the arguments that Marty and I used to have. And, as I look back, I suspect that much of his anger and frustration was also at not feeling heard, though he tended not to use those words.

MARTY: I was so out of touch with my feelings earlier in our relationship that I can't imagine having said, "I don't feel heard." I would have put it in some more "logical" framework like, "You're wrong!"

DOROTHIE: One day, after making a lot of progress, but still far from where we are today, we got into an argument over something so "important" that neither of us can remember what it was about. What both of us vividly remember, and what was really important, was the surprising way in which we moved past the previously insurmountable barrier of my not feeling heard.

MARTY: As the argument progressed, Dorothie told me what I'd heard a million times before: "You're not listening!" So I told her what I'd also said a million times before: that she was wrong, and that I had heard every word she'd said.

We went through a few more iterations of her exclaiming, "You're not listening!" followed by my loudly asserting, "Yes, I am! My ears are open. What do you want me to hear? Just say it."

In the past, each such iteration would have made both of us more frustrated and angry. But we had made enough progress at this point that, while Dorothie was determined to be heard, she did not get mad at me. She dug her heels in but did not attack me.

DOROTHIE: Operating at that more mature level allowed Marty to do something that created a crack in the old dam of resentment. He asked me how I knew that he wasn't listening. I told him that, if he were listening, he'd be behaving differently.

MARTY: At first, Dorothie's reply didn't seem to help, since I had no idea what I could do differently. Exasperated, I told her, "I'm doing everything I can humanly think of to hear you, but there must be something else I could do, since you're still not feeling heard. What *is* it?"

I didn't really expect an answer, but to my amazement, Dorothie replied, "You just did it."

My immediate reaction was confusion and disbelief. What had I done to make her feel heard?

DOROTHIE: Initially, my response surprised me every bit as much as it did Marty. I had thought I wanted him to hear whatever I'd been saying about the source of the argument—the thing both of us have since forgotten. But what I really wanted was for him to stop denying my reality. I didn't need him to agree with me since I, too, can be wrong. But I needed him to be open to what I was saying and feeling. I needed him to have compassion for my point of view. I needed him to "get curious, not furious."

MARTY: After a moment of disbelief that such a small shift could have cracked this seemingly uncrackable nut, I realized the genius of what Dorothie had just said. As long as I told her that she was wrong about not feeling heard, I might be hearing the words coming from her mouth, but I was not listening to the deeper message coming from her soul. I really was not listening.

DOROTHIE: What you just said highlights another important point in the resolution of this argument. I had said, "You're not listening," but what I really meant was, "I don't feel heard." In a way, you were right. You were listening to my words. But as you just pointed out, you were deaf to the deeper message coming from my soul. Thanks for translating for me.

Now that I finally felt heard, the original argument evaporated, and an important moment in our journey was born. It's a lesson from which we've both benefited immensely because I also had to be open to what Marty was saying and feeling. Before, when I was feeling unheard, I was so focused on my own pain that *he* felt unheard. When he finally dropped his insistence that he was listening (which I knew he wasn't), I could become more open to his perspective, as well.

Asking questions when you don't understand your mate and really listening to one another is key to creating a successful relationship. In our old maps, we thought we were listening if we heard one another's words. In the new map we were piecing together, listening involved far more than just hearing words. It required being open to new ideas that, at first, might seem crazy since they came from outside our existing frames of reference. Sometimes, we would cooperatively decide that the new idea was, in fact, crazy. But that was a joint decision, not an imposed ultimatum.

MARTY: And sometimes the seemingly crazy idea turns out to be brilliant. Ironically, I'd known that in my technical work, but had failed to see its applicability to my personal life.

When I first started working in cryptography, my colleagues all told me I was crazy. They pointed out that the National Security Agency (NSA) had a head start measured in decades, as well as a huge budget. How could I hope to discover something they didn't already know? And, my colleagues continued, if I did anything good, NSA would classify it.

Both arguments had validity and both later came back to haunt me. But the success of that work shows that sometimes it's wise to be foolish. (The later section on "The Wisdom of Foolishness" has more examples.)

DOROTHIE: There's another important difference between our old and new maps. Before we made that shift, we believed we had to fight to get what we wanted into the final agreement—if we ever reached agreement. In our new maps, the ultimate destination is to find a solution that meets both our needs. It takes patience to find what, at first, seems impossible—but our experiences show that it can be done.

MARTY: In our old approach to disagreements, each of us was so busy thinking of counter-arguments, while the other was speaking, that we could not really hear one another. That led to a counterproductive feedback loop in which each of us felt unheard and became ever more frustrated.

DOROTHIE: Another good example of the need to hear what the other person is saying occurred when we were in marriage counseling with Sheldon Starr. Marty was describing an incident in which I had done something that hurt him. His description was so different from my experience that I got hurt and I objected. I was *not* the witch I felt he was describing! Of course, my cutting him off only added to his pain. Fortunately, Sheldon stepped in and suggested that, instead of objecting to Marty's perspective on what had happened, maybe I could say, "That must feel terrible."

That honored Marty's feelings without violating my own sense of what had happened. I did that, and it worked. More magic.

That was such a powerful experience that we've decided, "That must feel terrible," may be one of the most valuable sentences in a marriage. At least, it became that important in ours. Once both people feel honored in their experience—even if they don't fully agree—a resolution of the underlying conflict can begin.

MARTY: The same problem exists at the international level, exacting a heavy toll in blood and misery.

The current civil war in Syria provides an example. The United States feels that Russia is deaf to our concerns about Bashar al-Assad killing his own people. In 2012, while still Secretary of State, Hillary Clinton summarized that American perspective when she decried Russia's and China's refusal to allow a UN Security Council Resolution condemning Assad's actions as "just despicable."[16] Secretary Clinton was right about needing to stop the bloodshed, but calling Russia "despicable" was no more helpful in accomplishing that than my telling Dorothie I was listening when she knew I wasn't. Just as my asking Dorothie how she knew I was not listening created a crack in her dam of resentment, we need to get curious—not furious—about why Russia has been unwilling to allow a UN Security Council Resolution.

Much of Russia's resistance to condemning the violence in Syria can be traced to what happened after it allowed a sequence of UN Security Council resolutions condemning the violence in Libya. Russia sees the West as having wrongly used those resolutions as the basis for a regime change that ended in Gadaffi's murder.

When Dmitry Medvedev, who was president of Russia at the time Hillary Clinton called his nation despicable, was asked whether Russia's experience with Libya was influencing its position on Syria, he replied:

Of course, this is influencing our position. ... When the resolution on Libya was adopted, we thought our countries would hold consultations and talks and at the same time we would send a serious signal to the Libyan leader. But unfortunately it ended up the way it did. [The West] kept telling us there would be no military operation, no intervention, but eventually they started a full-blown war that claimed many lives. ... So, what happened with Libya has definitely affected my position and continues influencing Russia's position on the Syrian conflict.[17]

There is much more that could be said about the differing perspectives that the United States and Russia have on Libya and Syria, but the important point here is that both sides are talking past one another, just as Dorothie and I used to do. Each side needs to become more curious about the other's perspective if we are to avoid needless bloodshed.

DOROTHIE: Getting curious, not furious; learning how to really hear the other person; and not denying their experience of reality are some of the most important lessons we've learned in our marriage. They are also some of the most important things the nations of the world need to learn.

Mountain or Molehill?

MARTY: The last story, about Dorothie's feeling unheard while I insisted that I was listening, is ironic because, five years later, an almost mirror-image incident occurred with my father. But this time, I was the one not feeling heard and he was the one who needed to be curious instead of furious.

I had flown in from California to visit my father and my brother's family in New York. One evening, I took my then twenty-four-year-old niece to dinner. When I returned to my father's house for the night, he commented that she shouldn't use so much hair spray, because it didn't feel nice to touch.

As casually as possible, I told my father that it would be better not to touch her hair. She wasn't a little girl any more. I was careful about saying this because, while I knew that all his granddaughters preferred not being treated that way, he hadn't a clue. He was likely to go ballistic at what I'd said.

He started by denying what I knew to be true: "Ah, they like it."

I knew that wasn't the case because I had been told the exact opposite by my niece at dinner, as well as many times before both by her and my own daughters. But, at my niece's and daughters' requests, I had kept that information in confidence so that I wouldn't hurt their relationship with their grandfather.

I told my father that, while he might think they liked him to touch their hair—and although his granddaughters loved him too much to tell him otherwise—they actually preferred that he not touch their hair.

Now he did go ballistic. He came out with guns blazing: "How do you know? Who told you that? Who's talking behind my back?"

I told him that it didn't matter how I knew, but that I was sure. That led him to put away his blazing handguns and bring out the heavy artillery: "Are you calling me a dirty old man?"

Careful not to fall into the trap he had just set for me, I tried to bring the issue back to a more reasonable place and focus on dealing with the unwanted hair touching.

Unable to get me to back down on that issue, he next accused me of being disrespectful. To him, respect meant agreeing with one's elders even when they were wrong—but to me, a false agreement seemed disrespectful, because it assumed they were incapable of dealing with reality. As gently as possible, I tried telling him this.

In the first hours of that battle, he tried several tactics to get me to back down. First, he puffed himself up with anger. His temper used to terrify me when I was a small child and he held the power of life and death over me. But I'd worked through enough childhood traumas that I didn't fall into that trap. At this point in our lives, I was fifty and my father eighty-seven, so he wasn't a physical threat to me.

Then he threw a tantrum. Years before, he had tried this tactic, and it had worked; during one argument, he had actually lain down on the lawn and beat it with his fists. I went over and patted his back until he stopped. But I learned my lesson and I wouldn't repeat that mistake. If he was going to throw a tantrum now, I thought, let him. He'd snap out of it eventually.

Finally, he tried his ace in the hole. "I'm not a young man. You're going to give me apoplexy and kill me!"

This one was new, but I vowed silently that even this would not force me to agree that black was white.

After all these unsuccessful attempts to get me to agree that the girls—now young women—liked his touching their hair, my father retreated to saying that I was making a mountain out of a molehill. He suggested we just let the whole thing drop. I tried to tell him something like this, although it probably was broken into pieces as he objected to various parts:

Dad, I understand that my concern seems like a molehill to you. But you're right that, to me, it looks like a mountain.

I also understand that what I'm saying makes no sense to you. That's because five years ago, I was on the other side of a similar argument with Dorothie. She kept telling me that I wasn't listening, even though I was sure that I'd heard every word she had said. Initially, what she was saying made no sense to me—but eventually, by asking the right questions, I came to see that she had a valid perspective.

Having been in your shoes, I can relate to your frustration and confusion. But I had to drop my resistance before Dorothie's position made any sense to me, and for what I'm saying to make any sense to you, you need to be interested in why your molehill seems like a mountain to me. You need to stop telling me I'm wrong and start asking me more questions.

Whenever you're ready to do that, let me know. But I'm not willing to continue our relationship on the old basis that it's been on for too long. I want to be able to talk to you about more than the weather. I love you, and I want us to have a deeper relationship than that.

My father's reply to that last part was telling, "It's better not to go too deep. It can get dangerous down there." In the world in which he grew up, that was true. Unfortunately, it's still true for far too many people. But I was sure my father and I could do better, although I had no idea how we would get there. I did know that I couldn't agree when he was flat-out wrong on something this important.

Our argument erupted just one day before I had to return home to California, and our impasse continued to the very end of my visit. I had to leave with my father still mad at me, which was hard.

Over the next several months, I tried different things to break the ice. Then Dorothie suggested that I write him a letter telling him how I felt—not that he was wrong, just how I felt. I tried telling him how sad it made me that we still were at odds, and how much I wanted a real relationship with him. I said that, although I knew it didn't feel that way to him right then, I loved him deeply.

A few days later, we came home to find a message on the answering machine. In a voice dripping with sarcasm, my father told me, "You poor little boy. You're sooo sad. Grow up and be a man!"

Dorothie and I agreed that it was best not to reply, so I just let it go. I was beginning to wonder if this argument would ever resolve itself. Then, less than a week after that answering machine message, my father called again. This time, I was home. I picked up the phone and heard my father say words that even now, twenty years later, make me misty: "I'm sorry. How could I have been so stupid? I love you and don't want to hurt you. What do I need to do?"

I told him the same thing Dorothie had told me five years earlier: "You just did it."

Our argument over his touching his granddaughters' hair was more important than whatever Dorothie and I had been arguing about and cannot now remember. But, as with Dorothie and me, the first step in resolving the underlying conflict was not to deny the reality of the other's experience. My father did that when he asked, "What do I need to do?"

He told me that he'd be more respectful of his granddaughters' wishes, and he treated them differently for those last eleven years of his life. Not only did he become more respectful of them during that time, but he and I had a relationship for which I'll be eternally grateful. It wasn't just the inappropriate hair touching that we could deal with in a new way. Issue after issue came up. While those things used to throw me for a loop, it now felt like I was surfing a monster wave. What a ride!

Several things had changed in our relationship to make that possible. My actions had made it clear to my father that I was no longer willing to play the role of a small boy over whom he held the power of life and death. Perhaps even more importantly, my actions had shown him that I was not out to have power over him. Instead, just as in my relationship with Dorothie, I was committed to finding a solution that worked for both of us—a holistic solution.

As an example of my "surfing the wave," one of my father's favorite verbal traps was to tell me or my brothers, "The parent is successful when the child is more successful than the parent." How do you respond to that? Any answer feels inappropriate.

Because of our new relationship, I just smiled and teased, "Well then, Dad, you must be a very successful parent." He would smile back, usually laughing—this happened more than once—and tell me, "You don't let me get away with anything!" To which I replied (truthfully), "You're right." More good-hearted laughter from my father.

My father had a reputation as being a bit cantankerous. But when I remember him, what comes first to my mind is the phone call that ended our argument.

Yes, he could be cantankerous. But when nothing else worked to restore our relationship, he loved me enough to do what must have seemed insane to him. And he did that at eighty-seven years of age. Who says you can't teach an old dog new tricks? No, change that to, "Who says an old dog can't learn new tricks?" Because no one can teach someone else anything they don't want to learn.

So Dad, if you can hear me, please know how much I appreciate what you did. It was the best gift a son could ever ask for.

MARTY: This story reinforces several important points. First, and reflecting the title of this chapter, it demonstrates the value of "get curious, not furious." My father initially got furious with me, but he was able to resolve the conflict merely by asking what I wanted him to do. Second, it shows the importance of having faith that a solution will be found when compassion is brought to bear on the problem. I didn't know how my father and I would resolve this conflict, but I had faith that, somehow, we would.

If, during the conflict, a voice had boomed out of the heavens and asked me to write a script for how I'd like it to end, I'd never have come up with as good an ending. But by treating my father with love and compassion instead of anger, and remembering how I had been in his shoes five years earlier when Dorothie told me I wasn't listening, a miracle occurred. The third point this story emphasizes is the importance of having patience. If I'd pushed my father to resolve the conflict before he was ready, it would not have ended the way it did. I had to wait three months for him to come around.

Patience is a Virtue

In the last section, we described a three-month-long conflict that Marty had with his father that had a miraculous ending as a result of his having the patience to ride it out. This section tells the story of Dorothie's twenty-fifth anniversary ring. Patience also proved critical to successfully resolving this conflict, which occurred in 1992, several years earlier than the last story.

But before we jump to our twenty-fifth anniversary, it helps to know how we decided to get married in the first place.

MARTY: When I met Dorothie in June 1966, just after graduating from college, I had decided that marriage was for idiots—at least at that point in my life. I had lived with my parents while commuting to New York University to earn my bachelor's degree and finally had a place of my own in Los Angeles, where I was working for the summer. Now I could operate. After playing the field for ten or fifteen years, there would be plenty of time to settle down. But not now.

DOROTHIE: Almost as soon as I met him, Marty told me that he wasn't going to get married for at least another fifteen years. I thought he protested too much. Also, I'm very intuitive, and I somehow knew from that first day that this was the man I was going to marry. It wasn't so much, "I want to marry him" as just knowing that it was to be. But I was smitten, so my intuitive insight was not unwelcome.

MARTY: I had fallen hard, too, but was so out of touch with my feelings at that point in my life that I was unaware of what was going on inside me—at least on a conscious level. But something was clearly going on, as you'll soon see.

When the summer was over, Dorothie left Los Angeles for her freshman year at the University of California at Santa Barbara, and I started my graduate work at Stanford. Being three hundred miles apart was really hard. After a week or two, I called and asked if I could pay her a visit.

DOROTHIE: I jumped at the possibility of being together again, and Marty drove down that weekend. Sunday, as we ate lunch at a Taco Bell, Marty casually asked me, "What would you think about getting married this summer?" Just as casually, I replied, "Sure."

Then, we looked at each other in some disbelief. Had we really just agreed to get married? A more serious discussion concluded that, in fact, we had. It may not have been the most romantic proposal ever, but it was fine by me.

MARTY: In my heart, I knew this was the woman I wanted to share my life with, but my head was still telling me that marriage was for idiots. Having just asked Dorothie if she would make me an idiot, my second question was, would she please not tell anyone?

I guess I wanted to keep my "idiot-hood" secret, at least a little while longer. I did relent slightly and agreed that she could tell her parents and sister.

My head and my heart were in different places, and fortunately, my heart won out. But it would take a while for me to resolve that inner battle. A couple of months later, I surprised Dorothie with a diamond engagement ring when I spent Thanksgiving with her and her family.

DOROTHIE: I wasn't the only one surprised by the ring. Everyone in my family, except my parents and sister, had been in the dark about our engagement, so Marty's coming out of the "idiot closet" (from his point of view) surprised everyone else. The family was happy at the news, but a bit startled.

MARTY: While I never would have admitted it at the time, and probably wasn't even aware of it at a conscious level, I missed Dorothie terribly. Early in January, I called her and asked what she would think about moving up the wedding from the summer to spring break. That way, we'd be together three months sooner.

DOROTHIE: That sounded great to me, and we were married in my parents' home on March 24, 1967. As you can tell from our whirlwind courtship—we knew each other only three months before getting engaged and only six more before our wedding—we were head over heels in love. But then life took over. Our "maps" were out of sync, and childhood traumas intruded on our relationship in ways we were unaware of and will discuss later.

Things got so bad that, if we hadn't started the process that got us to where we are today, we might well have ended up getting divorced. The wear and tear on our marriage was mirrored on my engagement ring, which got chipped. So, as our twenty-fifth anniversary approached in 1992, I told Marty I'd like a new diamond ring.

MARTY: I figured our budget could withstand a replacement diamond of about the same size. So I said, "Sure." But after Dorothie looked at rings for a while, she came back with a slightly sheepish look and said, with what I later learned was hyperbole, "I hate to admit it, but I want a big one."

DOROTHIE: I could tell that Marty was upset at this news. He'd be a lousy poker player, the way he telegraphs his angst.

MARTY: Earlier in our relationship, Dorothie probably would have let me have it. She could easily have said, "Don't be such a cheapskate. I've bought almost no jewelry in the twenty-five years we've been married, and you're always saying you can't figure out what to buy me. Well, I just told you!" And it all would have been true.

DOROTHIE: Fortunately, we had made enough progress that, instead of going ballistic, I calmly told Marty, "I don't know how we're going to work this out. But we're not going to do anything about the new ring until we can find a way that makes us both happy—no matter how long it takes."

MARTY: And she really meant it. Dorothie didn't have a shred of anger or frustration as she told me this. Somehow, she had faith that it would work out. And it did.

It took me about a month to realize that I'd never asked Dorothie what she meant by "a big one." When I did, it turned out that my fears had gotten the better of me. She wanted a larger diamond than I'd bought her when I was a semi-starving graduate student, but nothing outrageous. I could have kicked myself.

Dorothie's patience was crucial in this process. It gave me time to realize all of the things she could have told me when I first raised objections. But there's a huge difference between my realizing I was being ridiculous, and Dorothie telling me that in anger.

That ring, which Dorothie still wears, twenty-four years later, was a double gift. Of course, there is the beautiful ring itself. But even more of a gift was my realization that I needed to have faith in Dorothie and not jump to conclusions without first finding out what she means. That's a gift that keeps on giving. We've avoided many needless arguments because I learned that.

DOROTHIE: And I had to have faith in Marty, too. That's the only way I could have had the patience to wait for him to come to his senses. Marty's had faith in me, too, over the years, and it's made a huge difference in our relationship.

MARTY: Only after the conflict was resolved did I learn just how much faith Dorothie had to have. It was only then that she told me the ring she'd fallen in love with was a one-of-a-kind antique. I had assumed it was a solitaire, like the first one I'd given her. Fortunately, the antique ring was still in the store a month later when I came to my senses.

DOROTHIE: The theme of this section—"patience is a virtue"—reminds me of some advice my great-grandmother gave us soon after Marty and I were married: "Never go to bed mad." I loved my great-grandmother and had learned many valuable lessons from her. But on this point, she was wrong. When a couple is in the middle of a fight, trying to force your feelings into a box just doesn't work. You need to have patience.

I'm not saying that you should stay mad as long as you want. Just stay out of each other's way as long as is necessary to treat your partner with the love, respect, and compassion he or she deserves.

MARTY: As we noted earlier, Dorothie and I even made a rule about that. If one of us was afraid they were going to say something hurtful, they had not only the right, but the obligation, to leave the room. They also had the obligation to come back and help make things right when they'd cooled down.

DOROTHIE: Having patience—giving ourselves time to work things out—made us much more effective at resolving our conflicts. That's why we titled this installment, "Patience is a Virtue." We've already seen another example in which our therapist, Sheldon Starr, helped me realize that things were going too fast for me.

MARTY: Patience is also a virtue at the international level, with the Cuban Missile Crisis providing a great example. That incident was the closest the world has ever come to nuclear war, and the fact that President Kennedy was able to keep the Soviet Union's Cuban missiles secret for a week played a key role in avoiding catastrophe. It gave him and his advisors time to consider what to do without the pressure of the public and press demanding immediate action. Two months later, on December 17, 1962, in a television interview, he observed that "if we had to act on Wednesday in the first twenty-four hours, I don't think we would have chosen as prudently as we finally did."

When a group of Kennedy's advisors met, years after the crisis, one of them (George Ball) put it more bluntly:

Much to our own surprise, we reached the unanimous conclusion that, had we determined our course of action within the first forty-eight hours after the missiles were discovered, we would almost certainly have made the wrong decision, responding to the missiles in such a way as to require a forceful Soviet response and thus setting in train a series of reactions and counter-reactions with horrendous consequences.[18]

What Kennedy and Ball probably had in mind was that, early in the crisis, there was strong support for a surprise attack on the Soviets' Cuban missiles, to be followed by a massive American invasion of Cuba to remove "the communist cancer" from the Western Hemisphere once and for all. Only decades later did we learn that the Soviets had battlefield nuclear weapons on the island for repelling just such an invasion.

DOROTHIE: Too many couples and too many nations fail to take time to calm down and think things through before taking risky actions. At an individual level, the worst that usually happens is a divorce. At an international level, it literally could be "the end of the world."

Making Decisions With the New Map

A disagreement that we had a couple of years ago illustrates that far better decisions can be made with the new map by getting curious instead of furious. It also shows how a holistic approach to conflict resolution usually produces solutions that are better for both of us than what we each thought we wanted going into the conflict.

DOROTHIE: When Marty brought one of our cars to the local service station the owner told him that, if we ever wanted to sell the car, he would love to buy it for his wife. We weren't in the market for a new car, so Marty mentioned this to me in an offhand way when he got home.

MARTY: So imagine my surprise when Dorothie started looking at new cars. We usually keep cars for at least ten years, and the car in question was not much over six years old. It ran perfectly, so Dorothie's actions made no sense to me. You don't buy a new car just because someone wants to buy your old one!

Fortunately, I'd learned to "get curious, not furious." So I told Dorothie that, while her behavior seemed crazy to me, I must be missing something. What was it? She then reminded me that our other car had a backup camera and blind spot warning that this one did not have, and she told me those safety features made her feel much more comfortable driving. Anyone might appreciate features like that, but Dorothie's migraines and the meds she takes for them make her more cautious about driving than usual. The new cars she was looking at had even more safety features that would make her feel comfortable about driving more places, increasing her independence.

As soon as she explained that to me, I could see the limitations of my former perspective. I had thought that we had two perfectly good cars, so why buy a new one? But while our cars were mechanically perfect, they—and especially the car in question—were far from perfect for our needs.

That was true not only for Dorothie, but for me, too. I had just turned sixty-nine. I'd commented several times on how much I was hoping that self-driving cars would come on the market before I had to give up driving. But that seemed to be years in the future from the perspective of both availability and our needs. I hadn't thought in terms of an intermediate step, then available in some cars.

DOROTHIE: After a bit of research, we decided on the safety features that we wanted. Not many cars had them, and some versions weren't as good as others. The car I found that best met our needs was a Mercedes. At first, the idea of buying a luxury car was a barrier. We'd never spent that much on a car, and it felt uncomfortable. But once I got over that internal barrier and allowed myself to pick the car we needed, I surprised myself by liking the idea of owning a Mercedes. I suppose everyone has a bit of that hidden somewhere in their psyche.

MARTY: I love bargains, so I had even more of an issue with buying a Mercedes. But I had to agree that Dorothie's research indicated it was the right car for our needs. Then I read a review of the Mercedes that mentioned the 2015 Hyundai Genesis as a worthy competitor. I looked into the Genesis, and it seemed to be an even better car for our needs. Its collision avoidance system was rated one step above the Mercedes. It also had a "head-up display" that creates the illusion of key information being projected about ten feet in front of the windshield, so you didn't have to take your eyes off the road to see that data. This feature was on no other car we were considering.

There was an added plus for my bargain-loving brain. The Hyundai Genesis was thousands of dollars less than the Mercedes. But I love bargains so much that, sometimes, I'm penny wise and pound foolish. When I told Dorothie about the Genesis, I asked her to make sure I wasn't fooling myself about it being the safer car, which after all, was the reason we were buying a new car.

DOROTHIE: As I've already mentioned, after getting over my angst at becoming a Mercedes owner, I had come to like the idea. So this Hyundai Genesis didn't excite me at first. But, as I looked at the features, I had to agree that it was the better car for our needs. We bought one, and I love it.

MARTY: In analyzing how I handled this conflict, I found it startling that, initially, I *felt* like Dorothie's looking at new cars was crazy, even though I *knew* from prior experience that could not be the case. She is far from crazy. Only after she explained the logic of her actions did that feeling go away. Earlier in our marriage, before I learned the value of being introspective and open, that feeling would have overwhelmed me and led to an argument. Feelings have a logic of their own that cannot be denied, but they must be tempered with reason.

That same problem—letting strong feelings overpower our ability to reason things out—affects many other people and society as a whole. At a societal level, the "drumbeat to war" is an excellent (meaning horrible) example. Not asking enough questions and letting ourselves be carried away by feelings of anger, got us into needless wars in Vietnam and Iraq—and could do the same with Iran, North Korea, or Russia today.

DOROTHIE: Returning to the more positive example of resolving our conflict over the new car, it's also important to recognize that each of us got more out of that resolution process than we had thought we wanted going in.

MARTY: Initially, I wanted Dorothie to stop looking at new cars. Now I thank her repeatedly, because this car makes driving so much more relaxing for me. If I look down at the radio and the driver of the car in front suddenly hits his brakes, the adaptive cruise control will automatically apply my brakes to maintain a safe distance. That hasn't happened yet, but it takes a load off my mind to know this safety feature is there.

DOROTHIE: And I love the head-up display, which is something I wouldn't have had on the Mercedes. We each got more than we thought we wanted.

MARTY: The same was true with our disagreement over Dorothie's twenty-fifth anniversary ring, described in the last section. Going into the conflict, I thought I wanted her to get a smaller diamond. It's true that the ring we got cost more than I'd originally budgeted—but in the grand scheme of things, it had no real effect on our finances. The successful resolution of that conflict was worth far more than the ring's extra cost. We both learned to trust the new map, and we even discovered new paths on it that we didn't know existed. I also earned additional love and respect from Dorothie because of how I eventually handled the conflict.

DOROTHIE: And I got far more than the ring. Marty's learning to ask questions when I seem to be doing something crazy is a far more valuable gift, and it keeps paying dividends year after year.

Acting holistically—doing what's right for the whole instead of what you thought you wanted to do—really does work miracles. Surprisingly, the Rolling Stones said it in their 1969 song, "You Can't Always Get What You Want," which concludes that, if you look carefully, "You just might find you get what you need."

Chapter 4

The Power of Belief Systems

"They did not know it was impossible
so they did it."
—*Mark Twain*

As we've discovered during more than thirty years of working this process, we each had a vast store of untapped capacity for love and "right-living." But societal belief systems that we had adopted as our own prevented us from tapping into that potential. To follow a new map for our relationship, first we had to become open to a new belief system. We had to believe that true love at home and peace on the planet might, in fact, be possible. Overcoming outmoded belief systems was one of the most important steps in saving our relationship. It also is key to saving the world.

Inconceivable Does Not Mean Impossible

The words *inconceivable* and *impossible* are used interchangeably by many people. But, as the dictionary shows, inconceivable merely means *unbelievable*, not *impossible*.

DOROTHIE: If you've ever stormed out of the car in a rage, as I did in the first section of this book, it may seem inconceivable that you can recapture the bliss you felt when you first fell in love. But I can tell you from personal experience that it is possible to get there, if you will do the hard work that's required. But first you have to believe it's possible.

Something that happened recently shows how hard it is for people to entertain that possibility. I was talking with a new friend who marveled at how tenderly Marty treated me. Alice (not her real name) asked me, "Where do you find men like that?" I replied, "You don't find them. They evolve." To which Alice responded definitively, "People don't change!"

Here she was, confronted with living proof that her last statement was not true. But her existing belief system—her old map—told her this was impossible. She resolved her conflict by denying my experience. In doing so, she robbed herself of possibly achieving this kind of happiness herself, even though it was something she clearly craved.

MARTY: You have to be courageous enough to break with the conventional wisdom and believe in the seemingly impossible. For the longest time, I didn't, and that added to our conflicts. I remember telling Dorothie time and time again, "What do you want from me? I've done more than any husband I know, and you want more!"

What Dorothie wanted seemed impossible, but her vision was really only *inconceivable* for me at that point in time. I had never experienced a relationship in which disagreements were truly resolved. In my family of origin, when the fighting stopped, at least one, and often both, of my parents went off feeling beaten down. Yet here we are, married for forty-nine years (as of March 2016) with no anger between us in more than a decade. I thank Dorothie constantly for believing I was a better man than I thought I was.

DOROTHIE: What Marty just said highlights another very important point. Not only do most people, like Alice, believe that others are incapable of radical change. They also believe that they, themselves, can't make that kind of change. But they could, if they would question their existing belief system.

Sometimes, people recognize their own shortcomings, but their belief system sees those faults as an unchangeable part of human nature. Time and time again, they've seen people respond in anger or some other ineffective way. Rarely, if ever, have they seen truly mature behavior in emotionally-charged conflicts. So it's understandable that they believe they are incapable of great change. It's understandable, but regrettable, because it prevents them from getting out of needless pain and becoming the best that they can be.

Their life experiences have taught them—incorrectly—that when their desires are thwarted, they will become frustrated and angry. If those emotions don't work, they might even become threatening and belligerent. That belief is so ingrained that they usually do not even see it as a belief. They consider it just part of life.

It took both of us a long time to recognize the error of that conviction. In both our families of origin, and in almost all of our other interactions, frustration, anger, and belligerence were modeled as the natural consequence of not getting one's way. But some thought will show that reacting that way rarely, if ever, produces the desired result.

Another barrier to people making radical, positive changes in their lives is when they want so much to be good that they cannot face their faults. They believe that being human is not acceptable, so they hide their humanity, often even from their own conscious minds. Paradoxically, that belief consigns them continually to mistreat people.

My deep-seated fear of making mistakes created a problem of this nature in our relationship. Often, when Marty said he wanted to talk with me about something, my immediate reaction was to ask him, "What did I do wrong?" Most of the time, he wanted to talk about something totally different. Sometimes, he even wanted to tell me how much he loved me. With a great deal of personal work on my part, and patience and love on Marty's, I'm largely over believing (and worrying) deep down that I am a bad person. I'm not completely convinced yet. It is a process.

A related problem at a national level is that valid criticism of one's own nation is often seen as unpatriotic.

Most people would say they want a more peaceful world, but they see that as inconceivable. Believing that change is impossible is one of the biggest impediments to creating the kind of world we yearn for. I can't count how often people have told me, "War is a part of human nature, and you can't change human nature."

Yet the changes we've implemented in our relationship that allowed us to avoid needless arguments are the same ones the nations of the world need to make to avoid getting into needless wars.

MARTY: That concept of "needless wars" is an important one. Even people who believe that peace is impossible would agree that we should avoid needless wars. They're too expensive in blood, treasure, and international prestige—plus each needless war entails needless nuclear risk, since every war has some chance of escalating out of control. As we will document later in this book, a good case can be made that every war our country has gotten into in recent years was needless.

The frequency with which we've stumbled into needless wars may make things seem hopeless, but there are hopeful signs as well. The world's nuclear arsenal has fallen by more than a factor of four since the peak of the arms race: from more than 70,000 weapons to roughly 16,000. We still have a long way to go, but we are making progress.

There's also evidence that the world is getting much more peaceful. Several years ago, two books came out within months of one another that argue that war is going out of style. When I first read Joshua Goldstein's *Winning the War on War* and Steven Pinker's *The Better Angels of Our Nature*, I was tempted to discount their data. But I had to reconsider because the data came from a highly respected source and seemed undeniable.

During the Cold War, battle deaths averaged around 200,000 per year. In the 1990s, the first decade after the Cold War ended, they dropped to about 100,000 each year. And in the first decade of this century, they decreased to 55,000 per year. In spite of the

Syrian civil war pushing 2014's death toll back to 100,000, 2011's battle death toll of only 25,000 provides hope that the world will continue its trend to becoming increasingly less warlike.[19]

Sticking to ten-year averages, which smooth out such variations, both the number of nuclear weapons and the number of people killed by war each year has fallen by about a factor of four. If we keep up those trends—even better, if we accelerate them—we'll have a world we can be proud to pass on to future generations.

Borrowing from the titles of those two books, I sometimes say that—contrary to popular belief and the perception you get from the news—the better angels of our nature are, in fact, winning the war on war.

But I also point out that there's another entrant in that race, who is almost invisible to most people: the nuclear threat. He's running in the shadows, where almost no one is aware of him, hoping to trip up the better angels of our nature before they make it to the finish line and win the war on war. If he can do that, he then will leap ahead and win the race by destroying civilization.

If we can shine a spotlight on the nuclear threat and get people to realize that avoiding war is not just desirable, but necessary for our survival, a more peaceful world would become conceivable. That would give an adrenalin shot to our better angels and increase the odds that they will win the war on war.

You Can't Change Human Nature

DOROTHIE: People who think we're on a fool's errand often phrase their objection as, "You can't change human nature!" Since that's such a powerful belief system and a huge impediment to tearing up our old maps, let's explore it in more detail.

MARTY: We can't change human nature, *but it is human nature to change.* Adaptability is our species' hallmark characteristic. Through adaptations of clothing and shelter, we have extended our range from a small, tropical region to the entire globe. Through other adaptations, we have learned to fly higher than birds, outswim fish, and even walk on the Moon.

Another hopeful perspective on human adaptability was expressed by the late Prof. Yuri Zamoshkin of the Soviet Academy of Sciences' Institute on USA and Canada, in a book I co-edited in 1987:[20]

In the philosophy of twentieth-century German and French existentialists (notably K. Jaspers), the term grenzsituation *(border situation) has been used to designate an experience in which an individual comes face-to-face with the real possibility of death. Death is no longer merely an abstract thought, but a distinct possibility. Life and death hang in the balance.*

Different human beings respond to the grenzsituation *in different ways. Some become passive and put their heads on the chopping block, so to speak. Others experience something akin to a revelation and find themselves capable of feats they never before would have thought possible. In a* grenzsituation, *some timid individuals have become heroes; some selfish individuals have become Schweitzers. And sometimes, in so transcending their normal personalities, they cheat the grim reaper and survive where normally they would not.*

Until now, this notion has been applied only to individuals. But I am convinced that today it can be purposefully applied to the world as a whole. The present day global grenzsituation *resides in the possibility for global death and global life.*

This situation, for the first time in history, directly, practically, and not purely speculatively, confronts human thought with the possibility of death for the entire human race. The continuity of history, which earlier had seemed to be a given, suddenly becomes highly questionable.

As with the individual, this global grenzsituation *may contribute to a "revelation" in human thinking and to a positive change of character previously thought impossible for our species. ...*

Of course there is also the possibility that, faced with a grenzsituation, *mankind will go passive and put its collective head on the nuclear chopping block. But before we can learn our true mettle, we must bring the global* grenzsituation *into clear focus for all humanity. Society must see that it has but two possibilities, global life or global death.*

As Zamoshkin concludes so eloquently, the first key step in solving global challenges is to bring their existential risk into clear focus. Only after that has been accomplished can we learn whether human nature will succumb to those challenges or triumph over them.

Some people see adaptability as fundamental to human nature, even as others object to our goal by continuing to say, "You can't change human nature." Because of that, I was excited when the Stanford alumni magazine highlighted research of Prof. Carol Dweck in our Psychology Department that provided an explanation for those differing worldviews.[21]

Dweck studied how people respond when confronted with a challenge that exceeds their current abilities. She found that some people rise to the challenge, even though that might mean failing, while others shy away, fearful of being found wanting. Her research showed that much of this difference can be attributed to people having one of two mindsets. People with a *fixed mindset* see ability as something you are born with that cannot change. Others have a *growth mindset* that sees ability more like a muscle that can be developed by exercise and hard work.

Dweck found that people with the fixed mindset have a strong tendency to shy away from challenges that are above their current ability, since—according to their world view—trying would lead to failure. Conversely, she has found that people with the growth mindset tend to welcome such challenges as opportunities to learn.

She also found that it is possible to shift people's mindsets and change their response to new challenges. In one experiment, subjects read an article about geniuses such as Mozart and Einstein. Without their knowing it, the subjects were divided into two groups and given slightly different versions of the same article. One group's article emphasized the growth mindset by pointing to the hard work these men had undertaken to realize their potential. Einstein, for example, had struggled in school. The other group's article emphasized how Mozart was a child prodigy, reinforcing the fixed mindset that genius is born, not made.

Unaware of that different conditioning, subjects in both groups were given a test based on their reading and then offered an opportunity to take a tutorial to improve their test performance. Of those who scored lowest on the test—those who most needed the tutorial help—73 percent of the group that had read the growth mindset article took advantage of the opportunity, while only 13 percent of the other group did.[22] Reading an article that reflected the growth mindset got 60 percent more people who needed help to seek it.

This research, which dealt with an individual's mindset about his or her own abilities, has clear implications for improving personal relationships far beyond what most people think is possible. Encouraging people to believe they are capable of great change makes them more likely to tear up their old relationship maps, piece together a new one, and create true love at home. We hope this book provides that kind of encouragement.

Later research by Dweck's group extends that idea to societal change and implies that we are more likely to create peace on the planet if we believe humanity is capable of such change—the opposite of those who say, "You can't change human nature."

In one experiment,[23] Jewish Israeli test subjects were given what they thought was a reading comprehension test on an article about aggressive tendencies in groups in general. The article didn't specifically mention either Israelis or Palestinians. Again there were two versions of the article, with only minor wording changes. One version depicted groups as capable of change, for example when leadership changed. The other version depicted groups as unlikely to change.

Dweck notes that the researchers "found that simply reading an article that depicted groups in general as malleable ... led to more favorable attitudes toward Palestinians than did reading an article that depicted groups as having a more fixed nature." The researchers also found that "these more favorable attitudes went on to predict substantially greater willingness to make major compromises for peace." The same was found to be true for Palestinians who were test subjects in a similar experiment.

These results imply that, if someone believes "You can't change human nature," then bringing up global challenges, such as global warming and nuclear weapons, will tend to fall on deaf ears.

I had been hearing people say, "You can't change human nature!" for twenty-five years before I came across Dweck's research, and after I did, it gave that response a new context. People who claimed societal change was impossible were more likely to hold the fixed mindset, while those who believed we can successfully meet global challenges were more likely to hold the growth mindset.

This realization, coupled with the experiments on influencing mindset, highlighted the need to pose the challenges we face in a way that emphasizes both our individual and societal capacity for change. While we had been doing that at an intuitive level for years, Dweck's research brought the need into clearer focus.

Something I learned from another Stanford professor, the late Harry Rathbun, is also highly relevant to the question of whether human beings are capable of radical change. Harry often asked what harm there was in assuming what he called "the nobler hypothesis." Either we are capable of the great changes needed to make our relationships work and to ensure humanity's survival in the nuclear age—that's the nobler hypothesis—or we are not.

Harry pointed out that if we assume the less noble hypothesis, we have no chance of success, even if we really did have the capacity to change. But if we assume the nobler hypothesis, the worst that happens is we go down fighting, rather than meekly putting our heads on the nuclear chopping block.

"Why not assume the nobler hypothesis?" he concluded. It made sense to me then, and it still does today.

Plato's Allegory of the Cave

We feel as if we've been through what Plato described in his "Allegory of the Cave," a story that helps illuminate why belief systems can make this journey feel so scary at first. Plato describes how his teacher Socrates tried to show humanity its unenlightened state. Socrates tells his listener to imagine a tribe imprisoned in a deep cave. The members of the tribe are chained so they cannot move and can only look into the cave, away from its mouth. Behind them, a fire blazes, throwing its light on a wall, which is all the light the prisoners can see.

Other people walk behind the prisoners carrying statues of animals and other objects. Because of their constricting chains, the prisoners cannot see either these people or the objects they carry. All they can see are the shadows the objects cast on the wall in front of them.

Socrates argues that, in such an environment and never having experienced anything real, the prisoners naturally would confuse the shadows with the objects they represent. They would invent elaborate games and give honors to those in the tribe who were quickest to recognize each shadow.

Next, Socrates asks what would happen if the prisoners were to be freed from their chains. Those who turn around and face the fire and the distant mouth of the cave, where sunlight can be dimly discerned, would suffer temporary blindness because their eyes were accustomed to the deep darkness.

If one member of the tribe should venture further and actually exit the cave, initially, he would be totally blinded by the bright daylight. But if he stayed outside long enough, his eyes would adjust, and he would realize that there was much more to life than mere shadows. He would see depth and color. It would be better than the wildest imaginings of his former existence.

Socrates then describes what would happen if this member of the tribe should descend back into the cave and attempt to free his clansmen from their limited view of the world. His eyes would no longer be accustomed to the dark, and he would fail miserably at the games the tribe played. He would now appear blind to them. Socrates concludes that the members of the tribe would rule that if anyone proposed further such foolishness, "let them only catch the offender, and they would put him to death."[24]

Socrates was, in fact, put to death for "corrupting the youth of Athens" with such philosophy.

DOROTHIE: For me, there's another metaphor. While we were going through this transformation process, I felt so much like a fish out of water that I actually went out and bought a bronze statue of a fish to remind me of the state I was in. Sometimes, looking at the statue gave me the courage I needed when I felt like I was gasping for air while we figured things out.

MARTY: Returning to Plato's "Allegory of the Cave," it perfectly describes how I felt when I first opened up to the idea that my old map wasn't working. It took a long time for us to piece together the new map, and at first, some really smart things looked dumb—just like the member of Socrates' tribe who was initially dazed and knocked off balance when blinded by the sun's light.

That's how I felt during what I call my "*Last Epidemic* experience." This took place in 1983, when we were only a few years into this process.

We were working in a group called Beyond War, which had grown out of Creative Initiative. One way the group worked was for people like us, who were already involved, to invite friends into their homes for a "Beyond War Orientation." We'd show a video and then have a discussion about the need for a new mode of thinking about national security in the nuclear age—what we're now calling holistic thinking.

There was a popular half-hour video called *The Last Epidemic*, produced by a group of concerned physicians who later won the 1985 Nobel Peace Prize. That video felt like a propaganda piece to me, so there was no way I would use it. Maybe it worked for the general population, but not for people like me. And most of the people we invited to these orientations were other Stanford professors—people like me.

I had been deeply impacted by another video, *The Day After Trinity*, but it was ninety minutes long. Watching it with the group would leave almost no time for people to integrate their experience in a follow-up discussion. Dorothie kept encouraging me to use *The Last Epidemic* instead, and I kept saying, "No way." Finally, she pulled out the ace she keeps up her sleeve: "Why don't you try it as an experiment?"

Being unwilling to try an experiment would seem really closed-minded, and that's not something any scientist or engineer wants to admit to. So I said, "Okay. But just once."

The night we did "the experiment," our audience included Bill Kays, the Dean of Engineering, and several other powerful colleagues.

This was not the group I wanted to embarrass myself in front of! As each of *The Last Epidemic*'s thirty minutes slowly ticked by, I died thirty deaths. The video was even worse than I remembered it. Why had I let Dorothie talk me into this stupid experiment?

When the video finally ended and I turned off the TV, there was dead silence for what seemed like an eternity. I was so certain that my colleagues were quiet only because they were trying to figure out how to ask me why I'd wasted their time with such a propaganda piece that I nearly broke the silence to say, "Look, I know the movie has its faults. But there are some valid points, too!" Thank God I didn't say that.

Bill Kays was the first to comment: "We've got to do something, even if it's unilateral. This is too dangerous!"[25]

I was floored. I couldn't believe my ears. As we went around the room, my surprise was compounded. The silence had been because people were impacted, not offended. Person after person spoke positively about this movie, which just minutes earlier I had been so certain had offended them that I nearly broke the silence with an apology.

When Dorothie and I were alone later that night, I was hit by the full impact of what had transpired. For the first time in my life, I realized I could be 100 percent certain of something and be 100 percent wrong. Given how much I identified with my mind and being right, this was a huge blow to my ego. Yet there was no denying the experimental evidence.

I later figured out why I had been so wrong about *The Last Epidemic*. One of the speakers in the documentary impressed me as an arrogant, Jewish professor from New York. Three of those characteristics I can't deny: I'm Jewish, I'm a professor, and I'm from New York. But adding arrogance was too much. That man was my shadow or dark side, the part of me that seemed so abhorrent that I couldn't admit it existed. Watching this speaker tied me up in psychic knots, which ruined the whole video for me. Once I realized that, several very positive things happened.

Rather than being repulsed by *The Last Epidemic*, I came to like it. We used it in our Beyond War Orientations to good effect, since it fit so well with the format of the program. I also made friends with and embraced my arrogant, Jewish professor from New York shadow side. I came to see that I had benefited from his power. Back in the late 1960s and early 1970s, when I first started to work in cryptography, all my colleagues had told me I was crazy, and they had some very valid arguments. It had taken a certain amount of arrogance to ignore their naysaying, but that work later won me major professional awards.

While the Biblical injunction to love our neighbors as ourselves has tremendous value, it left off an important part: to love ourselves. Until I embraced my shadow, I reacted irrationally whenever I thought I saw those seemingly despicable traits in another person, often hating him with a red-hot passion. But the real battle was to have compassion for my own dark side. After I did that, my anger at the other person evaporated. Only when I loved myself, shadow and all, could I love my neighbor.

There was another important benefit to my not only admitting, but embracing, the potential for arrogance within me. Now I could accept Dorothie's pointing it out when my courage—a close cousin of arrogance—was starting to get out of control. Eventually, that wasn't even necessary. As I came to truly embrace my shadow, I could see him more clearly.

The night of my *Last Epidemic* experience, I left "the dark cave of having to always be right" and ventured out into the light, where I began to see things that I previously could not have imagined. It would take much longer for my eyes to adjust, but I had started the process.

This wasn't just an intellectual realization, either. That night, a big piece of my old self died, and an equally significant part of my new identity emerged. It was a powerful emotional experience as Dorothie and I talked about what I had come to see about myself. Even now, over thirty years later, emotion wells up as I write this. But now, I don't feel sadness at part of my ego dying, but gratitude that I was freed from my chains in the cave and allowed into the light.

I identify myself as a seeker of truth, but before that night, I'd had a huge blind spot. By embracing my shadow side, I took a big step closer to what I now realize is an ideal that one must constantly strive to approach ever more closely.

When I related what had happened to a close friend, he told me, "Realizing that you can be 100 percent certain, yet 100 percent wrong, is something every wife wishes her husband would realize."

DOROTHIE: And every husband wishes his wife would realize the same thing. I found a card in the stationary store that I kept taped to our bedroom door for many years. It said, "Do you just want to be right, or do you want to be happy?" Maybe that summarized it better than anything.

Try a New Experiment

When one of us is hurt by something the other has done, there is an understandable belief system that "the doer" needs to heal the relationship. While that is often true, the next story shows that sometimes, something else is needed.

DOROTHIE: I sometimes suffer from really bad migraine headaches, and when this story took place about twenty years ago, they had effectively disabled me. I'm much better now, but at that point in time, I couldn't drive at night or on the freeways. Often, even a five-minute drive on local streets felt like too much, so I'd ask Marty to drive me. He was doing most of the household chores and errands. My disability had become an impossible situation for both of us.

On top of everything else, the drugs I was taking to get some relief from the migraines clouded my brain. When Marty would ask me questions, it would take me forever to respond to what he'd said. Sometimes, I was so spacey that I wouldn't even hear his question.

MARTY: At a conscious level, I knew Dorothie appreciated how I'd turned my life upside down to take care of her. But when I'd ask her a question and get no answer, I couldn't help feeling like she was the queen and I was some lowly peasant whose time had no value.

I'd wait a long time for her to answer before repeating the question, because sometimes she had heard me, but her brain was working so slowly that she hadn't yet formulated an answer. If I repeated my question at one of those times, it would aggravate her, partly because it reminded her of how disabled she had become. For me, on the receiving end, it felt like she was aggravated with me.

There were other times when she hadn't heard me, so I had to repeat the question. But I had no way of knowing which it was. No matter how much we talked about it, and no matter how much Dorothie told me she appreciated me to the ends of the earth, I still felt unappreciated when this happened.

DOROTHIE: While it was clear that Marty didn't feel appreciated by me, it was hard for me to understand. The chasm between how deeply I appreciated all that he did for me and how unappreciated he felt seemed unfathomable.

A therapist who specialized in chronic illness told me that, in all her years of working with countless clients, she had known only two other men who had responded as positively as Marty. I felt like he was a saint. I relied on him for everything. Given that I felt that way, how could he not experience my appreciation? But he didn't.

I desperately wanted him to know how I felt, so I tried one thing after another. First, I told him how much I appreciated him. But, no matter how many times I said so, it didn't work.

Next, I tried asking Marty questions. What could I do to let him know I appreciated him? What would it look like if I was appreciating him? What was it that convinced him I didn't feel appreciative? He didn't have answers to any of those questions.

I must have asked those questions a million times—or at least, that's how it felt—all to no avail. Then a solution hit me that was shocking in its simplicity and boldness. I had to believe Marty when he told me there was nothing I could do to make him feel appreciated. He didn't use those exact words, but that was implied by his not being able to answer any of those questions.

So I gave up and told him that I wished there was something more that I could do, but unless he could help me with some new ideas, he would just have to believe me when I said that I appreciated him.

MARTY: Somewhat paradoxically, Dorothie's giving up worked. In our experience, giving up in an impossible situation often works much better than one might think. It cracks the old framework within which we had been working unsuccessfully, much like tearing up the map had forced us to piece together a new one.

I also realized that needing to feel appreciated by a woman who was in frequent, excruciating pain, and whose brain was addled by drugs, was incompatible with the high standards I'd set for myself in my new map. My goal was to be the most loving husband I could be, not the husband who felt most appreciated.

With the dynamic changed, I also remembered that feelings have a logic all their own, so my not feeling appreciated was not the same as my not *being* appreciated. That, in turn, reminded me of the important lesson I'd learned earlier in my "*Last Epidemic* experience": I could be 100 percent certain of something, yet 100 percent wrong.

Taken all together, these realizations allowed me to get over my hurt feelings.

DOROTHIE: This story illustrates an important path in the new map. If what you're doing isn't working, you need to get creative and try a new experiment. If that doesn't work, try something else. But don't keep repeating the same, failed approach. That's an exercise in futility.

MARTY: Often, as we went through this process, at first we couldn't see any possibilities for trying to solve the problem except for the same, old, failed one we had tried time and time again. In those situations, we had to face the hard reality that putting more energy into the failed approach was unlikely to change its outcome. We had to open up to new ideas that often made no sense from our old perspective—like Dorothie's giving up on trying to make me feel appreciated. But what really makes no sense is repeating an experiment for the 101st time after 100 negative outcomes and expecting a positive result.

DOROTHIE: Of course, you also shouldn't try the new experiment 100 times without seeing some sign of success. That would just be a new version of the old mistake. If the new experiment doesn't work, brainstorm some more until you come up with something else. If that doesn't work, go get some outside help.

Sometimes, there is no solution to the problem other than learning to live with a difficult reality. We've had to do that with my migraines. I tried many experiments: psychotherapy (hoping that some childhood trauma caused them), chiropractic (several versions), acupuncture, Chinese herbs, biofeedback, an elimination diet for possible food allergies, and a host of other remedies. None helped. Finally, I decided that I needed to use what little energy I had for enjoying life—especially my friends and family— rather than chasing yet one more cure that had worked magic for someone else. Maybe there is a cure for me that I missed, but after all the things I'd tried, attempting one more such remedy felt like doing the same failed experiment for the 101st time.

As much as I detest taking drugs and worry about side effects, I found a brilliant psycho-pharmacologist and went on a heavy regimen of medication. Over time, my condition improved considerably, both in terms of the migraines themselves and the "addled brain syndrome" that led to Marty's not feeling appreciated. Our lives are still greatly restricted, compared to most couples our age, but we've come to accept those limitations. We revel in the true love we brought back into our marriage through this process and how much fuller our lives are compared to when I was disabled. Some might call that denial. We call it acceptance of reality. Whoever is right, it's the experiment that worked for us.

The Wisdom of Foolishness

DOROTHIE: Recently, we were at a birthday celebration for a good friend and one of the other guests asked Marty what he did. When he told her that we were writing this book, her reply was polite, but she made it clear she thought we were on a fool's errand. To which Marty replied, "Thank you! That's the best compliment you could pay me." I'll let him explain.

MARTY: It's ironic that one of the last things most people want to be seen as is foolish, yet many great advances were initially derided as fools' errands before they paid off.

I had a personal experience of this. My work in cryptography (which today is called cybersecurity) has earned me some of the highest honors in my profession, but when I was starting out, all of my colleagues told me I was wasting my time. Luckily, one of them—former UCLA Professor Jim Omura—was standing near me when that birthday party guest basically told me that we were wasting our time writing this book. I asked Jim to come over and tell her what he had thought of my cryptographic research in the early days, and he obliged.

Jim had told me that I could quote him, so I knew that he would tell her how foolish my effort had seemed at first—which he did. In an interesting twist of fate, after my work panned out, Jim left UCLA and co-founded a Silicon Valley startup that capitalized on it and later sold the company for $35 million.

My experience is far from unique, and may actually be the norm for breakthroughs. In 2013, when I was inducted as one of Stanford's "Engineering Heroes," I gave a talk on the wisdom of foolishness that also used examples from several of my colleagues:[26]

Vint Cerf, who received a Presidential Medal of Freedom for his pioneering work creating the Internet, told me that the underlying technology "was regarded as crazy" at first. Brad Parkinson, chief architect of the GPS system, related that, when he first proposed the idea, "The Air Force thought GPS was foolish."

The same is true of major societal shifts. For more than thirty years, when people ask me how societal changes to solve our global challenges might come about, I've had a constant answer: "If I had a crystal ball and could tell you, I wouldn't dare. Based on how major societal changes have occurred in the past, I would sound crazy."

If, in the 1850s, someone had had that crystal ball and had told people that slavery would be ended by a war in which white men would die to free black men, he would have been seen as a fool. Sixty years later, the National American Woman Suffrage Association thought working on a constitutional amendment was a waste of time, and that women would only get the vote state by state.[27] If the crystal ball had predicted the 19th Amendment at that point in time, it would also have been seen as a joke. There is a mystery to the process that is well to keep in mind when people discount the possibility of radical change.

If people were more open to the wisdom of foolishness, the "seeming fools" who questioned the Johnson administration's false claim that the Tonkin Gulf incidents were unprovoked aggression might have saved us from the Vietnam War. Those who questioned the Bush administration's claims about Saddam Hussein's weapons of mass destruction (WMDs) and links to al-Qaeda might have prevented the Iraq War and the ascendance of ISIS. And those who today question the prevailing, overly simplified narrative about Ukraine might save us from an armed conflict with Russia, with all the nuclear risk that would entail.

In spite of those failures of vision, there are signs of hope. While we haven't yet fully solved the nuclear threat and other global challenges, the Cold War did come to an end. Imagine what people would have said if, before Gorbachev came to power, anyone had predicted that kind of event. They would have been dismissed as out of their minds. In fact, soon after the Berlin Wall came down, a friend told me that instead of saying, "That will happen when pigs fly" to dismiss ridiculous sounding ideas, he used to say, "That will happen when the Berlin Wall comes down." He then told me that he was going to have to re-examine many things to see if maybe they might be possible after all. So there's much more hope than people realize.

The wisdom of foolishness also applies at a personal level. Dorothie's tearing up the map, described in the first section of this book, initially seemed unhinged to me. But, in hindsight, it was brilliant.

Most people will see it as foolish if you set a lofty goal with no idea of how to get there, but that's what happens when you tear up the old map. You need to try new paths, one after another, until you find one that works, and not get discouraged by the seeming failures.

This fits with something Dorothie told a friend: "I can pick my goal, but I can't pick the timing or how to get there." At that point in time, her goal was inner peace. She had no idea how to get there. She just knew that she had to.

The same is true for world peace. We can pick that goal, but not the timing or the method. We will have to try a lot of experiments, most of which fail, before we achieve success. But we can't lose sight of the goal, or get discouraged by the experiments that don't work. And, even if we never achieve world peace, we'll make a much better world just by trying.

Deeply Held But Mistaken Societal Beliefs

In February 2016, as this book was nearing completion, we learned that Marty and his colleague Whit Diffie had been chosen as the recipients of the ACM Turing Award. (ACM is the Association for Computing Machinery, the world's largest computer science professional society, and the Turing Award is their highest honor.) We quickly agreed to use Marty's half of the million dollar prize that goes with the award to further our efforts to build a more peaceful, sustainable world, with promotion of this book being our initial focus. But there's another important connection between the award and this book.

The award's namesake, Alan Turing, was the hero of the recent movie, *The Imitation Game*. This brilliant mathematician laid one of the cornerstones of modern computer science. He also played a key role in breaking the German "Enigma" cipher during World War II, an intelligence breakthrough that is credited with saving countless lives.

In spite of his wartime contributions, when Turing's homosexuality was discovered by a police officer in 1952, he was arrested and given the choice of prison or chemical castration via female hormone treatments. Turing chose the latter and died of cyanide poisoning two years later—a death that an inquest attributed to suicide.

While there are alternative theories, Turing appears to have been hounded to death by the 1950s' belief that homosexuality was a crime worthy of severe punishment. Today, we look back with horror at the injustice perpetrated by that deeply held but mistaken societal belief. We wonder how our parents or grandparents could have been so blind.

This was not the first time that deeply held societal beliefs were found to have been mistaken or caused grievous harm. Four hundred years ago, the Church threatened Galileo with torture over his support for the theory that the Earth revolved around the Sun, instead of the other way around. One hundred sixty years ago, slavery was the law of the land. As with Turing's persecution, roughly sixty years ago, we now wonder how a supposedly civilized society could be so certain, yet so wrong. The same is true when we look back a hundred years to the fight over women's suffrage.

These four deeply held but mistaken societal beliefs that caused such injustice occurred roughly 400 years ago, 160 years ago, 100 years ago, and sixty years ago. If an area experienced major earthquakes at those points in time, wouldn't it be reasonable to assume that more will occur? In the same way, isn't it reasonable to assume that, even now, society has deeply held but mistaken beliefs that some years in the future will be seen as both laughable and tragic? While we cannot be sure what those mistaken beliefs will turn out to be, we suggest four possibilities for your consideration:

First, the belief that fighting is intrinsic to both marital and international relations, and only a fool would try to envision a world in which such conflicts are resolved peacefully.

Second, the belief that a nation can wage a war that kills millions of people and destroys the flower of its youth, yet still think of itself as civilized.

Third, the belief that thousands of nuclear weapons are essential to both national security and world peace.

Fourth, the belief that the science of global warming is so uncertain and the risks of inaction low enough that we should take no remedial action at this point in time.

While deeply held but mistaken societal beliefs have significant inertia, history proves that they can be changed by courageous individuals breaking with the norm and saying with conviction that "the emperor has no clothes." Whether or not you agree with any of the four possibilities suggested above, we hope you will join the effort to accelerate society's process of rooting out its mistaken beliefs.

Chapter 5

A Journey of Healing and Reconciliation

Out-of-control anger was one of the biggest impediments to recapturing true love in our marriage. Hurtful things we said and did to one another out of anger added new wounds to those that had produced the anger in the first place, creating an ever-escalating war, until we tried something new: tracing the anger back to its hidden source.

Tracing problems back to their sources also allowed us to move beyond fear and overcome what used to be frequent fights over money, sex, and power. Once we healed the underlying wound, we were able to move beyond the problem it created.

In December of 1981, about a year into the process of rebuilding our relationship, an incident sent Marty into an overpowering rage. Working that process of healing had a profound effect on both him and our marriage.

Healing Anger by Finding its Source

MARTY: We were at a Creative Initiative event in San Francisco—that's the organization we were working with that later morphed into Beyond War. At first, I had kept the organization at arm's length out of skepticism and mistrust, thinking, "What could they possibly have to teach me, and what was in it for them that they hadn't yet revealed?"

But after about a year of Dorothie's almost dragging me to meetings, I came to see that these people knew something I had to learn if my marriage was to survive. I dropped my resistance, threw my lot in with the group, and opened up to new possibilities that, earlier, I would have rejected as outlandish. I had begun the process of piecing together a new map.

Thus we found ourselves on that December evening in San Francisco's Masonic Auditorium, part of a large Creative Initiative gathering. The Masonic can seat over 3,000 people and the auditorium looked packed. We had made friends with a number of people in "the Community," as the group often called itself, and I was really enjoying seeing them and feeling the positive vibe. Although I enjoyed being at the event, I felt a gnawing anxiety eating away deep inside me. What could that be?

We had done enough personal work in the past year that, instead of pushing the anxiety away, I made a conscious effort to understand it. That didn't take long.

I had grown up in a close-knit Jewish community in the Bronx and, while it was okay not to go to synagogue—my parents almost never did, nor did I, after my bar mitzvah—it would have felt traitorous to go to church. In Hebrew School, I had learned how

Jewish martyrs had died rather than convert. To my mind at that point in time, going into a church would not only desecrate the sacrifices of my martyred ancestors, but it also would feel like putting my life in jeopardy. That last fear clearly was not based in current reality, but it was a powerful, unconscious force from my childhood.

I had grown up as the only Jewish kid my age in a neighborhood of primarily Irish Catholic children. We played together, but we also fought, and sometimes when I got beaten up, I was told in no uncertain terms it was because I was a Christ-killer. This was the early 1950s, before Vatican II made inroads into the Church's long-standing, anti-Semitic teachings.

It was only a few years after World War II ended, and I had heard a heartbreaking story about one of my mother's cousins. He had emigrated from Poland to New York just before the war broke out, and his family was supposed to follow once he had established himself here. The war made travel impossible, but he faithfully wrote letters to them for six years even though he never received a reply. When the war ended, the letters came back with the horrible news that his wife and children had all perished in the Holocaust.

Some of my friends' parents were concentration camp survivors, with numbers tattooed on their arms so the Nazis could keep track of them the way a rancher tracks his cattle.

All these traumas led my child's mind to transform St. Nicholas of Tolentine, the local Roman Catholic Church, into an enemy fortress where Jesus' legions were taught to hate Jews, after which they streamed out to do me in. With that mindset, going into a church understandably made me more than mildly nervous.

While the Creative Initiative ceremony at the Masonic Auditorium was not "church," it clearly wasn't synagogue. Therefore, in my child's mind (which was active at an unconscious level), it must be church.

Going through that thought process consciously, I saw that my malaise was a combination of fear and guilt. I quieted down and started to enjoy the evening's program. But the tremor of that initial angst was soon followed by a major earthquake of rage.

Several people spoke about key decision points in their lives. I related well to the first few speakers, but then a Jewish woman described a time, just after the 1973 Yom Kippur War, when she realized that a pledge she had made to a Jewish charity was helping to support war in the Middle East. She rescinded her pledge. She also joined a group of Creative Initiative women who went to all the Arab and Israeli consulates in San Francisco and presented petitions asking them to lay down their arms.

Her talk disturbed me at a very deep level and, on the drive home, I told Dorothie how stupid it was for those Creative Initiative women to ask the Israelis to lay down their arms. Didn't they know that if the Israelis did that, the Arabs would drive them into the sea? Blood would flow like water!

Dorothie, who is not Jewish, tried pointing out that the women had also asked the Arab nations to lay down their arms, but I couldn't stop ranting and raving. While my outburst was coming from the deep recesses of my psyche, I had become conscious enough to recognize that I was out of control. It was like watching a movie in which I was also the actor.

When it was safe to pull the car over, I turned off the engine and decades of pent-up emotions came gushing out. Even now, as I write this, I am having a deep emotional response. But now it's not anger. Rather, it's sadness at all the inhuman things we humans have done to one another and are continuing to do. Instead of making me fearful or angry, those emotions now deepen my commitment to do all that I can to change the world so that such things never again happen to anyone, Jew or otherwise.

But that's not where I was that night in December 1981. The emotions coming up were raw and unprocessed. Before I could worry about repairing the world—a very Jewish notion, incidentally, which is at the heart of Jewish mysticism—I had to first repair myself. I was broken.

My ego had built high walls to protect my inner self from the "slings and arrows of outrageous fortune." But that process also had walled off what I and other human beings are in our cores—loving, compassionate, and kind—and hindered it from being expressed in my relationship with Dorothie and the world. When I felt threatened, I fought back, even if I was mistaken about being threatened. Better safe than sorry.

That mode of thinking—that old map—had been somewhat useful when I was a small child in the Bronx, but now it was destroying my marriage. As Dorothie and I sat in the car, engine off, on the side of the road, two things became clear to me.

First, I realized that, even though there were much greater risks to my life (nuclear war among them), my childhood exposure to victims of the Holocaust had made me fearful that what happened in Germany could happen here. Israel was my "get out of concentration camp free card," a safe haven if ever I needed one. Attacking critics of Israel, no matter how justified their criticism might be, felt like a matter of life and death at an unconscious level. That explained my animus toward the Jewish woman who spoke about rescinding her charitable pledge.

Second, I realized that when I was five years old and my parents moved from a Jewish neighborhood to that new one with all its Catholic kids, of course I didn't want to be Jewish. What kid in his right mind would not want a Christmas tree with presents under it? What kid in his right mind would want to be ostracized and beaten up as a Christ-killer? What kid in his right mind wouldn't want to go to the same school as all the other kids? (That was St. Nicholas of Tolentine Catholic School, of course.)

When I was five, I wanted all those things, and I was young enough and foolish enough to ask my parents for them. Probably thrown back to their own conflicted, childhood feelings about being Jewish, they told me that what we had was better.

From my five-year-old perspective, that was absolute rubbish. It was not better going without the pretty tree and presents, or going to a different school from all the other kids. And it certainly wasn't better getting beaten up as a Christ-killer.

But while I was young enough to ask for all those things, I was old enough to know that arguing with my parents would have ended in disaster, possibly punctuated by a slap on my face.

So I buried my feelings and outwardly adopted the prevailing attitude of my community. I became proud of being Jewish even though I now realized that, every time I said that, the child within me had cried out, "Bullshit!" That child was buried so deep, I could pretend not to hear him. But the deeper I buried him, the more powerfully he could act out at an unconscious level.

Now, sitting in the car, tears rolling down my face, I could have compassion for my five-year-old self for the first time in my life. I could admit that there was nothing wrong with him, at that tender age, for not wanting to be Jewish. That was, after all, the logical conclusion of all the things I'd asked my parents for. No kid in his right mind would want all the troubles that being Jewish had brought on me.

When I finally had compassion for my long-buried, five-year-old self, he quieted down and my adult self became truly and unreservedly proud of being Jewish for the first time in my life. Contrary to the Jewish community's unspoken fears, acknowledging that I had not wanted to be Jewish didn't cause me to leave the fold. Rather, I became more connected to my heritage and could embrace it completely.

My "internal peace agreement" resolved the lifelong war between my adult and childhood selves. It also resolved my anger at the Jewish Creative Initiative woman and transformed it from a strife-causing element in our marriage into a healing agent. In this case, I had to heal myself before I could heal the wounds created in our marriage by my internal war. And I had to heal my marriage before I could try to heal the wounds of the world. I guess it's a multi-step process.

DOROTHIE: Marty had to first have compassion for himself before he could have compassion for the woman who had made him so mad. When we think of compassion, we tend to leave ourselves out, and that's a huge mistake.

I knew Marty's history, so I was aware of his experiences growing up Jewish. Up to this point in our marriage I had danced around his sensitivities in an attempt not to cause him pain. But as we untangled the knots in our relationship, I came to see how dancing around Marty's sensitivities had led us to trample all over mine.

123

MARTY: When we got engaged, my mother was so upset that Dorothie wasn't Jewish that she barely talked to anyone for weeks. If Dorothie's family had been upset at my being Jewish—which they weren't—that would have been anti-Semitism, and I would have expected Dorothie to object in no uncertain terms to their inappropriate behavior. But it was supposed to be understandable that my mother was upset. She never told either of us about it directly, so I never confronted her about it. Because Dorothie was dancing around my sensitivities about being Jewish, she never pressed me to do otherwise. But her being walled out by my mother hurt her deeply. Her sensitivities were trampled on.

DOROTHIE: Another instance, in which trying not to hurt Marty had inadvertently caused me pain, concerned Christmas. As a small child, I loved Christmas, and one of my favorite memories was playing with the "dolls" we set up in the crèche. At least, that's how I thought of them back then. Of course, in Marty's culture of origin, those "dolls" had a very different symbolism.

MARTY: Growing up, crèches and every other symbol of Christmas were taboo. Jews saw those figurines, especially the baby Jesus, as reminders of the horrors done to us supposedly in his name: murders, forced conversions, and children torn from their families so they could be "saved" by being brought up as Christians.

DOROTHIE: Several years after Marty made peace with his internal conflict, it hit me that we were treating one of my fondest childhood memories as if it were somehow evil. All of the pain that I had stuffed away for all those years—not just about Christmas, but also how Marty's mother had never really accepted me and more—came pouring out. It's embarrassing to admit, but I told

Marty I was going to go out and buy the biggest, most expensive crèche I could find.

MARTY: I was in shock. Where had this come from?

DOROTHIE: Clearly not from my mature self. It was my five-year-old self demanding to be treated as precious, not some evil, taboo creature. Who I was wasn't okay in Marty's old map, and that had to change. I wish I could have said it more compassionately, but that's not where I was at that point in time.

MARTY: One of my biggest concerns was what my father would say when he came to visit. (My mother had died a year earlier.) But that concern just aggravated another of Dorothie's long-standing wounds: my putting my family's sensitivities ahead of hers.

It was a time of high tension, not so much between Dorothie and me (although that's how it looked on the surface), but between the various parts of each of our psyches that were in conflict. As you can see, we were far from perfect at maintaining a compassionate, holistic perspective, but being committed to that goal allowed us to successfully navigate this journey on our new map.

DOROTHIE: There were almost no Jews living in our little suburb of Los Angeles, so when I met Marty, his being Jewish fascinated me. I yearned for something more than the plain vanilla life that my town offered, and here was something exotic and different. I also knew that Jews were a tight-knit community, and I longed to belong to something like that. I wanted to convert to Judaism, but Marty was, at best, uncomfortable with that idea.

MARTY: While I didn't know it back when Dorothie wanted to convert, as I came to terms with my inner conflict, I saw that her not being Jewish was an added attraction to my inner child.

This relationship was an opportunity to run away from everything Jewish. Ironically, the difference in our religious backgrounds and the conflicts they produced eventually brought me closer to my Jewish heritage, but only after I had made peace in my own internal war.

Earlier, my unconsciously running away from Judaism while Dorothie was running toward it created an explosive mixture. It didn't help that the tight-knit community to which she was attracted had a huge wall around it—at least in the Bronx in 1967—saying: "no Gentiles allowed." We Jews were tight-knit, but Dorothie was not part of the fabric.

DOROTHIE: As long as we kept the sources of these land mines buried deep in our psyches, they were hidden from consciousness. Continually stepping on those buried land mines was a big part of how we had ruined our relationship. Now we were working at bringing what had previously been unconscious to a conscious level, where we could defuse the land mines. We were able to move beyond anger—and eventually heal our anger—by tracing it back to its sources and healing the wounds that had created it. Our new map was beginning to come together. It was taking us on a journey of healing and reconciliation.

From Anger to Reconciliation

MARTY: Tracing my anger at the Jewish Creative Initiative woman back to my conflicted feelings about being Jewish freed me to start healing wounds that had been buried for decades. Given how long they had been festering, it's not surprising that, ten years after my December 1981 experience described above, I realized I needed one more act of reconciliation.

By this point, I could enter a church without feeling like a traitor or as if my life was in danger. I could even enjoy the beauty of a church. As I was preparing for a business trip to New York, it hit me that I had never set foot in the neighborhood church where I'd grown up, St. Nicholas of Tolentine. Because that church had a special place of both horror and forbidden attraction in my inner child's mind, I resolved to visit it on this trip.

I called information, got the phone number, and dialed. After a couple of rings, a woman answered, "St. Nicholas of Tolentine." I asked to speak with a priest. A man's voice came on the line with the same greeting, so I again said that I would like to speak with a priest. "This is Father John," he replied.

To my surprise, I was speechless—literally. Somehow, I managed to squeeze out enough words to communicate that I needed time to compose myself. Father John was understanding and told me to take all the time I needed.

Although I had done a great deal of work to make peace with the Church and with my inner turmoil over being Jewish, Tolentine was an especially delicate land mine that still had not been fully defused. I can't be sure which feelings paralyzed me, but residual guilt and fear were surely part of the mix.

After a short time that felt like an eternity, I was able to talk again. I told Father John that I had grown up not far from Tolentine, that I was Jewish, and that I wanted to visit the church on my upcoming business trip as an act of reconciliation.

At first, he thought I wanted an apology—the Church by now had acknowledged its earlier anti-Semitism—and he started to sympathize with what I'd had to live through. I explained that was not why I had called.

Yes, the Catholic Church had made mistakes, and I had suffered from them. But I also had come to see how my own people were prejudiced against non-Jews. The way my mother reacted when she heard I was engaged to Dorothie is a good example. I told Father John that I neither needed nor wanted an apology. I wanted reconciliation. I wanted to visit the church. I wanted to go there and pray with him.

A few days later, I was in New York and the time came for our meeting. We met in his office and, after a while, went into the church proper. Far from the horror house of my childhood nightmares, it was stunningly beautiful. Sunlight streamed through stained glass windows, bathing the pews in an otherworldly light.

It was a weekday, so we were the only ones in this huge, beautiful church. I asked if we could say the Lord's Prayer together. While it is usually thought of as a Christian prayer—the prayer's name clearly is Christian—the prayer itself had been composed by a Jew named Jesus. There was nothing un-Jewish about it. On the contrary, it seemed (and still seems) quintessentially Jewish to me:

Our Father which art in heaven, Hallowed be thy name.
Thy kingdom come, Thy will be done, as in heaven, so on earth.
Give us day by day our daily bread.
And forgive us our sins, as we forgive those who trespass against us.
And lead us not into temptation, but deliver us from evil.
Amen.

In my mind, what this prayer refers to as the Kingdom of God is that ideal state of being in which a person puts doing what is right above what he thinks he wants to do. It requires that God, or Righteousness—doing what's right—is king, not my ego. In this book, we call that state of being holistic thinking and compassion. To dwell in that Kingdom, it was essential that I not let myself off the hook because ideals may be unattainable. If an ideal truly is unattainable, that just means that seeking to approach it is a lifelong journey.

As I write this, at seventy years of age—having worked this process for half my life and still finding new things to learn—I tend to side with it being a lifelong journey. But a journey that can transform anger into reconciliation, love, and joy is one well worth taking—*especially* if it lasts a lifetime.

You Have to Love Me Because I'm Angry

DOROTHIE: To stop being run around by my emotions and to integrate all the parts of my personality—to become a whole person, a holistic person—I spent time deeply exploring different feelings. As part of that process, I spent about six months focusing on anger.

It hadn't been okay for me to be angry in my family of origin, so I had learned to be ashamed of my frequent, angry outbursts. Up to this point in life, whenever I got angry at someone, I ended up being angry with myself for feeling that seemingly shameful emotion. That meant that I never got to heal the underlying source of the anger, which kept the cycle going. This endless loop was poisoning my life, including my relationship with Marty. It had to change. I was determined to get in touch with my anger and to make peace with it.

MARTY: Dorothie's getting in touch with her anger was a real struggle for me. She may be only five foot three, but when she got angry, she seemed like a giant monster who was going to eat me alive. Once, while she was in this phase of getting comfortable with her anger, I was really proud of myself for not letting it scare me. I told her that I loved her even though she was angry.

Instead of the appreciation I'd expected—which, now that I think of it, was not a likely response when someone is in touch with their anger—Dorothie came back forcefully and demanded: "You can't just love me *even though* I'm angry. You have to love me *because* I'm angry!"

I went off disappointed, but I thought about what she had said. I realized that, as scary as her anger was for me, there were important issues that, at that point in our process, she could only get in touch with when she was angry. They had been buried so deep, for so many years, that they were stewing in a pot of anger. Dorothie's getting in touch with those old wounds and healing them was clearly in my interest as well as hers, even if the first part of that process involved her being angry.

As I thought more about her seemingly unreasonable demand to love her *because* she was angry, I realized that, if I had a magic wand and could make her anger disappear, I wouldn't. She needed to get in touch with the wounds that were causing her anger, and I had to better understand them as well. Only by each of us learning how to respond compassionately to the other, even when we were angry—no, make that *especially* when we were angry—could we heal those old wounds and reach true intimacy. It's an integral part of the journey to loving each other unconditionally.

Also, we had progressed enough that Dorothie's anger was not aimed at me the way it used to be. Rather, she was using anger to better understand her own inner psychic processes in an effort to learn from them and heal our relationship. Although it seemed paradoxical at first, she was using her study of anger as a tool to move beyond it.

My old expectations were like a statement in a computer program: "IF Dorothie is angry THEN I am going to get clobbered."

But now I saw a new possibility: "IF Dorothie is angry AND IF I honor that emotion THEN both our lives will get better."

I came back and told Dorothie that she was right: I loved her not *even though* she was angry, but *because* she was angry.

DOROTHIE: While I had demanded this of Marty, it was so revolutionary that it still surprised me when he agreed. It also helped—in fact, it was critical—that I had told Marty that, whatever I demanded of him, he also had the right to demand of me.

MARTY: That made a huge difference. On top of the direct benefit to me—Dorothie's moving beyond her own anger—what a relief it was to no longer have to pretend that I wasn't angry when I really was.

DOROTHIE: One of the key ingredients in our successfully traversing this previously mine-strewn path was the other side of "You have to love me because I'm angry," namely: "I have to love myself when I'm angry." I had to move beyond my childhood lessons that had taught me to be ashamed of my anger.

MARTY: Before we made this shift, back when we saw anger as an unforgivable sin, arguments would often end up with one of us accusing the other of being angry. Not surprisingly, the accused then turned the tables, damning the accuser with the same charge.

Fights like that now seem insane: two angry people, each getting madder at the other for being angry. The old map is full of crazy, endless loops like that.

DOROTHIE: That's the argument that goes, "You're angry!" followed by the other angrily insisting, "No, I'm not. You are!"

In the old map, only bad people got angry, so it was really difficult for either of us to take responsibility for our anger. We each became the "pot calling the kettle black." In the new map, anger is a normal human emotion, so when I told Marty he had to love me because I was angry, I was able to do it without blaming him, and with owning—rather than hiding from—my anger.

MARTY: You can see the power of that shift. Once Dorothie became comfortable with her own anger, she was able to demand that I love her when she was angry. She did it without rancor. She wasn't angry in the same way she used to be. It was more of an introspective anger, but very powerful and determined.

As the above stories on anger show, and as later ones will also demonstrate, a seemingly negative emotion such as anger can have a positive effect in a relationship if we own it rather than letting it take us over and blaming our bad behavior on those who we think made us mad. Making that shift allows us to embrace our anger and transform it into compassion for ourselves and the world.

We couldn't just excise anger from our souls. We had to replace it with compassion and love.

Moving From Anger to Compassion

Whole books have been written about managing anger so that it won't poison a relationship. Even though this book has only a few sections on anger and therefore cannot be all-encompassing, our goal goes far beyond just controlling anger: the goal is learning to move beyond anger by first embracing it and then transforming it into compassion.

MARTY: Not everyone may choose to adopt our goal of moving beyond anger. In fact, many people we've talked with say that they wouldn't want to give up anger—that it makes them feel alive. Of course, if they were to try our goal as an experiment, they might find even more excitement in the joy of living beyond anger and being deeply in love again.

People who say they don't want to move beyond anger also may be missing that we first embraced anger as our friend, or they may be confusing anger with passion or power. We are dedicated to living beyond anger, but other forms of passion now motivate us. Passion emanating from love is far more creative and effective—and far more powerful—than passion derived from anger.

Even people who don't want to move beyond anger ought to think about *how* they want to be angry. Do they want to be uncontrollably angry and mistreat those around them? Or do they want only to be in touch with their anger, while still being respectful of others? Do they want their national leaders making decisions in anger, or in a clear-headed, thoughtful manner?

DOROTHIE: While our goal of moving from anger to compassion may sound revolutionary, it's an old idea. Religious geniuses have been espousing it for thousands of years, although most of us are far from living it. Why is that?

We see two main obstacles. The first is the belief that it's impossible to move beyond anger—that anger is an immutable part of human nature. We discussed this idea in depth in the previous chapter on belief systems. As seen from our stories, anger was a necessary tool in the early stages of our process, but we no longer need it. Compassion is a much better tool for producing needed change. So, unless we aren't human, anger is *not* an immutable part of human nature.

The second obstacle to moving beyond anger is a lack of totality of commitment. If you go halfway, you will never get there. That's a scientific fact. You can't let yourself off the hook. Your anger is yours alone. No one else can make you angry, and it's your responsibility to deal with it. You need to be in the driver's seat—not your anger.

If you follow this path, early on in the process you will experience anger, and it will be extremely useful—just as it was to us. Treated properly, anger was like a flashing red light telling us to stop whatever we were doing, pay attention, and figure out what needed to change. When we had the same angry argument over and over again, it was often because we mistakenly saw anger as a sign that we needed to fight for what we thought we wanted, rather than as that flashing red light telling us where we need to bring about positive change.

There were times when my anger seemed uncontrollable. When that happened, I'd ask Marty to please stay out of my way for a while, since I didn't want to mistreat him but was not yet capable of living up to that standard. While that was far from what we wanted in the long run, it was much better than pretending my anger was entirely his fault.

When I told a good friend that we were writing this part of the book, she objected that anger often was necessary to produce desperately needed change, especially if the person she was dealing with was not committed to this process—which most are not. I can sympathize with her perspective because I used to think that way earlier in my relationship with Marty. But the resolution of Marty's three-month-long conflict with his father shows that not getting angry, and rather acting compassionately, can lead to a miraculous resolution even with a person who has a reputation as being cantankerous.

Before I understood that, I thought that Marty only heard me when I got angry, and I even told him that. But I was wrong. The problem was that I didn't know how to be powerfully assertive without also being angry. In that mindset, not being angry meant being a wimp.

MARTY: I can attest from repeated, direct experience that Dorothie's moving from anger to compassion has not made her a wimp. On the contrary, it's made her much more effective at getting what she needs. Now that she doesn't have to puff herself up to be heard, she can produce needed change in a more compassionate way. It's much easier for me to hear her, so she gets what she needs much more quickly.

Uncontrolled anger is an attempt to deny an unpleasant reality, so it makes us less effective at changing that reality. *You can't change something you pretend doesn't exist.* For that reason, and because it involves a state of being, our effort to move beyond anger has expanded far beyond our relationship. Today, our goal is to move beyond anger in all situations. It has become a total commitment.

It can be as trivial as when I'm driving and someone cuts me off or does something else that I don't like. Getting mad is likely to make a bad situation worse. It might even cause an accident. If I can think about what happened instead of responding reflexively in anger, I often find that what the other driver did to me is something I've also done to others—a good example of projecting my dark side on an enemy.

DOROTHIE: As always, the solution to that problem is to own your dark side and to have compassion for that part of yourself. If you do that, you'll find your anger at the other driver evaporating. Getting mad at him also isn't healthy for you, psychically, physically, or spiritually. Anger is a roadblock to experiencing joy, and joy is an emotion we all can use more of.

MARTY: Another key to our successfully moving from anger to compassion was patience. Putting the problem on the back burner often produced a creative solution that would not have come to me if I'd tried to force a quick resolution. It also got me out of the heat of the moment, where I might have exploded. I couldn't just force my anger to go away. I had to process it and replace it with compassion.

The section "Patience is a Virtue" has a great example in which patience was critical to resolving a potentially explosive disagreement. In that case, it was Dorothie having patience with my resistance to buying her the twenty-fifth anniversary ring she wanted. Now we both cherish the process that led to that successful resolution, which gives the ring beauty far beyond its physical appearance.

The section "Mountain or Molehill" has another good example. By that time—several years after our twenty-fifth anniversary—I'd also learned the value of patience, and that allowed me to resolve a major disagreement with my father in an unbelievably positive way. The tension in our relationship evaporated. But it took three months to get to the point where that was possible.

DOROTHIE: There's another important rule we used for moving from anger to compassion. Once Marty and I were both committed to this process, we made an agreement that we had to give one another the benefit of the doubt. We had to believe what the other told us about their state of being. I can't count how many times I was sure that Marty was mad or upset with me, but he assured me he wasn't. As hard as it was to accept, I was committed to act on what he told me about himself.

Often, it turned out that I was wrong. Other times, I was right, and Marty just wasn't aware of how he was feeling. But even then, there were two reasons it was far better for me not to argue with him about his state of being. First and perhaps most basically, I couldn't tell when I was right and when I was wrong. Second, when he was wrong and didn't recognize that he was upset, not arguing with him gave him space in which he might recognize that himself. Then he could come back and tell me what he'd realized.

MARTY: Remember that Dorothie prefaced all of the above with the condition: "Once Marty and I were both committed to this process." That's really important because, before we did that, when we got into disagreements, each of us was out to win rather than to find the truth. That's a huge difference. You can't always believe what the other person tells you about their state of being if they're out to win at all costs. You can only do that after they've committed to seeking the truth, including the truth about their own mistakes.

DOROTHIE: Even in conflicts with people other than Marty, I found that it helps to start by giving them the benefit of the doubt. We have very active imaginations, and sometimes misinterpret a harmless interchange as a direct assault.

MARTY: I'll never forget one time when that happened to me. We were just a couple of years into this process, and I was at a conference on cryptography. One of the encryption algorithms I'd developed was under attack, and another researcher gave a talk about how to break it. To demonstrate his technique, he set up an Apple II computer—which gives you an idea of how long ago this was—and let it churn away attacking my algorithm while he talked. At the end of the talk, the computer was supposed to produce a result proving that his method worked (which it did).

He started his lecture by saying, "First the talk, then the public humiliation." I was livid! Cryptography is more an art than a science, and all of the top researchers had come up with at least one system that had been broken. Why did he have to say he was going to humiliate me?

Later, I realized he was talking about himself, not me. He was afraid the computer would crash or some other problem would prevent him from proving that his approach worked. This experience of mine is a great example of why Dorothie is right about giving everyone the benefit of the doubt, at least initially.

DOROTHIE: Now, when we make things up, we try to make up things that are helpful and positive—things that won't start a fight.

I call giving each other the benefit of the doubt "unconditional positive regard." If my assumption of unconditional positive regard for the other person turns out to be wrong, as the interaction progresses, he will give me plenty of evidence to change my mind. But going into an interaction, I've found it extremely helpful to have an open, positive mind.

When I was angry, sometimes it meant that I needed to change, sometimes that Marty needed to change, and most often that we both needed to change. Early on, sometimes one of us was unable to change in a way the other needed. We were too hurt or too stubborn or something. In that case, whichever of us had asked for change only had the ability to change him or herself. But even if that's all that was possible at that point in time, our lives became far better. Uncontrolled anger is not good for a relationship.

After we developed more compassionate ways to ask for change, anger became a nightmare of the past. We've healed ourselves and each other through acceptance of our humanity, by having compassion not only for one another, but also for ourselves.

After I moved beyond anger, I could see what a waste of time it had been. Anger had caused me needless pain, anxiety, and discomfort, and I'd had to spend time dealing with its aftereffects on our relationship. But the most basic, most personal reason I found for moving beyond anger was that it prevented me from being in a state of compassion that brought joy and peace into my life. From my current vantage point, moving from anger to compassion is a no-brainer.

Moving Beyond Fear

MARTY: Learning to move beyond fear was just as important to our marriage as learning to move beyond anger. It used to drive Dorothie up the wall when I'd get what she called "squirrely" around her—acting afraid of her and desperately searching for an exit: "How do I get out of here?" But there was no way out. I felt like a trapped squirrel about to be eaten alive.

DOROTHIE: Whenever that used to happen, it devastated me. I'm a bit of an odd duck and, especially in childhood, I often felt alienated because I saw the world through such different eyes from most of my friends and family. I frequently came home from school in tears because it was too overwhelming.

I longed to be seen for who I was, not what other people thought I was. When Marty and I met and fell in love, it felt like, "At last! Finally I have found my soulmate who will see me for who I am and love me."

So it was excruciatingly painful when Marty was fearful of me. It actually caused me physical pain. My heart hurt. I suppose that's what it means to feel heartbroken. Here was the person who, more than anyone else in the world, was supposed to love me, and it felt as if he was treating me like a witch. The vision I had of finally having found my soulmate evaporated before my eyes. I would get self-protective and pull back into my shell.

MARTY: The difference in our experiences is astounding. Dorothie saw my squirrely behavior as proof that I thought she was a witch, whereas to me it felt like I'd made a terrible mistake and could not find a way to correct it. It was about me being unacceptable, not her.

Similarly, while Dorothie's pulling into her shell felt self-protective to her, it came across as rejection to me. In fact, her pulling into her shell had much the same effect on me that my being squirrely had on her. It made me feel like I was a terrible, unlovable person.

DOROTHIE: Of course! If I had to retreat into myself, I must be seeing Marty as a scary person—his own kind of witch. Unfortunately, back then, I was so deeply hurt, I couldn't see that. I couldn't take the holistic perspective.

Our writing this section of the book reminded me of something else that's really important, but that I'd almost forgotten. My inability to respond appropriately back then was partly due to a deep-seated belief that I really was unlovable.

Toward the end of our first year in Creative Initiative, we took a course designed to trace our personal journeys. We did a number of exercises to reconnect us with old experiences that we had largely forgotten at a conscious level, but that were running us around unconsciously. In one of those exercises, we found pictures from our childhood and spent time writing about and remembering what life had been like back then.

Another exercise was to draw a self-portrait. Mine surprised and shocked me and clearly emanated from deep in my unconscious. It was a grotesque monster, with the caption "I AM UNLOVABLE." So Marty's treating me like I was unlovable fed into one of my deepest, darkest fears. His fear became a trigger for one of my own. So long as my fear of being unlovable operated only at an unconscious level, it ran me around. Drawing that self-portrait brought the feeling into my consciousness and allowed the healing process to begin.

MARTY: Ironically, my fear of Dorothie became a self-fulfilling prophecy. The more fearful I became, the angrier and scarier she became and the more she demanded that I change. Having no idea how to change, I became ever more fearful, she became ever more hurt, and the cycle spiraled downward—until we started dealing with it on a more conscious level.

DOROTHIE: That's how the early stages of this process work. Our "new map goal" was to reach the top of the tallest mountain, where we could see the beauty of the world spread before us in a totally new light. But we had to start our journey where we were, bogged down in the swamp of self-involvement by all those old

141

hurts. The first step in reaching the mountain was to extricate ourselves from that swamp by moving through fear, anger, and hurt.

MARTY: Because my fear affected Dorothie so negatively, and because it was incompatible with my goal of becoming the best person I could be, I set to work on cutting it out of my life. It had to go. I was determined. But then I discovered a glitch in my plan.

Because I was trying to learn how to deal with the more emotional, less logical side of life, I also had started working on getting back in touch with my feelings. As a result of the deep personal work we had done, I had come to recognize that, when I was a small boy, my emotions and feelings had gotten me in trouble with the other kids. Nobody wants to be ridiculed as a "cry baby."

When I reached adolescence, my rational mind had developed enough that I was able to use logic and rationality as a shield against being tossed around by my emotions. Doing that saved my life back then, but now things were different. Being locked in the cold, hard, Spock-like world of logic was ruining my marriage and my life. It was time to get back in touch with my emotional side.

After a while, what should have been obvious hit me: I can't get in touch with my feelings when I'm trying to cut fear out of my life. Fear is a feeling. I had to get back in touch with it, too.

That realization finally allowed me to do what previously I had found impossible: move beyond fear. Trying to excise it from my life wouldn't work. I'd tried for decades, without success, to suppress fear. I had to embrace fear before I could move through it.

The next time I started to feel fear come up during a conversation with Dorothie, instead of getting squirrely, I welcomed the feeling. Without knowing why I was about to step on a land mine,

I moved the conversation in a slightly different direction. A few seconds later, my conscious mind caught up with my intuition, and I understood the nature of the land mine. But if I had waited for it to make sense logically before taking evasive action, the explosion would have already occurred and it would have been too late. Fear really was my friend.

As I continued working with fear, I came to see that my biggest fear was that I would be afraid. In this sense, Franklin Delano Roosevelt was right when, in his 1933 first inaugural address he said, "the only thing we have to fear is fear itself." My childhood experiences had taught me that, whenever I felt fear, something really bad was sure to follow. So I understandably became afraid of that feeling and confused a useful warning sign with an alarm signifying impending disaster. But now I had the tools that allowed me to recognize that feeling as a friend, not an enemy, and to use it to my advantage.

It also was critical that Dorothie, unlike the kids I had hung out with, was not out to get me in these interactions. (In fairness, I was out to get them too. Most of us were into one-upping one another and trying to be at the top of the pecking order.)

DOROTHIE: Marty's making this shift had a huge, positive impact on our relationship, but I had my work cut out, too. I came to realize that I had to stop getting so upset when Marty got squirrely or did something else that drove me up the wall. In fact, I realized that Marty couldn't drive me up the wall. I was letting his behavior do that to me, and I had to take back control of myself.

So I thought about why his being afraid of me hurt me so much. That's when I realized it was resonating with my own childhood wounds. Marty wasn't being cruel to me the way the other kids sometimes had been, but when he became afraid of me, it threw me back to those situations and I felt he was being cruel.

My part in resolving this long-standing conflict was to bring compassion into the process, which also made it easier for Marty to do his own work. Once I saw how my fear of being an unlovable witch was hurting Marty, I couldn't allow myself to be taken over by that feeling.

I also had to have compassion for my own fear of being unlovable. So long as I pushed that fear down, it ran me around and fed my part of the vicious cycle we had been locked in for years. Ironically, my fear of being an unlovable witch made me less lovable, although nothing like the grotesque monster I had drawn as my self-portrait. Once I faced that fear consciously, I could see what a ridiculous caricature it was. Between that and Marty's working to love me "because I was angry," my fear of being unlovable has largely evaporated.

MARTY: The fact that Dorothie's fear was a self-fulfilling prophecy is not unique to her or this particular conflict. The same was true of my fear that something bad was going to happen. When I got squirrely, it sure did! And we've found that happening time and time again in working this process. Fearing something tended to bring about the very disaster we were afraid of. And, as with anger, only by bringing our fears to consciousness—which, at first, was a very scary thing to do—were we able to move beyond fear.

Sometimes It Only Takes One

When we were first married, we encountered in-law problems, which at the time seemed insurmountable. But as you'll see in this section, those problems were resolved in an almost miraculous way by bringing compassion to bear. As in Marty's three-month-long conflict with his father, it only took one party doing that to work a miracle—and hence, the title of this section, "Sometimes it Only Takes One."

MARTY: When we got engaged, Dorothie had never met my parents. Our initial plan was to visit them over Spring Break and get married that summer, when they could travel to Los Angeles for the ceremony. But then we accelerated the wedding so we could be together three months earlier. We were married on Good Friday 1967 and flew back to New York the following day. That's when Dorothie first met my parents. She's joked that I was smart to marry her before she met them, since otherwise she might have changed her mind.

DOROTHIE: That first day in New York, Marty's dad told me that I reminded him of his mother. Flattered, I said, "Why, thank you." To which he replied: "I never liked my mother. We didn't get along." I stood there mute. How do you respond to something like that?

MARTY: That incident was indicative of the personal and culture shock Dorothie experienced in New York. She'd grown up in the Southern California Gentile culture and here she was, playing Annie Hall in a real-life Woody Allen movie.

Another, big factor in Dorothie's in-law problems was mentioned earlier. My mother was so upset that Dorothie wasn't Jewish that she barely talked to anyone for weeks after she learned of our engagement. By the time of our visit to New York, my mother had recovered enough that she could try to pretend she was okay with my marrying Dorothie, but it hurt her at a very deep level. She'd been brought up in an Orthodox Jewish home in which a child who marries outside the faith is dead to his parents—they literally go into mourning as if he'd died. While my mother had broken with her parents' Orthodoxy, she still carried many of its taboos deep within her.

Dorothie came to me early in this visit, seeking comfort. My brothers and I—who, out of necessity, had learned as children not to challenge our parents—told her to not let it bother her. "It's annoying, but that's how they are," we said. "You can't do anything about it. Just let their craziness slide off you, like water off a duck's back."

DOROTHIE: I was in shock. Even normal people would have difficulty letting such insults "slide off their backs," and I'm not normal. I'm "the Princess and the Pea of relationship conflict." I was deeply hurt, and I felt abandoned. Marty was supposed to be my knight in shining armor, and here he was pretending the dragon wasn't there and telling me to ignore its fiery breath as it burned me to a crisp.

But I was even more in love than I was hurt so, somehow, I managed to get through that visit without blowing up, melting down, or trying to annul my marriage. But it was no honeymoon, and I mean that literally, since we'd just been married.

Over the ensuing years, I tried everything I could think of to improve my relationship with my in-laws, but nothing worked. On one visit, I even took Valium. Being tranquilized allowed me to view things as if I were watching a movie. I didn't take their misbehavior personally, and the visit went much better than in the past.

Not being present psychically didn't seem any worse than not being present at all, so after that visit, I told Marty that, on future trips to New York, he should take our daughters but go without me. In addition to avoiding being hurt, I didn't want to come between him and his parents or between our girls and their grandparents. I was afraid that continuing to subject myself to the agony of these visits would have those effects.

MARTY: While I could see Dorothie's point, at first I was resistant. My family, like many, held itself together by ignoring the elephant in the room. Remember that, in an earlier story, my father told me, "It's better not to go too deep. It can get dangerous down there."

Dorothie's not coming to New York would violate that rule by shining a spotlight on a problem that everyone else was trying to pretend didn't exist. My parents would not understand Dorothie's absence, at least at a conscious level. What would I tell them? But a combination of Dorothie's resolve and the wisdom of her decision eventually prevailed, and I took the girls to New York without her for our next few visits.

And then a miracle happened.

DOROTHIE: As Marty and I started on our process of reconciliation, I took responsibility for my relationship with his parents. I searched out ways that I could reclaim power to heal the relationship while taking care of myself, in spite of their mistreating me. I found the answer in compassion.

When I'd first met them, when I was eighteen years old and a new bride, I had needed them to love me and I was devastated that they did not. Now, in my mid-thirties and armed with compassion, I didn't ask anything of them or expect anything from them. By loving them as they were, I finally was able to "let it roll off my back," as Marty and his brothers had first advised, but in a totally different way.

Now my goal was not to have them love me, but to love them. How they treated me was irrelevant to that goal, so it didn't hurt me. I was coming to them from an entirely new place where how they treated me couldn't hurt me. All that mattered was that I loved them. That was my whole focus. If I could succeed in loving them, the visit was a success.

They were amazed at the change in me and were so appreciative that the tension which had always been there in the past just evaporated. Compassion gave me that kind of power.

Marty's parents weren't bad people. They just couldn't help themselves, and up to this point, I had kept the cycle going by reacting to their behavior. Once I refused to do that and stood my ground, compassion ruled ... and won. It's amazing what bringing compassion to a conflict can do.

A couple of years later, something happened that helped me to see how impossible my earlier fight to be loved by Marty's parents had been. His mother attended a Hadassah meeting—that's the Women's Zionist Organization of America—at which a woman, known as the Jewish Billy Graham, had spoken. His mother bought a copy of the speaker's book, *The Jewish Soul on Fire*, and sent it to Marty. The author had inscribed it, "Martin, the Jewish people need you!"

Among other things, the book stated that marrying outside the Jewish faith was worse than recreating the Holocaust. It argued that the Jews who had been marched into the Nazi gas chambers had no choice, but Marty was destroying Judaism by choice when he married me, and that's why it was worse. When I read that, I realized how impossible my quest to be loved by his parents had been. If the message etched in Marty's mother's identity was that deep, I didn't have a chance, except through compassion. Compassion worked where nothing else had.

Compassion can often work miracles, even if, as here, only one party to the conflict brings it to bear. Sometimes it only takes one.

You won't always get that kind of outcome and, if you expect it, it probably won't happen. That's not how compassion works. You have to love for the sake of loving, with no expectations, and see what the universe sends back. Isn't it worth the experiment?

Money, Sex, and Power

So many arguments in intimate relationships are about money, sex, or power that this book would be incomplete if we didn't say how we eventually resolved the many fights we had over those issues. Dorothie used to say that all fights in a marriage are about money, sex, or power, and she clearly was basing that on personal experience.

This section reinforces many of the lessons illustrated earlier. You'll see compassion playing a key role in resolving our conflicts over money, sex, and power, as well as the importance of tracing those conflicts back to their otherwise hidden sources. You'll see processes at work, transforming what were initially unattainable goals into reality. And you'll see how insisting on holistic solutions that work for both of us gained each of us more than we could possibly have hoped for when we fought over those issues.

Finally, and somewhat surprisingly, you'll see how the lessons we learned about money, sex, and power carry over to international relations, making an excellent segue to Part 2 of this book, which emphasizes that global context.

MARTY: Both of us came from environments in which there was enough money for the necessities of life, but not much more. Although our families' financial situations were comparable, we had developed very different approaches to money. Even as a kid, I'd save up to the point that I sometimes had $25 to $50. Today, that $50 would be like several hundred. Not bad for a thirteen-year-old who was overjoyed to get a twenty-five-cent tip for delivering groceries up five flights of stairs.

I liked money for the power it gave me to buy whatever I wanted. Once I bought something, I lost that power. So, while I occasionally bought things with my savings, I tended to hold onto my money much longer than most kids.

DOROTHIE: I liked to save money too, but with a specific acquisition in mind. When I was nine years old, it seemed like all the other girls were wearing pink, Angora, bobby sox warmers. They were purely decorative, but they were so soft and so beautiful that I desperately wanted a pair. They cost many months of my allowance, so I saved and saved and saved, and as soon as I was able to, I bought a pair. I was so happy. I couldn't stop looking down at my ankles to marvel at the gorgeous pink fluff that money had allowed me to buy.

When we were first married, those differences in our perspectives didn't matter, perhaps because we didn't have any money. Once Marty was working, and especially after our kids were born, that changed. Our income was greater, but our desires—which often felt like needs—exceeded what we could afford. Deciding how to apportion our money between those competing desires and how much to save became a major battleground.

MARTY: Our fights were exacerbated by a powerful dynamic from my family of origin. My father taught high school, and in those days, teachers were even more underpaid than they are today. He was into enjoying life, while my mother focused more on the things she wanted the family to have.

When summer vacations came and he'd talk about going somewhere, she'd want him to get a summer job so we could buy whatever the immediate need of the day seemed to be. These disagreements often led to fights, so I grew up with the belief system that, if the wife wanted something, the husband had better provide it or he'd be in the doghouse.

That belief system played itself out in our marriage—unconsciously, of course. I could dream about vacations we couldn't afford, or other luxuries I had no intention of actually buying. But if Dorothie did that, it would trigger a deeply rooted fear and I would try to stop her from dreaming by pointing out the practical impediments.

DOROTHIE: I felt so controlled by Marty's doing that, that sometimes I'd go out and buy something just to prove to myself that he didn't have control over me. My need to convince myself that I wasn't powerless was overpowering.

MARTY: When Dorothie bought things, it made me feel powerless and reinforced my fears, keeping that vicious circle going for years. The old map is full of blind alleys like that, and the only way out was for us to think in a new way—holistically.

DOROTHIE: After Marty brought his fears to consciousness and stopped trying to control me, it freed me up to appreciate how good he is at managing money.

MARTY: And I came to appreciate Dorothie for bringing beauty into our lives. I've often joked that, if it weren't for her, I'd be living on orange crates instead of real furniture. And that's not as much of an exaggeration as it might first appear.

Of course, transforming our fights over money into appreciation for one another was far from simple. Unconscious, deeply ingrained beliefs take time, hard work, and courage to bring to consciousness where they can begin to change.

DOROTHIE: Our conflicts over sex followed a related pattern. Each of us brought experiences into the relationship, some going all the way back to childhood. But we did so unconsciously, making it impossible to resolve the arguments they produced. The arguments seemed to be about events that had just happened, but in reality, they were rooted far in the past.

My most traumatic experience—being molested as a small child—was so repressed that I tearfully confessed it to Marty three times, years apart, and each time thought it was the first time I had even remembered it.

MARTY: While my heart went out to Dorothie and I told her that she had nothing to confess—she had done absolutely nothing wrong—sexual baggage that I brought to the relationship caused me to be unloving in other ways. Suffice it to say that Dorothie understandably ended up feeling like sex was more important to me than she was. And what woman—especially one who has been molested—wants to give herself to a man who feels like that?

The more I pressured Dorothie, the less responsive she became and the more frustrated I became—another of the old map's vicious circles.

Once we brought the conflict to a more conscious level and were committed to doing what was right for the relationship, I came to see how blind and unloving I had been. Determined to put things right, I told Dorothie that, if it was the right thing to do, I'd even be willing to live our marriage celibately. It wasn't what I wanted, but if that was what she needed, I would do it.

DOROTHIE: I was overwhelmed. My first thought was, "He loves me that much?" But I also knew that celibacy was not what I wanted and wasn't right for our marriage. I wasn't asexual. I was just tired of feeling pressured and unloved.

We couldn't ignore the problem by avoiding sex. We had to find a way for it to work for both of us. We needed to move beyond the power struggle over sex and have it become an act of love once more. Treated properly, sex can be what it has become for us again: a way of expressing how much a couple loves and appreciates one another.

With the power struggle out of the way, I was free to explore my own sexuality in a totally new way. For me to be a whole person, I needed to become comfortable with that part of myself, in spite of my childhood trauma.

Later in my healing process, I had an "Aha!" moment when I realized that being sexually molested was something that just happened to me. It had nothing to do with who I am at my core. Looking the abuse "in the eye," so to speak, instead of running away from it, allowed me to reclaim my power and stop it from running me around.

MARTY: Each of us had much more power to improve our sexual relationship than we thought, but we had to use our power in ways that our old maps saw as useless. Dorothie's old map told her that facing her abuse would be devastating, whereas in reality, it led to freedom. My old map said I had a right to pressure her when I felt inadequately loved. Our new map tells me that's a sure-fire way to push her away.

My old map also made another mistake with respect to sex. It saw sex as separate from the rest of our relationship, which is the opposite of holistic thinking. I expected Dorothie to be receptive, even though I did not treat her with the love and respect she deserved and craved. Now I understand that cherishing and honoring her is key to all aspects of our relationship, sex included.

DOROTHIE: I summarize that truth as, "sex begins at breakfast." When we used to fight on a regular basis, Marty's pushing for sex made me angry. Who wants to make love with someone who's angry at you, unappreciative, and generally unloving? Not me. For Marty, sex made the relationship better. For me, the relationship had to be right for me to want sex.

MARTY: Looking back, I wonder how I could have been so blind. If we had been dating and I'd treated Dorothie that way, I'd have expected her to end the date early. Somehow, because we were married, it was supposed to be different?

DOROTHIE: At the start of this section, we said that I *used* to say that all fights in a marriage were about money, sex, or power. We used the past tense because, as I looked beneath the surface of our conflicts about money and sex, I found that usually they were really about power. After I realized that, I started saying, "All fights in a marriage are about power, power, and power." If you look back over what we've said about our conflicts over money and sex, you'll see the words "power" and "powerless" occur repeatedly.

MARTY: We used to believe there was a fixed amount of power to be divided between us. The more I gained, the less Dorothie had. That model was, in many ways, the guiding star of our old relationship maps. It explains why we repeatedly fought for power.

Our new map sees power as expandable. In the earlier story about Dorothie looking at new cars long before it seemed reasonable to me, instead of trying to squelch her—as my old map would have directed me—I asked her why she was doing that. When she pointed out how the innovative safety features available on some new cars would enhance both our lives, I totally changed my perspective.

I lost no power in admitting the truth of this new information. On the contrary, it improved my life. Similarly, when I discovered a car that met our needs better than the one Dorothie had fallen in love with, she was open to this new information, again benefiting both of us.

Earlier stories show the same dynamic with money and sex. Giving up on trying to control Dorothie got me more of what I wanted; in fact, I got all I wanted and more.

If the guiding star of the old map is amassing as much power as possible at the expense of the other, true north on our new map is to empower one another in ways that benefit the relationship—which, of course, benefits each of us. As we noted in an earlier section of this book, re-examining the nature of power is a big part of the shift from the old map to the new, at both the personal and international levels. That section showed how I gained the power to end an excruciatingly painful argument by seeking out and then admitting my part in creating it, rather than blaming it all on Dorothie. That proves that the old map is wrong when it says that admitting error is a sign of weakness. On the contrary, admitting such truths conveys great power.

Nations make many of the same mistakes that we did, and even though sex doesn't figure directly into their interactions, there still are analogies. "Sex begins at breakfast" becomes "avoiding wars requires starting long before the spark that might set them off." As we'll soon see, the best time to have avoided the Vietnam War was in 1945, two decades before it started. That's when we should have refused to support France in its futile effort to re-impose colonial rule on Indochina. When France was defeated, we stepped in out of misplaced pride and fear of Communism—and eventually lost our own war.

The old map gauges a nation's power by its military might, as can be seen from the current tendency to call the United States "the world's sole remaining superpower." The new map provides a very different picture. First, it recognizes nuclear weapons as a great equalizer, so that Russia, which spends only one-seventh as much on weapons as we do, is for all practical purposes our military equal. Second, it recognizes that destructive power is not the only kind a nation can wield, and usually it is not the most useful.

If we measure American power by how we are perceived by the rest of the world, our military power has even had a negative impact. A 2013 Gallup worldwide poll found that, "The US was the overwhelming choice for the country that represents the greatest threat to peace in the world today," with 24 percent of those polled naming us. Pakistan came in second at 8 percent. China was seen as the third greatest threat to peace at 6 percent, followed by North Korea, Israel, and Iran, all tied at 5 percent. When we are seen as a significantly greater threat to peace than North Korea, something needs to change.[28]

DOROTHIE: Our military might also reduces our other forms of power by narrowing our field of vision. "When you are a hammer, everything looks like a nail." The relative importance of diplomacy and the military in American foreign policy can be seen from the fact that, in fiscal year 2015, the Defense Department budget was well over ten times that of the State Department.

Our prodigious military might reduces our power in other dimensions by limiting our ability to steer clear of dangerous conflicts. When military power is sought, we are the "go-to nation," as happened with Libya in 2011. President Obama was initially reluctant to attack Gaddafi—with good reason, as shown by the resultant rise of Islamic jihadists in Libya. But once other nations dragged us into their military intervention, we ended up doing most of the heavy lifting, reinforcing the hatred that the more violent elements within the Islamic world feel toward us. Similar anger at US military actions in the Middle East played a key role in motivating the 9/11 attacks, so this unintended consequence of our military power can have significant, negative repercussions to our national security.

Astonishing new horizons would be opened if our nation were to critically re-examine what kind of power benefits it. Many will see such hope as simplistic or naive, but in the nuclear age, sticking with the old model for power will eventually lead to devastation.

Rethinking international power is not just desirable, but necessary for survival. Doing so is therefore far from simplistic or naive.

Becoming Best Friends

If you're not treating your mate like your best friend, you need to change. End of section, end of chapter, on to Part 2!

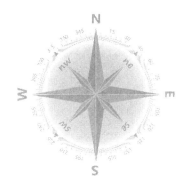

Part 2

Healing International Relationships in a Personal Setting

Chapter 6

The Shadow Side
of Our Nation

Part 1 of this book showed how important it was for the two of us to face our shadow or dark sides—those parts of ourselves that seemed so repulsive that they were hidden even from our own conscious minds. Before what Marty calls his *Last Epidemic* experience, his "arrogant, Jewish professor from New York" shadow side ran him around. Only after he accepted that part of himself—only after he embraced his shadow—could he function properly.

For the same reasons, the nations of the world need to face their shadow sides. As Americans, it is not our job to point out Russia's, or even Britain's, shadow side. In fact, doing so would only make them madder and drive their shadows deeper. That's why this chapter focuses on our own nation's shadow side, even though all nations need to undertake a similar self-examination.

Projecting Our National Shadow

The 1930s radio program *The Shadow* unwittingly described one of the key steps in resolving many seemingly insoluble interpersonal and international conflicts. By day, the Shadow posed as a wealthy *bon vivant*. By night, he became a superhero, using his psychic powers to defeat otherwise invincible criminals. Episodes often started with eerie music, followed by the announcer asking in a sinister voice, "Who knows what evil lurks in the hearts of men?" After an ominous pause and a spine-chilling cackle, he answers: "The Shadow knows!"[29]

Much of the hate, anger, and fear that we feel for others, at both an individual and national level, comes from projecting our shadow or dark side onto them. Even though our negative emotions seem to be directed outwardly, what we really hate is part of ourselves.

Despising those qualities in others is often an unconscious attempt to prove that we don't suffer from them. Consciously, we are unaware of our shadow side. That's why only "the Shadow knows what evil lurks in the hearts of men (and women)"—namely ourselves—and why we need to harness its psychic powers in combatting evil—again, within ourselves.

Just as Marty had to make peace with his "arrogant, Jewish professor from New York" shadow side to stop it from running him around, our nation needs to make peace with its shadow side so we can stop making the same mistakes over and over again.

MARTY: Two political cartoons that I saw in the 1980s illustrate how nations project their shadow sides onto one another.

One, in an American newspaper, showed the Russian bear, its fangs bared menacingly with rabid slobber dripping from its mouth. This fearsome beast was clawing madly at a map of Eastern Europe, leaving it torn to shreds. I saw the second political cartoon when I visited Moscow in that same time period. It showed the American eagle staring ominously out from the poster, its talons dripping with blood, clutching at a rolled-up map marked "Latin America."

Each cartoon had some truth in its message, but each made a major mistake that made it totally ineffectual: It focused its hatred on the mistakes of the other, where it had no power to produce change. Even worse, if you showed either political cartoon to citizens of the other nation, most would have objected that they were blameless and merely responding to the kind of aggression depicted in their own cartoon.

DOROTHIE: That reminds me of arguments we used to have in which each of us was out of control, attacking the other for the horrible injustices we had suffered and paying no attention to the pain we were inflicting.

MARTY: Unfortunately, little has changed in the years since I saw those cartoons. A recent political cartoon depicted a menacing Russian bear about to eat a frightened rabbit labeled "Ukraine." I haven't been to Russia in almost thirty years, but I'd bet that they now have political cartoons depicting some vicious caricature of America preying on Iraq or Libya.

When nations project their dark sides onto enemies, it produces a distorted "image of the enemy." This was exemplified by a 2015 *Newsweek* cover showing Putin with fiery hot coals where his eyes should be, glowing through dark sunglasses and making him look like the devil incarnate. A huge headline declares him to be

"THE PARIAH," and the subtitle reads: "Inside the bullet-proof bubble of the West's Public Enemy Number One." The magazine cover's message that Vladimir Putin is a devil is implanted at an unconscious level, where it is free to work mischief in ways that our conscious minds would dismiss as paranoid hysteria.[30]

Projection of our national dark side also appears to be involved in this passage from Bob Woodward's 2002 book, *Bush at War*. Interviewing President George W. Bush at his ranch in Crawford, Texas, the conversation turned to Kim Jong Il, then the leader of North Korea:

> *The president sat forward in his chair. I thought he might jump up he became so emotional as he spoke about the North Korean leader. "I loathe Kim Jong Il!" Bush shouted, waving his finger in the air. "I've got a visceral reaction to this guy ... I have seen intelligence of these prison camps—they're huge—that he uses to break up families, and to torture people. I am appalled. ... It is visceral. ... I feel passionate about this."*[31]

Bush's reaction strikes me as a likely case of projection for two reasons. First, his administration engaged in "enhanced interrogation" that many see as no different from the torture he claimed to abhor in Kim Jong Il. Second, Bush's "visceral reaction" is a sign that projection is likely at work, since seeing our shadow side in others tends to tie us up in psychic knots.

Our nation's reaction to Russia's 2008 invasion of Georgia and its ongoing military action against Ukraine also appears to involve projection of our national dark side, since those actions have similarities to what we did in Iraq and Libya. Going back in time, our over-reaction to the Soviet Union's 1979 invasion of Afghanistan may well have involved projection of our own repressed guilt over Vietnam.

DOROTHIE: As early as the 1960s, the noted psychiatrist Carl Jung recognized the danger of nations projecting their dark sides onto one another:

> *Mankind is now threatened by self-created and deadly dangers that are growing beyond our control. … Western man, becoming aware of the aggressive will to power of the East, sees himself forced to take extraordinary measures of defense, at the same time as he prides himself on his virtue and good intentions.*
>
> *What he fails to see is that it is his own vices … that are thrown back in his face by the communist world, shamelessly and methodically. What the West has tolerated [in itself] … comes back into the open and in full measure from the East and ties us up in neurotic knots. It is the face of his own evil shadow that grins at Western man from the other side of the Iron Curtain. …*
>
> *But all attempts [to resolve the problem] have proved singularly ineffective, and will do so as long as we try to convince ourselves and the world that it is only they (i.e., our opponents) who are wrong. It would be much more to the point for us to make a serious attempt to recognize our own shadow and its nefarious doings. If we could … we should be immune to any moral and mental infection and insinuation.*[32]

While Jung wrote that at the height of the Cold War, unfortunately it is still true today, with Russia, China, Iran, and North Korea replacing Communism for projection of our dark side.

Both at an individual and at a national level, pretending that our shadow sides do not exist condemns us to repeatedly act out in abhorrent ways we despise. Only by embracing our shadows and admitting that we, as well as they, suffer from those qualities can we break the cycle and become the people and nations that we aspire to be.

Moving Beyond Fear, Anger, and Hate Internationally

It would be ludicrous and dangerous for a nation to base its foreign policy on fear, anger, or hate instead of cool-headed logic. Yet that happens far too often as a result of projecting our national shadow side onto other nations. The results are disastrous—just like when both of us used to let fear and anger rule our attempts to reshape our marriage. Of course, it's a far greater disaster when nations are involved. Literally millions of unnecessary deaths can be traced back to fear, anger, or hate trumping reason in international relations.

MARTY: Our lives started to improve only after Dorothie and I stopped trying to force one another to change and instead focused on changing ourselves. Only I can change myself, and I am the only person I have the power to change. For the same reason, this book focuses primarily on mistakes our own nation has made. We recognize that criticizing one's nation in that fashion is illegal and even dangerous in many parts of the world, and we appreciate the freedom of expression in the United States that allows us to do that. Where possible, we encourage readers from other countries to undertake a similar soul-searching.

We see working to bring our nation ever closer to its founding ideals as an act of patriotism, a love of country. That view was expressed by President Obama when he visited Selma, Alabama, on March 7, 2015, the fiftieth anniversary of "Bloody Sunday." Speaking of the civil rights protesters who were attacked and beaten by Alabama state troopers, he said:

> *As we commemorate their achievement, we are well-served to remember that at the time of the marches, many in power condemned rather than praised them. ... Their faith was questioned. Their lives were threatened. Their patriotism challenged.*
>
> *And yet, what could be more American than what happened in this place? ... What greater expression of faith in the American experiment than this, what greater form of patriotism is there than the belief that America is not yet finished, that we are strong enough to be self-critical, that each successive generation can look upon our imperfections and decide that it is in our power to remake this nation to more closely align with our highest ideals?*

Just as the next sections highlighting America's mistakes are intended as an act of love for our country, their demonstrating the needlessness of our nation's various wars does not denigrate the losses suffered by our military forces in those wars. On the contrary, it hopes to redeem them. Our soldiers only died in vain if we fail to learn from our mistakes and keep getting into needless wars. If we learn from those mistakes, their deaths will prevent many more such losses in the future, and the wars in which their lives were sacrificed will become the greatest victories our nation has ever achieved.

DOROTHIE: There are a number of other, very good reasons for focusing on the mistakes our nation has made. We already know about Iran's bad behavior in getting its mobs to chant, "Death to America!" But too many Americans are surprised to learn that the CIA instigated a coup in 1953 that overthrew a democratically elected Iranian government. Learning about our mistakes turns what otherwise appears like a black and white situation—a conflict between good and evil—into one with shades of gray. That, in turn, can transform hatred into compassion, an important step toward holistic thinking and a more peaceful world.

America is the most powerful nation in the world, and its preeminent leader. But how will we use that power, and where will we lead the world if we don't correct our own mistakes? Nowhere good. Conversely, if we face our shadow side and correct our errors, we can use that power and that leadership position to transform the world in positive ways that, today, would be dismissed as mere wishful thinking. Now that's the kind of "American exceptionalism" I can go for.

As we've noted earlier, even if your primary concern is improving your personal relationships, there is real value in seeing how distorted our picture is of the international situation. As you see how wrong we, as a nation, can be about the international conflicts covered in the next seven sections, it will raise questions about how wrong we, as individuals, can be about our conflicts with one another. And it's easier to open up to such new ideas internationally, where you are not as emotionally invested as you are with your partner.

MARTY: Since the new information we'll present on these international conflicts flies in the face of conventional wisdom, our evidence needs to be solid. I have therefore used formerly classified information and confessions or other "declarations against interest" by authoritative individuals as much as possible.

For example, you'll hear the man who helped Colin Powell craft his speech to the UN just before the 2003 Iraq War deplore what he did as "a hoax on the American people."

You'll hear President Johnson tell a friend that, contrary to what he was telling Congress and the American people, the North Vietnamese attacks on US destroyers in the Tonkin Gulf were not unprovoked aggression on the high seas. Rather, he tells his friend, "There have been some covert operations in [North Vietnam] that we have been carrying on—blowing up some bridges and things of that kind, roads, and so forth. So I imagine they wanted to put a stop to it."

DOROTHIE: The next seven international case studies will explore how fear, anger, and hatred led our nation, and in some cases are still leading it, to make disastrous mistakes. We'll also look at how holistic thinking, which worked wonders in our marriage, would do the same internationally as well.

International Case Studies

Iraq

We chose Iraq as our first example because it is the worst mistake America has made in recent memory, and holistic thinking would have prevented it. Its full cost is estimated to be trillions, not billions, of dollars. Islamic fundamentalists, who had virtually no power in Iraq under Saddam Hussein, now control large swaths of the country under the ISIS banner. And the chaos in Iraq has spilled over into Syria, creating more human misery, more power for ISIS, and more threats to our nation's security. Even Britain's former Prime Minister Tony Blair, who led his nation into joining the invasion of Iraq, has agreed that it was "pretty much of a disaster."[33]

DOROTHIE: Even though Iraq's leader, Saddam Hussein, had nothing to do with the terrorist attacks on 9/11 that ruthlessly killed 3,000 Americans, the Bush administration was able to use our fear, anger, and hatred over that event to cast blame on him.

Our baser emotions needed to strike at someone—"to do something." But Saudi Arabia, which supplied fifteen of the nineteen hijackers, was supposedly our ally and therefore an unacceptable target. Egypt and Lebanon, with one hijacker each, and the United Arab Emirates, with two, were no better. Saddam was the ideal target, not based on the facts, but based on our hatred for him that stretched back to 1991's First Gulf War.

Our desire to overthrow Saddam predates the Bush administration and was enshrined in The Iraq Liberation Act, signed by President Clinton in 1998. Its first sentence, "declares that it should be the policy of the United States to seek to remove the Saddam Hussein regime from power in Iraq and to replace it with a democratic government."[34]

Members of the Bush administration, who already were looking for a reason to topple Saddam, played on that hatred to create a drumbeat to an unnecessary and costly war. But we can't just blame the administration. Their subterfuge wouldn't have worked if we, the people, hadn't also harbored hatred, causing us to uncritically accept the story our leaders were telling.

MARTY: Notes taken by one of Secretary of Defense Donald Rumsfeld's aides at a meeting only hours after the 9/11 attacks show that Rumsfeld was looking for an excuse to attack Iraq: "Hit Saddam Hussein at the same time—not only Osama bin Laden … Go massive. Sweep it all up, things underlined and not." (The underlining is in the aide's original, handwritten notes.)[35]

Thus began a successful attempt to shift blame for 9/11 onto Saddam Hussein, a task made easier because he was a man Americans already loved to hate. A week before the invasion of Iraq, the *Christian Science Monitor* noted how President Bush continually and falsely tied Saddam Hussein with September 11:

> *In his prime-time press conference last week, which focused almost solely on Iraq, President Bush mentioned Sept. 11 eight times. He referred to Saddam Hussein many more times than that, often in the same breath with Sept. 11.*
>
> *Bush never pinned blame for the attacks directly on the Iraqi president. Still, the overall effect was to reinforce an impression that persists among much of the American public: that the Iraqi dictator did play a direct role in the attacks. A New York Times/CBS poll this week shows that 45 percent of Americans believe Mr. Hussein was "personally involved" in Sept. 11 …*
>
> *Sources knowledgeable about US intelligence say there is no evidence that Hussein played a role in the Sept. 11 attacks, nor that he has been or is currently aiding Al Qaeda. Yet the White House appears to be encouraging this false impression,*

as it seeks to maintain American support for a possible war against Iraq ...

Polling data show that right after Sept. 11, 2001, when Americans were asked open-ended questions about who was behind the attacks, only 3 percent mentioned Iraq or Hussein. But by January of this year, attitudes had been transformed. In a Knight Ridder poll, 44 percent of Americans reported that either "most" or "some" of the Sept. 11 hijackers were Iraqi citizens. The answer is zero.[36]

Several years after the invasion, when President Bush again linked Iraq to 9/11, Ken Herman of Cox News pinned him down: "What did Iraq have to do with ... the attack on the World Trade Center?" Bush's reply was stunning: "Nothing ... nobody's ever suggested in this administration that Saddam Hussein ordered the attack."[37]

While Bush's reply was technically correct—his administration had never said Saddam ordered the 9/11 attacks—it overlooks the obvious impact that repeatedly linking Iraq with 9/11 had on the nation's beliefs.

Initially, Secretary of State Colin Powell and his Chief of Staff, Colonel Lawrence Wilkerson, had serious doubts about the administration's claims of a link between Saddam Hussein and al-Qaeda. But in the 2007 video documentary *Taxi to the Dark Side*, Colonel Wilkerson explains how the administration got him and his boss on board after a terrorist named al Libi was captured in Afghanistan in November 2001:

The moment al Libi was waterboarded, he started blurting things out. ... [and] rather than questioning what he was

saying and ... [seeing if it] could be corroborated, they imme-
diately stopped and ran off to report what al Libi had said.
... And all of a sudden Colin Powell is told, "Hey, you don't
have to worry about your doubts anymore, because we've just
gotten confirmation that there were contacts between al-Qaeda
and Baghdad."[38]

But, as often happens with information obtained by torture, al Libi was telling his captors whatever he thought they wanted to hear, in order to stop the torture. And a connection between Saddam Hussein and al-Qaeda is what they wanted to hear.

Fear was added to the mix by the Bush administration's claim that Saddam possessed weapons of mass destruction, an allegation that also proved to be false. Secretary of State Colin Powell's UN speech—in which he held up a vial of simulated anthrax—was one of the administration's most powerful levers for generating public support for the invasion.

But things weren't as straightforward as they seemed. Colonel Wilkerson now regrets the role he played in helping craft Colin Powell's UN speech. While he and his boss were misled by CIA Director George Tenet and others, both of them had significant doubts about the CIA's findings. They put their misgivings aside, probably because doing otherwise would have been political suicide. Wilkerson later confessed:

My participation in that presentation at the UN constitutes
the lowest point in my professional life. I participated in a hoax
on the American people, the international community and
the United Nations Security Council. How do you think that
makes me feel? Thirty-one years in the United States Army

and I more or less end my career with that kind of a blot on my record? That's not a very comforting thing.[39]

While the *Christian Science Monitor* and a few others raised questions about going to war, most of the media bought into the anger, fear, and hate. Bill Moyers' *Buying the War* video documents this abdication of responsibility by the press, including an interview with Phil Donahue, one of the few media personalities to question the administration's allegations. Donahue tells Moyers that he was instructed to have at least two supporters of the war on his show for every person raising questions: "You could have the supporters of the President alone. And they would say why this war is important. You couldn't have a dissenter alone. Our producers were instructed to feature two conservatives for every liberal."[40]

In spite of following that rule, Donahue's show was canceled several weeks before the invasion. While NBC denied a connection between the cancellation and Donahue's raising questions about the war, Moyers cites a leaked, internal network memo that stated: "Donahue presents a difficult public face for NBC in a time of war. At the same time our competitors are waving the flag at every opportunity."

Moyers' documentary also has a February 2003 clip of Fox News commentator Bill O'Reilly creating an emotionally charged atmosphere designed to repress any questions about going to war: "Anyone who hurts this country in a time like this. Well, let's just say you will be spotlighted. ... I will call those who publicly criticize their country in a time of military crisis, which this is, bad Americans."

Letting fear, anger, and hate take us over as a nation resulted in a war that has caused more American deaths than the 9/11 attacks, and many times that number of dead Iraqis. The emotional outburst that spawned this war also has done tremendous harm to our national security by creating the chaos in which ISIS has thrived.

DOROTHIE: Fear and anger work no better for our nation internationally than they did for Marty and me in our marriage. When hate is added to the mix, it becomes even more toxic.

I recently saw a television ad for a charity raising money to aid wounded veterans. A man who had suffered a horrendous brain injury while serving in Iraq asked viewers to donate money. His face was contorted as he struggled to speak. His grievous injuries clearly were going to affect him and his loved ones for the rest of his life. My chest tightened as I recoiled in horror at how needless his sacrifice had been.

What are we doing sending our young people off to needless wars, when far too many come home traumatized, maimed, or in coffins? It's inhuman. Why don't we think things through before putting our soldiers in harm's way?

I want to go far beyond the old map's goal of making things better for our wounded veterans once they return home. I want to stop putting our soldiers in harm's way for no good reason. As this section makes clear, this war did not have to happen. To use Colonel Wilkerson's words, we didn't have to buy this "hoax on the American people." Holistic thinking could have avoided all that human misery by rescuing us from fear, anger, and hate. Those are self-involved states of being, incompatible with a holistic perspective. All by itself, that could have saved us from this disaster.

Holistic thinking also would have required us to try to understand alternative perspectives that conflicted with our deeply held (but, in this case, incorrect) beliefs. Being open to that "opposing point of view" would have led us to ask more questions rather than blindly accepting a false story. We needed to get curious, not furious.

MARTY: Holistic thinking also would have caused us to consider the impact of our invasion on the Iraqi people—to have greater compassion for their fate. That would have led us to learn something about Iraq's ethnic and religious diversity. Saddam Hussein was a minority Sunni who had subjugated the majority Shiites.

Holistic thinking thus would have shown us how wrong Vice President Dick Cheney was when, four days before our invasion, he told *Meet the Press* that, "we will be greeted as liberators." To the 42 percent of the population who were Sunnis,[41] we were an invading force that reversed the roles and let the Shiites subjugate them. Not surprisingly, they fought our soldiers. While many Shiites initially welcomed us for freeing them from Sunni subjugation, that feeling soon evaporated as we came to be seen as an occupying military force.

Yet another way holistic thinking would have saved us is its requirement to do what's right, instead of what we think we want. If we had thought things through before invading, we would have recognized that we were creating a horrible situation for large segments of the Iraqi population, which was clearly not the right thing to do. As just one example, over two-thirds of the 1.5 million Christians who lived in Iraq under Saddam Hussein have had to flee the chaos we created.[42]

Just as Dorothie and I found that doing what's right often produces better solutions for each of us than if we'd gotten what we initially thought we wanted, the same would have been true here. We thought we wanted to invade Iraq, but as we've seen, not invading would have been far better for our nation.

DOROTHIE: Of course, we're not implying that if you apply holistic thinking to Iraq or other international conflicts, that will, all by itself, resolve them. Only when enough of us do that will our nation's policies change. But that process has to start somewhere, and you are as good a starting point as anyone.

Also, as we pointed out earlier, applying holistic thinking to international and global issues is excellent practice for learning to do the same in our personal relationships—and often, it's far easier because we're not as personally involved in the conflict.

Vietnam

MARTY: Tragically, the Iraq War was not the first time that the American public let anger, fear, and hatred blind us to misrepresentations by our government and media. The mistakes we made in Iraq were, in many ways, carbon copies of those we made in Vietnam—a debacle from which we should have, but did not, learn a painful lesson.

Back in the 1950s and '60s, our fear was Communism, not terrorism, but the effect was the same. Fear helped propel us into a needless war in Vietnam, at a high cost in blood, treasure, and national prestige.

The "domino theory" said that we had to fight the Communists in Vietnam or we would end up fighting them on our own soil. President Bush stated almost exactly that same idea—but with terrorism replacing Communism—when he said, in his August 2007 speech to the American Legion: "We're using all elements of American power to protect the American people by taking the fight to the enemy. ... We will fight them over there so we do not have to face them in the United States of America."

Too few people questioned why we were getting into a war in Vietnam based on the domino *theory*, without our officials first checking to make sure that the theory was correct—which, of course, it wasn't. Eventually, the Communists won in Vietnam, but rather than a Communist wave lapping at our shores, that ideology largely died after Gorbachev came to power. Yet the Secretary of Defense who presided over much of the Vietnam War, Robert McNamara, referred to the domino theory as "the primary factor motivating the actions of both the Kennedy and the Johnson administrations."[43]

Anger, which played an important role in creating public support for the Iraq War, did the same in Vietnam—even though it was later established that the Johnson administration lied. To understand the nation's anger, it helps to first hear the false story the Johnson administration told Congress, the American people, and the world. Here's that false story as we heard it in 1964:

On August 2, 1964, North Vietnamese PT boats made an unprovoked attack on the USS Maddox *as it cruised through international waters in the Tonkin Gulf. In an effort to prevent war, America restrained itself and fired only on the attacking PT boats. But the US government warned North Vietnam that further such aggression would bring a swift American response.[44]*

Two days later, on August 4, the North Vietnamese made a second attack on the Maddox *and another American destroyer that had been sent to reinforce her. Johnson ordered devastating air strikes on North Vietnamese targets in reprisal.*

If that story we and Congress had been told by the administration had been true, American anger would have been understandable, but still dangerous. It's always safer and more effective to plan how to respond to a provocation after you've cooled down. But we now know from declassified documents that the whole story was false.

The first attack did, in fact, occur. But far from being unprovoked aggression, this attack was a response to our own, covert attacks on North Vietnam. That's what President Johnson told a former Treasury Secretary the day after it occurred:

> *There have been some covert operations in that area that we have been carrying on—blowing up some bridges and things of that kind, roads, and so forth. So I imagine they wanted to put a stop to it. So they come out there and fire and we respond immediately with five-inch guns from the destroyer and with planes overhead. And we cripple them up—knock one of them out and cripple the other two. And then we go right back where we were with that destroyer, and with another one, plus plenty of planes standing by. And that's where we are now.*[45]

Two days after the first attack, on August 4, the *Maddox* and another American destroyer sent to reinforce her reported a second attack. Following up on his earlier warning of "grave consequences" for such aggression, Johnson ordered major air strikes on North Vietnamese targets in reprisal, with strong approval from the American media and public.

There was just one problem: In the words of a formerly top-secret NSA history of the event, "no attack happened that night." The NSA history goes on to explain, "In truth, Hanoi's navy was engaged in nothing that night but the salvage of two of the [PT] boats damaged on 2 August."[46]

In light of what we now know, the media coverage of the second non-attack is stunning. *Newsweek*, then America's second largest-circulation weekly news magazine, described it in terms worthy of a war movie script:

> *At 9:30 p.m., the* Maddox *reported that enemy craft, identified as Soviet-built 50- and 100-ton PT boats, were closing in. By 9:52 p.m., both destroyers were under continuous torpedo attack. In the mountainous sea and swirling rain, no one knew how many PT boats were involved as they rose and fell in the wave troughs. The US ships blazed out salvo after salvo of shells. Torpedoes whipped by, some only 100 feet from the destroyers' beams. A PT boat burst into flames and sank. More US jets swooped in, diving, strafing, flattening out at 500 feet, climbing, turning 90 degrees at 8,000 feet, and diving again.*[47]

Newsweek, having bought the administration's fictitious account, went on to announce self-righteously, "Now it was time for American might to strike back."

In Johnson's defense, I should note that he didn't just invent the second attack. The commander of the *Maddox*, Captain John J. Herrick, initially did think he was under attack, and he reported that up the chain of command—and those reports did reach the president. But after several hours of believing he was under continuous attack, serious doubts crept into Captain Herrick's mind and he cabled his superiors: "Review of action makes many recorded contacts and torpedoes fired appear doubtful. Freak weather effects and overeager sonarman may have accounted for many reports." Captain Herrick concluded that cable with a caution: "Suggest complete evaluation before any further actions."[48]

Unfortunately, Herrick's advice was not heeded, partly because information sent to Johnson and his advisers downplayed such doubts[49]—probably because it was known that Johnson wanted a reason to attack North Vietnam. To cite one piece of evidence of that mindset within the Johnson administration, on June 5, two months before the Tonkin Gulf incidents, our Ambassador to South Vietnam, Henry Cabot Lodge, sent a cable to Washington that proposed lying to allow us to attack North Vietnam. After proposing that American planes fire rockets into North Vietnam "on the pretext that they had been fired on and were firing back," Lodge wrote:

> *We want a scream from them that they had been hit by something coming from our side. I would not object if they blamed us. They could prove nothing. We could either be totally silent, or challenge them to provide proof, or say we are looking into it.*[50]

Given that elements within the Johnson administration were proposing blatant lies as a pretext for striking out at North Vietnam, it makes sense that subordinates would downplay information that questioned the second attack.

Why that bias existed is related to another important question: Why—to use Johnson's own words—did he agree to send the *Maddox* and the other destroyer "right back where we were" when the *Maddox* was attacked? Right back where Johnson knew we were "blowing up some bridges and things of that kind, roads, and so forth"? Right back where they were likely to be attacked?

I can't be sure, but I believe that Johnson wanted North Vietnam to attack the destroyers in order to rally the nation around him and ensure a landslide victory in the presidential election, which was to be held three months later.

Several weeks before the Tonkin Gulf incidents, the Republicans had nominated Barry Goldwater to run against Johnson in November. Goldwater advocated a more forceful approach in Vietnam, even suggesting that we should use nuclear weapons to win the war.[51] Johnson's campaign used that against Goldwater, suggesting that a vote for Goldwater was a vote for nuclear annihilation.

But Johnson had another problem. The Republicans had accused him of being an indecisive Commander-in-Chief. A month before the Tonkin Gulf incidents, the *New York Times* reported: "The Senate and House Republican leaders said today that the Vietnamese war would be a campaign issue this year because 'President Johnson's indecision has made it one.'"[52]

A week later, another *Times* story stated: "Senator Barry Goldwater confirmed today that if he were President he would order a 'win policy' in South Vietnam and would then tell the military commanders 'that it was their problem and to get on with solving it.'"[53]

Johnson needed to appear aggressive and restrained at the same time—quite a tall order. The deceitful account of the Tonkin Gulf incidents that Johnson presented accomplished those two otherwise incompatible goals. In his TV address of August 4, after calling the second attack—which we now know never happened—"an outrage," Johnson turned black into white:

182

Yet our response, for the present, will be limited and fitting. We Americans know, although others appear to forget, the risks of spreading conflict. We still seek no wider war. ... but it is my considered conviction, shared throughout your Government, that firmness in the right is indispensable today for peace; that firmness will always be measured. Its mission is peace.[54]

By claiming a false national emergency, Johnson was even able to get Goldwater to publicly support the "retaliatory" air strikes that he announced in that speech. Johnson won the 1964 election by a landslide. But far from his promise that "we still seek no wider war," he escalated the armed conflict soon after the election. A later interview with Johnson's National Security Adviser, McGeorge Bundy, gives the strong impression that Johnson did not escalate until after the election in order to maintain his self-created image of restraint.[55]

DOROTHIE: How could holistic thinking have saved us from the Vietnam War? In much the same way it could have saved us from the Iraq War, four decades later.

A holistic approach would have prevented fear, anger, and hatred from determining our actions. We could have ended up with the same situation we have today—Communist control of all Vietnam—but without the loss of 58,000 American lives and somewhere between one and three million Vietnamese lives.

As with Iraq, holistic thinking also would have required us to consider the impact of our actions on the people of the country involved, rather than just worrying about our own security—a concern that, as we've seen, backfired by costing us tens of thousands of American lives while making us no safer.

Learning more about the South Vietnamese people would have showed us that only a minority of them supported the American-backed government. The 1954 Geneva Accords had temporarily divided the nation into North and South Vietnam and called for elections within two years to reunify the nation. The American-backed ruler of South Vietnam, Ngo Dinh Diem, knew that his northern rival, Ho Chi Minh, would win a free election, so with our backing, he refused to allow it.[56]

Also as with Iraq, holistic thinking would have required us to do what's right instead of what we thought we wanted to do. Again, doing what's right would have been far better for us than acting out of our exaggerated fear of Communism.

Russia

MARTY: Russia is an important case study because its 8,000 nuclear weapons[57] make it the nation most capable of destroying us. The poor state of Russian-American relations makes that risk larger than it needs to be. But how can we improve relations with a nation that forcibly annexed Crimea, leading Hillary Clinton, among others, to compare Putin to Hitler?[58] By the end of this case study, you'll have seen how.

The typical American perception of Russia is captured in the January 2015 *Newsweek* cover described earlier, in which Vladimir Putin is depicted as the devil incarnate. In such an environment, it might seem like a fool's errand to suggest that Americans need to develop more compassion for Russia, but that is precisely what is needed to arrest a dangerous slide toward a new Cold War, with all the nuclear risks of the old one. It's also what is needed if our nation is to live up to its claimed ideal of dealing fairly with all. Putin is not Mr. Nice Guy, but neither is he the devil.

Having compassion for Russia does not mean overlooking its faults. Rather, it means understanding how that nation's traumatic history has contributed to its behaving in ways that otherwise would mystify us. If we see Russia more clearly, our actions will be more effective in meeting our nation's goals, while also reducing the risk of Russia acting like "a bear in a china shop."

Russia has been repeatedly invaded, with horrendous consequences, making it extremely sensitive to turmoil or foreign troops near its borders. Today, when we expand NATO or speak of bringing Western values to Russia and its environs, we think in terms of expanding democracy and human rights. But Russians tend to see our actions as a renewed attempt at religious, cultural, and political subjugation.

They also see democracy very differently from us. The Yeltsin era, which is celebrated in the West as the most democratic period in Russia, today is held in disdain by most Russians. Life savings were wiped out by hyperinflation and the country's most valuable assets were stolen by oligarchs.

While other invasions hold an important place in the Russian worldview, World War II is the 800-pound gorilla pounding on Russia's brain. That's understandable, given that over fifty times as many Soviet citizens died in that war compared to America's losses. Even their name for that war shows the difference in our perspectives. Russians call it The Great Patriotic War, a much more Russo-centric view of events.

We have our own Amero-centric perspective on the war, with D-Day being the prime example. That June 6, 1944, Allied invasion of France, which opened the Western Front, is seen in the West as "the battle that won the war." That's even the subtitle of a 2013 article in *Foreign Affairs*.[59]

But the Russian view is very different, since roughly 80 percent of the German "permanent losses" (dead, missing, or disabled) occurred on the Eastern Front, at an even greater cost in Soviet lives.[60] Russians are infuriated at the way the West overlooks their painful sacrifices in defeating Nazism, making it seem as if Russian lives don't count.

Aside from the fact that Germany was on the way to defeat by D-Day, many Russians view our opening this second front as coming far too late. The web site of the historian of the US State Department explains:

> *Stalin's troops struggled to hold the Eastern front against the Nazi forces, and the Soviets began pleading for a British invasion of France immediately after the Nazi invasion in 1941. In 1942, Roosevelt unwisely promised the Soviets that the Allies would open the second front that autumn. Although Stalin only grumbled when the invasion was postponed until 1943, he exploded the following year when the invasion was postponed again until May of 1944.[61]*

Putin's personal account of his family's World War II experiences, written on the 70th anniversary of the Allies' victory over Nazism, also helps explain why that war plays such a large role in Russia's worldview.[62] His parents lived in Leningrad (now St. Petersburg), where more civilians died during the war than all American military losses. Five of Putin's six uncles were killed, his father was seriously wounded, and his older brother died of diphtheria. Such tragic personal losses must have made the West's boycott of Russia's 70th anniversary victory celebration all the more painful. (We boycotted the event to protest Russia's annexation of Crimea.)

Russia's perspective is also influenced by the 1941 US Senate debate on whether to extend Lend Lease to the Soviets, during which then-Senator Harry Truman stated: "If we see that Germany's winning we ought to help Russia, and if Russia is winning we ought to help Germany, and that way let them kill as many [of each other] as possible."[63]

Words like that coming from the man who became president before the war ended help explain why many Russians believe that we repeatedly delayed D-Day in an effort to bleed them dry. That Russian belief fit with earlier fears generated right after the 1917 Bolshevik Revolution, when the United States, Britain, and France sent troops into Russia. The Russians saw this as an invasion, while we saw it as aiding the anti-Bolshevik Russians in a civil war.

Russia's fear of the West can be better understood in light of Churchill's "Operation Unthinkable." Developed as World War II was drawing to a close, "Unthinkable" proposed that, within months of Germany's surrender, Britain and the United States should form a new alliance with Germany and together attack the Soviet Union.[64] Fortunately, the British military had the good sense to point out the unworkability of Churchill's unthinkable plan.

Jumping forward four decades, President Reagan's first term was marked by extreme hostility toward the Soviets, with loose talk of fighting and winning a nuclear war creating a war scare within the Soviet Union. Reagan's labeling it as "the evil empire" didn't help matters, nor did his praise for *The Late Great Planet Earth*,[65] a highly popular book of that era among Evangelical Christians. The book described a nuclear war as a probable precursor to the Second Coming of Christ and cast Russia in the role of leading the armies of the Antichrist.[66]

Fast-forwarding to current times, a 2013 article by the noted Russian international relations expert Fyodor Lukyanov gives an excellent view of the current Russian perspective. Lukyanov, editor of the Russian equivalent of *Foreign Affairs*, is highly regarded by some of the top people within the American diplomatic community. His article was titled, "What Russia Learned From the Iraq War":[67]

The conclusions drawn by Putin from ... Iraq were ... [that the] strong do what they want [so the] ... only rational way of behaving ... is to increase one's own power and capabilities, so that one can fight back and exert pressure, if necessary. ...

In the 10 years since the Iraq war, Putin's worldview has only strengthened and expanded. Now he believes that the strong not only do what they want, but also fail to understand what they do. From Russian leadership's point of view, the Iraq War now looks like the beginning of the accelerated destruction of regional and global stability, undermining the last principles of sustainable world order. Everything that's happened since—including flirting with Islamists during the Arab Spring, US policies in Libya and its current policies in Syria—serve as evidence of strategic insanity that has taken over the last remaining superpower. ... Moscow is certain that if continued crushing of secular authoritarian regimes is allowed because America and the West support "democracy," it will lead to such destabilization that will overwhelm all, including Russia.

Lukyanov's analysis was written a year before the February 2014 change of government in Ukraine, and it helps explain why that event is of such concern to Russia and Putin. The West sees that revolution as the replacement of a corrupt government by popular demand, while Russia sees it as a violent coup that empowered neo-Nazis in Ukraine. Each perspective has some validity, but each becomes a dangerous myth when it ignores the truths present in the other.

Viktor Yanukovych, the president of Ukraine who fled to Russia in February 2014 out of fear for his life, was extremely corrupt and had become highly unpopular. But in 2010, he had won the presidency in an election that international observers called "transparent and honest."[68]

The protests that led to Yanukovych's ouster started as peaceful demonstrations, but turned violent in February 2014, leading to approximately 100 deaths from sniper fire. The West blames Yanukovych's forces for the deaths, while Russia claims they were a "false flag" operation by violent extremists within the protestors.[69] Evidence has been presented to support both theories, and both may have some truth: There may have been snipers on both sides. Unfortunately, we are unlikely to ever know what happened, since the Ukrainian General Prosecutor's Office bungled its investigation of the massacre.[70]

This blame game only prolongs the horrendous suffering of Ukraine's population. Every nation involved in the conflict, but especially Russia and the United States, needs to stop focusing on its adversaries' mistakes, where it has no power to bring about positive change. Instead, each nation needs to take a hard look at itself, figure out what it's been doing wrong, and focus on changing those behaviors. That's where it has power to stop the violence. A first step would be to admit that the other side has some valid concerns.

While Russia overplays the role of ultra-nationalists and neo-Nazis in the current Ukrainian government, those groups have more power than the West usually admits. A notable exception was a September 2015 Radio Free Europe report that noted, "No longer can the post-Maidan government of President Petro Poroshenko deny it has a problem with a small but dangerous ultranationalist contingent that has served as a useful ally in the past, but that also has repeatedly shown a willingness to use violence to push its own agenda."[71]

Russia also sees our actions in Ukraine as a further attempt to encircle it with hostile NATO forces. Before Gorbachev allowed the peaceable breakup of the Soviet Union and the dissolution of the Warsaw Pact, Moscow had a huge buffer separating it from NATO forces. That distance shrank in 1999 when Poland, Hungary, and the Czech Republic became NATO members, and again in 2004 when Lithuania, Latvia, and Estonia joined. If Ukraine were to join NATO—something both it and the United States are on record as supporting—Moscow's buffer would be reduced once again.

An article written in 2007 by Vice Admiral Ulrich Weisser (Retired), who was head of the policy and planning staff in the German Ministry of Defense from 1992 to 1998, helps explain the Russian perspective:[72]

Prior to admitting Poland, Hungary and the Czech Republic, NATO had indeed stated to Russia that there was no need, no plan, and no intention to undertake such stationing [of

NATO troops in Eastern Europe]. The alliance has not held this promise. On the contrary, the US has even secured rights in Romania to establish forward bases for its air force. Moscow also feels provoked by the behavior of a number of newer NATO member states in central and Eastern Europe. Poland and the Baltic states use every opportunity to make provocative digs at Russia; they feel themselves protected by NATO and backed by the US.

Having gone over a number of reasons we should have more compassion for Russia, there's an important caveat I need to add. The evidence presented in this section occasionally may make it look like the Russians are saner than we, but that's only because I focused on our mistakes—the ones over which we have control. If I were Russian and writing for a Russian audience, the same result could be produced in reverse by highlighting people like Vladimir Zhirinovsky.

Zhirinovsky, a Russian ultranationalist, reportedly advocated using tactical nuclear weapons against Chechen rebels and setting off nuclear weapons in the Atlantic to flood Great Britain.[73] Zhirinovsky's extremism is of particular concern because he was twice elected Deputy Speaker of the Duma and garnered almost 7 million votes in the 2008 presidential election—roughly 10 percent. The Russian population showed a bit more sense in the 2012 presidential election, giving him only 6 percent. But that amount of support is still worrisome, given his extreme positions.

I'm not saying that Russia is never wrong. What I am saying is that Russia is not *always* wrong, we're not *always* right—and contrary to *Newsweek*'s cover, Putin is not the devil incarnate.

For civilization to survive in the nuclear age, greater maturity and a more holistic, more compassionate perspective is needed from all nations. As Americans, we are most effective when working to bring that about in our own country, which is why this section focused almost exclusively on our mistakes.

If we succeed in developing that more inclusive perspective, the world will become far less violent, whether or not Russia and other nations also grow up. Even one adult in a room full of unruly children is better than none. It is our hope that one nation acting maturely will set an example, spread, and create a room full of adults.

North Korea

MARTY: North Korea's dictator, Kim Jong-un, presents another example of how our own hatred has caused us great harm. By the end of this section, you'll have seen how our failing to take in the bigger picture—failing to think holistically—played a role in North Korea building its nuclear weapons and is unintentionally encouraging that nation to expand its arsenal. You'll also see how mistakes on all sides increase the risk of a second Korean War that could bring China and Japan into the fray. Should that happen, the United States would be treaty-bound to come to Japan's aid—even though doing so would risk nuclear war.

As always, I'll focus on places where our nation has power to improve what appears to be an impossible relationship—in other words, I'll focus on mistakes our nation has made and therefore can correct. But my focus on our mistakes is not to excuse the many despicable acts committed by the rulers of North Korea. Rather, that focus recognizes that we do not have direct control over their actions, and scolding them tends to make them dig in their heels. I see it as a hopeful sign that we have options for improving relations even with a regime as abhorrent as North Korea's. The sad part is that, thus far, we have squandered those options by allowing repugnance to override our national interests.

Most Americans' main concern about North Korea is its nuclear weapons program, so let's look at its history. Our media gives the impression that nuclear diplomacy with the North is a waste of time because the country is too untrustworthy. But the historical record tells a more nuanced story.

Back in 1994, the United States prepared to go to war if North Korea did not rein in its nuclear program. Fortunately, former President Jimmy Carter flew to Pyongyang and was able to defuse the situation. This resulted in the 1994 Agreed Framework, under which North Korea froze its production of plutonium, the most dangerous element of its nuclear weapons program. You didn't hear me wrong. They really did freeze it.[74] They didn't do any nuclear tests until several years after that agreement fell apart in 2002.

Here's what they did from 1994 to 2002 to freeze the program:

- They shut down their only nuclear reactor, a small Magnox research reactor—a type of reactor that is well suited to making bomb-grade plutonium.
- They put the fuel rods from that reactor under lock and key, so that the plutonium already produced could not be extracted to make an estimated four to eight nuclear bombs.
- They stopped construction of a larger Magnox reactor that would have made enough plutonium for ten bombs a year and was estimated to be within a few years of completion.[75]

- They also stopped construction of an even larger Magnox reactor that would have made plutonium for forty bombs a year and was expected to be completed in about five years.

In return for those significant concessions on North Korea's part, we agreed to provide it with two light water reactors or LWRs. Substituting LWRs for Magnox reactors was a real win because the plutonium they produce is not as useful for making bombs. The target date for delivery of the LWRs was 2003.

Until the LWRs were delivered, we agreed to make annual shipments of heavy fuel oil to make up for the energy that the larger Magnox reactors would have produced. From our perspective, the Agreed Framework worked well from 1994 to 2002, as can be seen from several incontestable facts:

- North Korea did not conduct any nuclear tests during that period.
- North Korea stopped construction of both larger Magnox reactors and never put them into operation. If those reactors had been completed, North Korea today could have an arsenal of at least 100 nuclear weapons, instead of the much smaller number they are estimated to possess.[76] [77] [78]
- We were often late in the required heavy fuel oil shipments, and President Bush stopped them completely in 2002.[79]
- We never completed the promised LWRs to replace the Magnox reactors North Korea stopped building. Thus, when we cut off the heavy fuel oil shipments, North Korea lost the energy that their reactors would have produced.

In 2002, after we stopped the heavy fuel oil shipments, North Korea withdrew from the Nonproliferation Treaty, kicked out the international inspectors, and started extracting plutonium from its previously locked-up fuel rods. Four years later, they conducted their first nuclear test. What killed the 1994 Agreed Framework?

North Korea and the United States saw the agreement through very different eyes from the beginning. Our emphasis was on its ability to keep North Korea from getting a bomb. A *Washington Post* article even claimed: "Clinton administration officials have privately said that they agreed to the plan in 1994 only because they thought the North Korean government would collapse before the project [construction of the LWRs] was completed."[80] I have heard both supporting and contradictory statements from first-hand participants, and my overall conclusion is that some within the American government were of the mind described in the *Post* article, while others were working in good faith trying to fulfill our obligations.

In contrast to our focus on nuclear nonproliferation, North Korea saw the Agreed Framework as the first step toward improving relations with the United States, a goal that had increased in importance three years earlier when the Soviet Union fell apart in 1991. The resultant lack of Soviet support made North Korea more fearful of its giant neighbor, China, and it sought improved relations with the United States to fill the void. If successful in that effort, they also would reap a huge bonus by weakening our ties with their mortal enemy, South Korea.

That difference in perspectives laid a shaky foundation for the Agreed Framework. Then, in January 2002, President Bush worsened relations when he included North Korea in his "axis of evil" speech, with Iran and Saddam Hussein's Iraq being the other two members. North Korea's fears were heightened by President Bush's September 2002 *National Security Strategy* [81] and its emphasis on our right to preemptively attack nations that we considered rogue states.

Later that year, the Bush administration accused North Korea of cheating on the Agreed Framework by enriching uranium, which led to our ceasing shipments of heavy fuel oil. There is evidence that they were experimenting with uranium enrichment, but that is not technically forbidden by the Agreed Framework. In fact, neither *uranium* nor *enrichment* appears anywhere in the text of the agreement.[82]

However, an American diplomat who worked on the document told me that the North Koreans undoubtedly knew that we would regard any uranium enrichment as a violation. He told me that the only reason it was not prohibited in the text was because the State Department wanted an agreement that could be verified, and uranium enrichment is too easy to hide.

Having studied the matter, my own opinion is that both sides pushed the limits more than they should have, but that the Agreed Framework was doing a good job of preventing North Korea from obtaining nuclear weapons until President Bush took the actions he did in 2002.

My Stanford colleague and former Director of Los Alamos National Laboratory, Dr. Siegfried Hecker, has visited North Korea seven times on unofficial missions sanctioned by our government. In a 2010 paper, he gave his perspective on how the deal fell apart (emphasis added): [83]

The Agreed Framework was opposed immediately by many in Congress who believed that it rewarded bad behavior. Congress failed to appropriate funds for key provisions of the pact, *causing the United States to fall behind in its commitments almost from the beginning. … [In 2002,] the Bush administration killed the Agreed Framework for domestic political reasons and because it suspected Pyongyang of cheating by covertly pursuing uranium enrichment. Doing so traded a potential threat that would have taken years to turn into bombs for one that took months, dramatically changing the diplomatic landscape in Pyongyang's favor. … **We found that Pyongyang was willing to slow its drive for nuclear weapons only when it believed the fundamental relationship with the United States was improving, but not when the regime was threatened.***

Hecker's last sentence provides the key to defusing the Korean crisis. If we continue to engage in regime change around the world and encourage it in North Korea via crippling sanctions, that nation's leaders will maintain or increase their nuclear arsenal in order to deter such efforts. It's a matter of self-preservation for them. Regime change probably would result in their being killed.

Holistic thinking would require us to take in the perspective of North Korea's leaders. We don't have to like them, but we do have to understand them. If we were to consider their perspective, we would recognize that, as distasteful as the North Korean government is, encouraging regime change is not in our best interests, because it will lead to the North maintaining, and probably increasing, its nuclear arsenal. If we were to think things through more rationally, new possibilities would open up.

A lack of holistic thinking—not taking in the bigger picture—also led us to unwittingly add an additional barrier to dealing with

North Korea's nuclear weapons when, in 2011, President Obama helped topple Libya's dictator Muammar Gaddafi. What did attacking Libya have to do with North Korea's nuclear arsenal?

Eight years earlier, in 2003, when Gaddafi gave up his nuclear weapons program, President Bush promised that his good behavior would be rewarded and asked other nations to find "an example" in Libya's move.[84] When the United States attacked Libya eight years later, North Korea put out a statement which showed that they had learned a lesson from Libya's good behavior, but not the one President Bush had intended. The North Koreans saw us as coaxing Libya "with such sweet words as *guarantee of security*" so that it dismantled its nuclear weapons program, after which we "swallowed it up by force."[85]

Given how we treated Gaddafi, North Korea will be understandably hesitant to give up its nuclear weapons. Yet our current bargaining position is that we will not resume negotiations unless it's to talk about that very action. That means no talks, which means we have even less power to influence the North.

Our bewilderment over North Korea's seemingly crazy behavior bears a resemblance to how I sometimes used to see Dorothie. Earlier, I described a realization I had after a huge fight with her that seemed to me like it was all her fault. If my perception was correct, then I had no power to end the pain I was in. Nothing could happen until Dorothie came to her senses. But if my perception was wrong and I had played a role in creating the fight, then I might have the power to end it (and my pain) by apologizing for what I'd done. Reframing it that way helped me find the part that I'd played. I apologized to Dorothie for what I'd done, which led her to do the same to me. The argument was over.

How might that relate to North Korea? In 2013, the country seemed to throw a tantrum that had the West puzzling over "this crazy nation"—in the same way that I had been puzzled by "this crazy woman." North Korea conducted its third nuclear test, canceled the armistice ending the Korean War, threatened the United States with nuclear ruin, evacuated people to tunnels, cut its hotline with South Korea, and warned that "war may break out at any moment."[86]

The American government, media, and public saw this shrill, irrational behavior as confirming our conviction that North Korea is a rogue nation run by a nut job. In that perspective, there was little we could do, other than hope that it wouldn't be deranged enough to follow through on its threats.

But there are at least several other possibilities we might consider, each of which would give us some power to start resolving the conflict—but only if we would move from blame to responsibility. And of course, more than one of these possibilities may be at work.

First, North Korea's irrational behavior may come from our own nuclear strategy playbook. A 1995 report from the Strategic Advisory Group to the top American nuclear weapons command recommended that, in order to create the "sense of fear" needed to deter our adversaries, the United States should act in ways that make it appear "irrational and vindictive if its vital interests are attacked."[87] Doesn't that sound like North Korea?

A second possible explanation for North Korea's tantrum lies in noting that it occurred during the winter, and that it frequently acts threateningly during that season. This is not due to winter's long, dark nights causing seasonal affective disorder. Rather, winter is when the United States and South Korea announce their annual spring military exercises—war games that the North claims are "a rehearsal for an invasion" of their nation.[88]

Moving the troops and hardware needed for an invasion warns the intended victim, giving it time to prepare its defenses. Disguising preparations for an invasion as a war game helps cloak such maneuvers and maintain an element of surprise. North Korea must be aware that the Commander-in-Chief of the US Atlantic fleet suggested using that approach during the Cuban Missile Crisis when a war game was used to mask preparations for a possible invasion of Cuba.[89]

A third possible explanation is that we may have driven North Korea mad. Early in our marriage, I often did that to Dorothie by misunderstanding some of her legitimate complaints and treating them as absurd. The more frustrated she became at being ignored, the more irrational she appeared to me, and the less attention I paid to her demands—a vicious feedback loop. The first two possible explanations above show that North Korea has some legitimate complaints that we have ignored, possibly leading them to complain shrilly and causing us to see them as even more irrational than they are.

While we regard our military exercises with South Korea as defensive in nature, a holistic perspective would understand how, to North Korea, they appear aggressive and therefore offensive. A mirror image misperception occurred during the 1962 Cuban Missile Crisis. Khrushchev viewed his missiles on Cuba as defensive in nature, designed to deter a second American invasion after the Bay of Pigs fiasco. But we saw the Soviet missiles as offensive.

DOROTHIE: This international name calling, "You're being offensive!" followed by, "No! You're the one being offensive," reminds me of our old fights in which one of us would accuse the other by saying, "You're angry!" followed by the other angrily insisting, "No, I'm not. You are!" We were two angry people, each accusing the other of being angry.

I'm not saying that either of us back then was at all comparable to Kim Jong-un today. But it's amazing how similar some of the disagreements can be.

MARTY: And just as we used to not really listen to one another during those old fights, our nation paid no attention when, in January 2015, North Korea offered to suspend nuclear testing in return for cancellation of the joint US-South Korean military exercises.[90] Those war games started a month later, and North Korea conducted a nuclear test in January 2016. We don't know if suspending our war games would have prevented that test. Only if we had taken North Korea up on its offer would we have useful information on whether or not the country's leaders had been serious.

Iran

MARTY: Iran is yet another country where our nation's propensity for hatred has caused us great harm. If the growing number of nations on our "hate list" gives you the impression that we have a problem with how we conduct our foreign policy, you're right. Of course, we are not alone. Iran expresses its own hatred when it calls us "the Great Satan" or has its people chant "Death to America!"

But Iran's hating us does not negate the toxic effects of our returning the emotion. The history of Iranian-American relations provides some appalling examples of ways in which our actions often have caused grave harm to our national interests.

Part of the problem is the different perspectives our nations bring to the table. We view Iran through the prism of 1979 when, in violation of all international norms, Iranians stormed our embassy and held our diplomats hostage for fifteen months. In contrast, the Iranian viewpoint revolves around 1953, when a CIA-backed coup overthrew the democratically elected Mossadeq government and installed a police state under the Shah.

How could we help overthrow a popular, democratically elected government in order to put a police state in power? Part of the answer is that we fooled ourselves, but we also let fear get the better of us and cloud our judgment.

In 1953, Mossadeq was tired of the British getting the lion's share of the revenue from Iran's oil fields under an outdated, sweetheart deal negotiated decades earlier. When the British rejected Mossadeq's demands, he nationalized the oil industry. Britain then played on America's fear of Communism to enlist the CIA in fomenting a coup by the Shah. The CIA's involvement allowed Iran to feel justified later in its 1979 takeover of our embassy, since CIA agents often had "cover jobs" working there.

A formerly classified CIA history of the 1953 coup[91] details how the agency created "black propaganda"—false information—to justify Mossadeq's being overthrown. According to this CIA history, the agency created fake documents "proving" a secret agreement between Mossadeq and the Iranian Communist Party. Next, it describes how CIA collaborators bombed the houses of several Iranian religious leaders, but made the attacks look like terrorist acts committed by the Communists. This black propaganda allowed the hereditary Shah's forces to stage a coup, overthrowing the democratically elected Mossadeq while giving the appearance of a victory for democracy and law and order. The CIA's "black propaganda" transformed black into white.

This CIA history shows that the story Americans were told about the coup was based on lies. A *New York Times* article, written on the day of the coup, reinforced the myth that Mossadeq was a highly unpopular leader, running an illegal government, who was overthrown by popular demand:

> *TEHERAN, Iran, Aug. 19—Iranians loyal to [the] Shah ... swept Premier Mohammed Mossadegh out of power today in a revolution ... The troops and police that took part in the overthrow were led by huge mobs shouting for the return of the Shah ... [and] for the death of Dr. Mossadegh. ... A declaration ... had been circulated among army cadres ordering the troops not to obey the illegal Mossadegh Government on pain of severe punishment.[92]*

That *New York Times* article also falsely described the new government as planning to "re-establish a rule of law" and "restore individual freedom." In reality, the overthrow of Mossadeq in the CIA-inspired coup was the opposite of the "rule of law." And, once Mossadeq was out of the way, the CIA helped set up the Shah's feared secret police, known as the SAVAK, which used torture and executions to stifle dissent. Instead of "restoring individual freedom," the coup greatly curtailed it.

Because Americans have been told—and most have believed—that black was white, it should not be surprising that misperceptions still play a prominent role in the current, disastrous state of US-Iranian relations.

Our actions in helping overthrow Mossadeq were compounded decades later by our behavior during the eight-year-long Iran-Iraq

War. On September 22, 1980, Iraq's Saddam Hussein invaded Iran. We supported Saddam, the aggressor, instead of Iran, the victim of his aggression. One of the reasons was that our Tehran embassy personnel were still being held hostage. We didn't like Saddam, but we hated Iran with a passion.

The extent of our support for Saddam comes across in an affidavit filed by Howard Teicher, who served on President Reagan's National Security Council (NSC) staff during the Iran-Iraq war:[93]

> In June, 1982, President Reagan decided that the United States could not afford to allow Iraq to lose the war to Iran. ... President Reagan formalized this policy by issuing a National Security Decision Directive ("NSDD") to this effect in June, 1982. I have personal knowledge of this NSDD because I co-authored the NSDD with another NSC Staff Member, Geoff Kemp. The NSDD, including even its identifying number, is classified. ...
>
> Pursuant to the secret NSDD, the United States actively supported the Iraqi war effort by supplying the Iraqis with billions of dollars of credits, by providing US military intelligence and advice to the Iraqis, and by ... [making] sure that Iraq had the military weaponry required. The United States also provided strategic operational advice to the Iraqis to better use their assets in combat. For example, in 1986, President Reagan sent a secret message to Saddam Hussein telling him that Iraq should step up its air war and bombing of Iran. ...
>
> I personally attended meetings in which CIA Director Casey or CIA Deputy Director Gates noted the need for Iraq to have certain weapons such as cluster bombs and anti-armor penetrators in order to stave off the Iranian attacks.

You might be wondering why Teicher would reveal such damning information. He did it to help individuals who were being prosecuted for exporting weapons to Iraq during the war. Although US policy barred such exports, the Reagan administration turned a blind eye toward them.[94]

During the war, Saddam Hussein used chemical weapons to kill tens of thousands of Iranian soldiers. In spite of Iraq's violation of this international norm, the Reagan administration continued supporting Iraq, including providing intelligence that helped Saddam target Iranian troops with chemical weapons. A 2013 article in *Foreign Policy* adds an interesting wrinkle:

US officials have long denied acquiescing to Iraqi chemical attacks, insisting that Hussein's government never announced he was going to use the weapons. But retired Air Force Col. Rick Francona, who was a military attaché in Baghdad during the 1988 strikes, paints a different picture. "The Iraqis never told us that they intended to use nerve gas. They didn't have to. We already knew."[95]

Because the United States had so callously supported Saddam Hussein's use of poison gas against them, Iranians must have been shocked when we later used that as one of our justifications for overthrowing Hussein in 2003.

Holistic thinking would have saved us from such a diabolical performance by taking in the bigger picture. It requires us to be consistently fair, rather than excusing our bad behavior toward another nation because it wronged us earlier—in this case, Iran seizing our embassy. But that's what I used to do when I excused my mistreating Dorothie by pointing to some bad behavior on her part and blaming her for "making" me mad. Now I am committed to owning my anger, rather than blaming it on anyone else, and Dorothie is committed to doing the same. Imagine what would happen if nations were to make that shift.

As with North Korea, Iran's nuclear program is of greatest concern to most Americans, so let's take a look at the contentious nuclear agreement that the P5+1 (China, France, Germany, Russia, the United Kingdom, and the United States) reached with Iran on July 14, 2015.

Opponents of the agreement point to Iran's repeatedly threatening to "wipe Israel off the map;" the fact that the agreement does nothing to rein in Iran's ballistic missile program; Iran's history of untrustworthiness; and the fact that many of the agreement's provisions expire in ten to fifteen years, after which Iran will be unconstrained on those issues. Those are valid concerns, but they require more careful examination, so let's tackle them one at a time.

While there are Iranian zealots who want to wipe Israel off the map, there also are more moderate elements, and the question becomes which group this agreement helps to empower. I am convinced it is more supportive of the moderates. In a strange twist, hardline elements in both the West and Iran oppose the agreement.

Iran's ballistic missile program is of great concern, but including it in the agreement would have lengthened the negotiation process so much that Iran probably would have reached "nuclear breakout," the time when it could build a bomb if it chose to. A conscious decision was made to restrict the agreement solely to nuclear matters, since those were of greatest concern.

Supporters and opponents differ on how much the agreement has increased that breakout time.[96] But, given that Iran has reduced its enriched uranium stockpile by 98 percent and cut its working centrifuges by a factor of roughly three, there would seem to be little doubt that it has increased the breakout time. The value of the agreement becomes even greater if, as seems likely, Iran would have increased its enrichment capacity without it.

It is true that Iran's seizure of our embassy in 1979 and other actions are evidence of its untrustworthiness, but Iran would point to our overthrowing Mossadeq in 1953 and other misdeeds on our part to show that we are also untrustworthy. Evidence also shows that Iran can be trusted to do what is in its best interest, even if that requires working with Israel.

During the 1980s, after Iraq attacked Iran, the ayatollahs secretly did business with both the United States and Israel in order to get weapons needed to fight Saddam Hussein. This was part of what became known as the Iran-Contra scandal and was used to get around Congressional restrictions on using American funds to help the Contras in their guerilla war against the leftist Sandinista government in Nicaragua. While the details were a bit more circuitous and several variations existed, in essence, President Reagan secretly approved supplying weapons to Israel that were sold to Iran, with some of the proceeds used to fund the Contras.

Critics are correct that many restrictions that the 2015 nuclear agreement places on Iran end in ten to fifteen years, but without it, those restrictions never would have been in place at all. We need to use those years to improve relations between our countries so that when the restrictions lapse, Iran will not be motivated to expand its nuclear program. Unfortunately, at this point in time, hardliners on both sides make that positive outcome (and the success of the agreement) questionable.

That makes it vitally important for you to make yourself heard. The Conclusion of this book will suggest several ways for making that happen.

As an example of American hardline rhetoric, in March 2015, our former UN Ambassador John Bolton penned a *New York Times* OpEd arguing that "only military action ... can accomplish what is required" to prevent Iran from getting the bomb.[97] He noted that such action "could set back Iran's program by three to five years," and recommended "vigorous American support for Iran's opposition, aimed at regime change in Tehran." Such threats coming from former high-ranking American officials reinforce the beliefs of Iran's hardliners that we are not to be trusted.

One of Iran's most fanatical factions, its Revolutionary Guards (known as the IRGC), has a financial interest in maintaining the sanctions that will be dropped as part of the nuclear agreement. In a June 2015 talk that I attended, Dr. Abbas Milani, the Director of Iranian Studies at Stanford University, stated that the IRGC has made $20 billion a year from smuggling sanctioned goods into Iran. That income goes away if sanctions are dropped. When I later emailed Dr. Milani to confirm the amount, he told me: "That is the minimum. Iranian sources have indicated higher numbers."

What price have we paid for failing to think holistically about our relationship with Iran and for failing to see our own role clearly while focusing solely on Iran's sins? For starters, it allows Iran to call us "the Great Satan" without feeling the abject shame it should feel at such name-calling. Iranians find enough evidence in their favor that they can fool themselves. But talk about demonizing an enemy! It doesn't get any more direct than Iran's calling the United States the Great Satan.

Another price we pay for our lack of holistic thinking is that it empowers the most reactionary elements within the Iranian government, including those who want nuclear weapons. Iran, like all nations, is not a monolith. The country has both progressive and reactionary elements vying for power. A hardline attitude by the United States undermines Iran's moderates and aids the reactionaries.

Attacking Iran would do even more harm. In the Spring of 2015, when the budding nuclear agreement was under attack, I asked a colleague who had held high positions in the intelligence community what he thought of using military force to rein in Iran's nuclear program—the method John Bolton, among others, has advocated. My colleague replied that attacking Iran would have the opposite of its desired effect. Using military force would create a powerful consensus among Iranians for developing nuclear weapons to deter future American attacks—a consensus that now does not exist.

His exact words to describe our military option with respect to Iran: "It's a fantasy." He went on to explain that we don't know where all of Iran's nuclear facilities are, so some would survive an attack, and the Iranians would build new ones. Iran is stronger than Iraq, so going to war with Iran would be even costlier than what we've experienced in Iraq—and the chance of a military victory would be even less.

Having suffered through the 1953 CIA-inspired overthrow of Mossadeq, having been invaded by Saddam Hussein, having most of the world support Saddam the aggressor instead of Iran his victim, and having suffered Saddam's chemical weapons attacks with barely a peep from the so-called civilized world—given all those wounds and almost no attempts on our part to make amends, how can we expect Iran to work with us constructively? Our actions to date reinforce the conviction of its hardliners that deceit and military might are the gold standard in international relations. In short, our actions tend to produce a more militarized, aggressive Iranian government than we would face otherwise.

We've tried the same experiment over and over again with Iran, with the same negative results. Logic should be telling us that it's time we tried something new, and it's time we listened. For peace to have a chance, we need to tear up the old map and start trying to piece together a new one. I know because, for far too long, I made mistakes in my relationship with Dorothie that were similar to the ones that our nation is now making with Iran. Our marriage would not have survived if she and I had not found the courage to change. Our world may not survive if we, as nations, do not change.

Cuba

DOROTHIE: The October 1962 Cuban Missile Crisis was the closest the world has ever come to nuclear war, with President Kennedy later estimating the odds of war as having been somewhere between "one-in-three and even."[98] Neither Kennedy nor Khrushchev had intended to teeter at the edge of the nuclear abyss, so it's important to understand what happened and avoid repeating those mistakes.

MARTY: The seeds of the crisis go back to January 8, 1959, when Fidel Castro and his Cuban revolutionaries entered Havana in triumph—and the Eisenhower administration took an immediate dislike to him. Much as in the fights Dorothie and I used to have, a vicious circle set in, with negative actions by one party being magnified in the other's eyes, leading to an escalating conflict.

The United States refused to allow arms sales to Castro, causing him to buy Soviet-bloc weapons. This fed United States fears that Castro was sympathetic to Communism. While Castro later instituted a Communist government in Cuba, our fears were largely a self-fulfilling prophesy, as noted by Khrushchev's speechwriter, Fyodr Burlatsky:

> *[When he first came to power,] Castro was neither a Commu-*
> *nist nor a Marxist. It was the Americans themselves who*
> *pushed him in the direction of the Soviet Union. He needed*
> *economic and political support and help with weapons, and he*
> *found all three in Moscow.*[99]

DOROTHIE: That's what used to happen to us. When you were afraid of making me mad, I felt like you saw me as a witch, which made me mad, fulfilling both of our fears.

MARTY: At least our fears didn't start World War III, like Kennedy's and Khrushchev's almost did. A key step leading to the crisis had occurred a year and a half earlier, when roughly fifteen hundred CIA-trained Cuban exiles staged the Bay of Pigs invasion. Although it was intended as the first step in a popular uprising against Castro, the invasion instead turned into a rout. More than 100 of the Cuban exiles were killed, and most of the rest were captured.

President Kennedy was humiliated—a dangerous state for a world leader armed with nuclear weapons. He stepped up "Operation Mongoose," a series of covert CIA actions designed to topple Castro. The formerly top-secret minutes of a meeting that took place a week before the start of the missile crisis called for "considerably more sabotage" and stated that, "All efforts should be made to develop new and imaginative approaches to the possibility of getting rid of the Castro regime."[100]

In addition to more routine acts of terrorism like sabotaging a refinery, a later Senate investigation "found concrete evidence of at least eight plots involving the CIA to assassinate Fidel Castro from 1960 to 1965."[101] In one of these, the CIA prepared a box of Castro's favorite cigars "contaminated with a botulinum toxin so potent that a person would die after putting one in his mouth."

In March 1962, seven months before the Cuban Missile Crisis, all members of the Joint Chiefs of Staff approved a top-secret document known as Operation Northwoods. They recommended a number of operations that would allow the United States to invade Cuba while falsely making us look like the injured party.[102] The long list of suggested deceptions included: "A 'Remember the Maine' incident could be arranged ... We could blow up a US ship in Guantanamo Bay and blame Cuba. ... [Or] We could foster attempts on lives of Cuban refugees in the United States even to the extent of wounding [them]."

While President Kennedy had the good sense to reject these suggestions, he and his brother, Attorney General Robert F. Kennedy, pursued their own approaches via Operation Mongoose, and some were not so different. In a meeting with the president and his top advisers during the crisis, RFK suggested, "We should also think of whether there is some other way we can get involved in this through Guantanamo Bay ... you know, sink the *Maine* again or something."[103]

The Kennedy brothers' fixation on eliminating Castro was shared by much of Congress, the American public, and most of the media. A month before the crisis, *TIME* magazine had a cover story that concluded, "The only possibility that promises a quick end to Castro—if that is what is wanted—is a direct US invasion of Cuba, carried out with sufficient force to get the job done." The rest of the article left no question that military force was exactly what was wanted.[104]

With that background, it's not hard to see why Khrushchev would want Soviet troops on Cuba to act as a "nuclear trip wire" to deter the United States from invading its only ally in the Western Hemisphere a second time. American troops based in our European allies had long served a similar purpose. If the Soviets invaded Western Europe, thousands of American soldiers would be killed, automatically bringing the United States and its nuclear arsenal into the war. Khrushchev wanted the same to be true in Cuba, but with the roles reversed.

But why did Khrushchev add nuclear-armed missiles to that already dangerous mix? Much of the answer lies in Turkey, where the US had deployed similarly armed Jupiter missiles in the Spring of 1962. Khrushchev's speech writer, Fyodr Burlatsky, explained:

Khrushchev and [Soviet Defense Minister] R. Malinovsky ... were strolling along the Black Sea coast. Malinovsky pointed out to sea and said that on the other shore in Turkey there was an American nuclear missile base. In a matter of six or seven minutes missiles launched from that base could devastate major centres in the Ukraine and southern Russia. ... Khrushchev asked Malinovsky why the Soviet Union should not have the right to do the same as America. Why, for example, should it not deploy missiles in Cuba?[105]

In spite of the similarity between his Cuban and our Turkish missiles, Khrushchev realized that America would apply a double standard and be outraged to find Soviet missiles so close to the United States. He therefore deployed his missiles in secret, expecting to confront the United States with a *fait accompli*. Once the missiles were operational, America could not attack them or Cuba without inviting a horrific nuclear retaliation.

But Khrushchev's plans were foiled when photos taken by an American U-2 spy plane showed the missiles being deployed. President Kennedy was informed of these developments on Tuesday morning, October 16, 1962. He immediately formed a team of advisers known as the Executive Committee or ExComm.

Fortunately, Kennedy was able to keep the Cuban missiles secret from the public for almost a full week, giving him time to think things through. In the first few days of the crisis, the strongest support was for air strikes to destroy the missiles, followed by a massive invasion of Cuba. But over the next several days, Kennedy began to think through the likely consequences of those actions, and he hesitated. What would happen if we hadn't located all the missile sites, or if a Soviet officer were able to launch his missiles during the strikes? Even one or two thermonuclear warheads hitting Miami or Washington would kill more American civilians than all of our military losses in World War II.

There were two other, very serious risks that Kennedy over-looked. We learned of the first such risk thirty years after the crisis: The Soviets already had battlefield nuclear weapons on Cuba to repel an American invasion.[106] The second such risk became known forty years after the crisis: Three Soviet submarines near Cuba, which were attacked and forced to surface by American destroyers, had carried nuclear torpedoes. A crew member on one submarine later reported that his captain had given orders for that torpedo to be armed, but was calmed down by another officer on board.[107]

The possibility of Soviet battlefield nuclear weapons being on Cuba was largely ignored by ExComm members and the Joint Chiefs—a dangerous instance of non-holistic thinking. Only by putting blinders on and ignoring that possibility could they dare to think in terms of invading Cuba, which was their initially preferred option. And there is no evidence that they ever considered the possibility of the Soviet submarines carrying nuclear torpedoes.

Even without knowing about the Soviet nuclear torpedoes or battlefield weapons, Kennedy began to see the huge risk inherent in air strikes and an invasion. He began to favor a naval blockade of Cuba. The blockade would not remove the missiles already there, but it would show Congress and the American public that he was taking action—something both groups demanded of him once he went public with news of the missiles in a television address on Monday, October 22.

Two other glaring examples of non-holistic thinking are highlighted in a 2012 paper by one of the preeminent historians of the nuclear age, Stanford Professor Barton Bernstein:

> *Significantly, no ExComm member suggested that Khrushchev and the Soviets might have been acting, at least in part, to defend Cuba from a feared US-sponsored attack. … Surprisingly, aside from a few, rather oblique passing comments, no one in the ExComm concluded that Khrushchev and the Soviets might have been responding to the very recent US emplacement of Jupiter missiles in Turkey.[108]*

Instead of trying to understand Khrushchev's frame of reference, Kennedy and his advisers viewed the Cuban missiles solely through their own eyes. In that perspective, Khrushchev was a reckless madman threatening world domination who had to be confronted.

DOROTHIE: I was not quite fourteen at the time, but remember clearly how I felt. I was walking across my high school campus, talking to a friend about how the world was probably about to end. It's strange, but somehow I wasn't terrified, just resigned. There was nothing I could do. But now there is—which is one reason we're writing this book.

MARTY: I had just turned seventeen and was in my freshman year at New York University. I wasn't terrified either, but for a very different reason. Most of my friends shared Dorothie's belief that we were all going to die. I thought they were out of their minds. To me, it was inconceivable that anything like that could happen. With what I now know, I was the one not thinking straight.

DOROTHIE: And don't forget Castro's begging Khrushchev to launch the missiles preemptively.

MARTY: That's an important wrinkle that few people know about. On Friday, October 26, the day before what became known as "Black Saturday," Khrushchev's memoirs claim (emphasis added):

*We received a telegram from our ambassador in Cuba ... Castro informed him he had reliable information that the Americans were preparing within a certain number of hours to strike Cuba. ... **Castro suggested that in order to prevent our nuclear missiles from being destroyed, we should launch a preemptive strike against United States.** He concluded that an [American] attack was unavoidable and that this attack had to be preempted. ... When we read this I, and all the others, looked at each other, and it became clear to* *us that Fidel totally failed to understand our purpose. ... We had installed the missiles not for the purpose of attacking the United States, but to keep the United States from attacking Cuba.*[109]

Given the strong support in the United States for invading Cuba, Castro's fear of an imminent invasion was understandable, but fortunately wrong. Castro's belief was strengthened by the occurrence of CIA-sponsored sabotage operations during the crisis. These operations had been put in motion prior to the start of the crisis, and the CIA was unable to stop them.

Two other major risks occurred on "Black Saturday." At 11:19 a.m. Washington time, an American U-2 was shot down over Cuba, killing its pilot, Major Rudolph Anderson. Even though we had violated Cuban airspace on spying missions, had been carrying out sabotage operations under Operation Mongoose, and had given strong indications that we were about to invade Cuba, Kennedy's reaction, caught on his secret taping system, put all the blame on Khrushchev: "Well now, this is much of an escalation by them, isn't it?"

DOROTHIE: That sounds just like our old fights, in which each of us could only see how the other one was escalating the argument. We were blind to our own provocations.

MARTY: Secretary of Defense Robert McNamara went further than Kennedy and argued that, "We ought to go in at dawn and take out that SAM site," meaning the surface-to-air missile site responsible for shooting down our U-2.

The ExComm was in a bind because ongoing U-2 flights were needed to determine the status of the Soviet missiles, yet attacking the SAM sites would kill Soviet military personnel and increase the risk of war. Just as the ExComm felt that it had to retaliate for Major Anderson's death, Soviet casualties would put pressure on Khrushchev to do the same, producing a feedback loop with a high risk of escalation. Fortunately, Kennedy decided against taking that path, a decision that infuriated the Pentagon.

The second major Black Saturday risk also involved a U-2 spy plane, but this time in the Arctic. The U-2 got lost and strayed far into Soviet airspace. MiG fighters were scrambled to shoot it down, while F-102 interceptors from Alaska were sent to protect and escort it home. Due to the heightened alert level during the crisis, the F-102s' conventionally-armed, air-to-air missiles had been replaced with nuclear-armed Falcon missiles. If the F-102s engaged the MiGs, their only option was to go nuclear. Fortunately, the MiGs never reached the U-2 spy plane—or the nuclear-armed F-102s.[110]

DOROTHIE: Marty has told me about many other, unbelievably risky events during the Cuban Missile Crisis that helped me understand why I felt like the world was about to end. But let's jump to how the crisis was resolved.

MARTY: Kennedy worked out a deal with Khrushchev in which the Soviets agreed to immediately start removing their missiles from Cuba in return for our lifting the naval blockade and pledging not to invade Cuba again.[111] That part was public and satisfied most of Congress and the American public. A major exception was the Joint Chiefs of Staff, who were livid. Even though most Americans breathed a sigh of relief and felt like Kennedy had "won," Air Force Chief of Staff Curtis LeMay argued that we still should "go in and make a strike on Monday anyway."[112]

But there was another part of the deal that was kept secret from all but a very few people. Kennedy promised Khrushchev that we would remove our missiles from Turkey within four to five months. Khrushchev was warned that if he ever referred to this part of the deal, we would deny it.[113]

This secret was kept for years, even from Vice President Johnson, who assumed the presidency after Kennedy's assassination. The fact that Johnson was kept in the dark may have played a role in his decision to go to war in Vietnam. Too many Americans, possibly Johnson among them, learned the wrong lesson from Kennedy's handling of the Cuban Missile Crisis. Instead of learning that it was necessary to take the other side's needs into account to avoid a nuclear war, most Americans mistakenly concluded (based on the Turkish missile trade being kept secret) that, if you stand firm with the Russians, they'll back down.

Afghanistan

MARTY: Afghanistan is an important case study because mistakes we made there, starting in 1979, laid the foundation for al-Qaeda's 9/11 terrorist attacks twenty-two years later. A holistic perspective might well have prevented 9/11 from occurring by correcting the worldview in which we mistakenly saw the Afghan *mujahideen* rebels—including a young Osama bin Laden—as "freedom fighters." That led us to arm them, allowing them to overthrow the Afghan government and create the chaotic conditions that allowed the Taliban to come to power. While there is controversy as to whether the CIA directly funded and trained Osama bin Laden as part of that effort, it is unquestionable that the success of the US-backed rebels provided a safe haven from which bin Laden planned the 9/11 attacks.

By aiding the rebels, we shot ourselves in the foot. But instead of learning from that costly mistake to prevent repeating it, after 9/11, we shifted the focus of our fear, anger, and hate onto the radical Islamist terrorists we had helped create—a mode of operation that appears to be harming us yet again.

Fear caused us to see the Soviet's December 24, 1979, invasion of Afghanistan as a thrust toward the Middle East and its oil. The reality was very different, as Sir Rodric Braithwaite, Britain's Ambassador to Moscow from 1988 to 1992, explained:[114]

The Russians did not invade Afghanistan in order to incorporate it into the Soviet Union, or to use it as a base to threaten the West's oil supplies in the Gulf, or to build a warm water port on the Indian Ocean. They went in to sort out a small, fractured and murderous clique of Afghan Communists who had overthrown the previous government in a bloody coup and provoked chaos and widespread armed resistance on the Soviet Union's vulnerable Southern border.

And, contrary to the view that the Soviets' invasion was part of a carefully orchestrated plan to take over the world, Ambassador Braithwaite also noted: "For the previous nine months they had resisted repeated pleas from the Afghan Communists to send Soviet troops to help put down the insurgency."

In spite of their caution, eventually the Soviets wrongly concluded that they had to dispatch troops. Their error became clear as their death toll mounted, Afghanistan became more chaotic, and American-backed *mujahideen* crossed the Soviet-Afghan border in terrorist attacks *within* the Soviet Union, hoping to stir up a rebellion within its Muslim population.[115]

The American media, rather than exploring these aspects of the Soviet motivation, portrayed the invasion in fearful, angry, and hateful terms. The January 7, 1980, issue of *TIME* magazine called it, "the most brutal blow from the Soviet Union's steel fist since the Red Army's invasion of Czechoslovakia in 1968."

Two weeks later, *TIME* had a column by Strobe Talbott—who would later serve President Bill Clinton as Deputy Secretary of State—that referred to the invasion as "the Soviet army's blitz against Afghanistan," thereby evoking a vision of Communism as a new version of Nazism, whose *blitzkrieg* devastated Europe.

That bogeyman image was enhanced when Talbott went on to warn that "the Soviet jackboot was now firmly planted on a stepping stone to possible control over much of the world's oil supplies." In a private communication, Lieutenant General (US Army, Retired) Karl Eikenberry, Commander of the American-led Coalition forces in Afghanistan from 2005 to 2007 and our Ambassador to that country from 2009 to 2011, told me, "Given the geographic constraints and geopolitical realities, it is not at all clear why Talbott thought this was so."

A lack of such critical thinking, combined with our fear and hatred of Communism, magically transformed the *mujahideen* from the misogynist rebels that most of them were into something far nobler. On March 21, 1983, President Ronald Reagan gave a speech that called them "courageous Afghan freedom fighters," and saw them as "an inspiration to those who love freedom."[116]

In contrast to that wishful thinking, a May 15, 1987, *New York Times* article, written while the Soviets were trying to extricate themselves from their Afghan debacle, noted how the Soviet-backed government had improved gender equality in Afghanistan. Women were better off then than they are now under an American-backed government:

> Many diplomats, professionals and others say that the [Soviet-backed] Government has won support among working women because it appears to have gone out of its way to provide day-care services, literacy training and other benefits for women. ...
>
> A Western diplomat said that rights for women was one of the few areas he would concede had been an achievement of the 1978 revolution ... At Kabul University, where today 55 percent of the 7,000 students are women, many women recall that one of the insurgent leaders, Gulbuddin Hekmatyar, is an Islamic fundamentalist who used to oppose women's removal of their veils when he was a student there more than 20 years ago.
>
> "His people used to throw acid at women," said Jamila Takhari, a nineteen-year-old student. "They don't want women to have an equal role in society."
>
> She and her friends agreed that if Mr. Hekmatyar were to ever come to power in Afghanistan, women would have to struggle to retain their rights.[117]

Unfortunately, as a result of our support, Hekmatyar did come to power. He was one of the *mujahideen* "freedom fighters" supported by the CIA, and he served as Prime Minister after they defeated the Soviet-backed government.

When the United States invaded Afghanistan in 2001, Hekmatyar fought against us and, in an audio tape, made a direct threat on the life of Lieutenant General Karl Eikenberry, then commander of our military forces in Afghanistan: "I would like to kill you myself."[118] In 2015, Hekmatyar called on his followers to support ISIS.[119]

In addition to aiding al-Qaeda, Washington's desire to bloody the Russians by aiding the *mujahideen* played a role in Pakistan getting the bomb—one of today's greatest nuclear risks. The day after the Soviets invaded Afghanistan, President Carter's National Security Advisor, Zbigniew Brzezinski, penned a secret memo to the president which argued that we needed to stop opposing Pakistan's nuclear weapons program: "We must both reassure Pakistan and encourage it to help the rebels. This will require ... alas, a decision that our security policy toward Pakistan cannot be dictated by our [nuclear] nonproliferation policy."[120]

Brzezinski saw opposing the Soviets in Afghanistan as more important than preventing Pakistan from getting the bomb. He was wrong. When I organized a 2010 Stanford lecture series on nuclear weapons, former Director of Los Alamos Dr. Siegfried Hecker gave a talk on "The Greatest Nuclear Risks." He put Pakistan at the top of that list.

Chapter 7

Creating Peace
on the Planet

The seven international case studies of the last chapter provide a strong foundation for showing how our nation could take steps to produce a more peaceful planet. Of course, progress will be even more rapid if other nations implement similar changes in their foreign and military policies, but even all by ourselves, we here in the United States could accomplish much. This chapter integrates lessons from those case studies with things the two of us had to learn to bring true love back into our marriage.

Get Curious,
Not Furious Internationally

Just as getting curious instead of furious has prevented many needless fights in our marriage, the seven international case studies highlight the need for us as citizens to ask more questions before we join the drumbeat to what is likely to be yet another needless war.

With our recent success rate on military interventions being zero, why do we as a nation keep turning to them as our first option? Dorothie and I don't expect the nations of the world to love each other the way we do, but we do expect them to grow up enough to reduce the risk of global devastation to a more reasonable level.

If more Americans had gotten curious instead of furious in 2003 before the United States invaded Iraq:

- We would have questioned the Bush administration's giving the false impression that Saddam Hussein was involved in the 9/11 attacks.
- We would have questioned claims that Saddam had weapons of mass destruction—claims that were later proved false.
- The media would not have been so one-sided. For example, NBC would not have directed Phil Donahue to have at least two supporters of the war on his show for every person raising questions.

If we'd gotten curious instead of furious after North Vietnam's August 1964 Tonkin Gulf attack:

- We would have asked more questions before accepting the Johnson administration's bald-faced lie that the first attack was unprovoked aggression on the high seas.
- We would have asked more questions before accepting the Johnson administration's false portrayal of the second attack as requiring a forceful American response. A now-declassified top-secret NSA history of the event clearly states, "no attack happened that night."

- We would have questioned the now-discredited "domino theory" that said we had to fight the Communists in Vietnam in order to avoid fighting them later on our own shores.

If we were to get curious instead of furious at North Korea, Iran, and Russia, we would question whether we should write them off—and them alone—as "rogue nations." All are guilty of a number of despicable actions, but does the evidence show them to be uniquely deranged? Or do some of our allies, and even our own nation, sometimes behave like rogue elephants running wild, creating chaos in their wake?

Asking such questions would force us to confront the shadow side of our nation. As in our personal journey, seeing our nation clearly will be painful at first. But also as in our personal journey, embracing our national shadow will free us to come closer to the ideals that we hold and allow us to play a much more positive role in creating peace on the planet.

A Stitch in Time Saves Nine

DOROTHIE: In thinking about the seven international case studies, I was struck by how much easier it would have been to resolve those international conflicts early in the process of their formation. A stitch in time really does save nine. That's holistic thinking in time—resolving conflicts before they even occur. Marty will explain.

MARTY: The section on Vietnam showed how we could have avoided going to war in 1964 if we had abided by the 1954 Geneva Accords that called for free elections to unify North and South Vietnam. Even better, we should have started right after World War II by not aiding the French in their war to re-impose colonial rule on Vietnam—an effort at which they failed, so we then picked up the ball. Trying to extricate ourselves in 1964 was almost impossible because we had invested too much, we had propagated too many myths, and we had come to believe them. It would have been far easier to avoid the Vietnam War in 1945 or 1954 than in 1964.

The section on North Korea shows that we probably could have avoided that nation becoming nuclear-armed in 2006 if we'd abided by the 1994 Agreed Framework. Again, it would have been even better to start the process right after World War II, long before there were concerns about North Korea developing nuclear weapons. Partly out of fear that there were Communist sympathizers within the Korean population, we alienated most Koreans by using Japanese officials to govern South Korea immediately after the war.[121] We also installed Syngman Rhee as president of South Korea—although the title "dictator" would be a more apt description. Even though Rhee had spent the war years in Hawaii, we chose him over Koreans who had fought the Japanese because of his staunch anti-Communist credentials. A more reasonable and popular choice for president—ideally one elected by the Korean people—might have avoided not only a nuclear-armed North Korea, but the Korean War itself.

The section on Iran also shows how defusing international conflicts early in their formation would be much easier than trying to do so later. If we hadn't let fear of Communism fool us into overthrowing Mossadeq in the 1953 CIA-inspired coup, the ayatollahs who now rule Iran probably never would have come to power.

It was too late to stop the Cuban Missile Crisis in 1962, after the Soviet missiles were installed. It would have been far better to start in 1959 by not opposing Fidel Castro, which caused him to seek Soviet aid and led to his becoming a Communist.

A good time to stop the terrorist attacks of September 11, 2001, would have been 1979, when the CIA started giving covert aid to the *mujahideen* fighting the Soviet-backed Afghan government. The *mujahideen*'s success laid the foundation for the Taliban coming to power, which in turn allowed Osama bin Laden to plan the 9/11 terrorist attacks. Our aid to the *mujahideen* also erased the gains that Afghan women had made under that Soviet-backed government, so our recent attempts to improve women's rights in Afghanistan also would have been much more effective if we'd started in 1979.

To counter skeptics who might argue that all of the above examples benefit from hindsight, I'll include a forward-looking example. In 1984, four years before the Soviets started withdrawing from Afghanistan, I helped write *The Beyond War Handbook,* one of whose FAQs was:

What about the Soviet invasion of Afghanistan? Doesn't that show they are bent on world domination?

No. To understand why, we must better understand the Soviet view of the world. ... Over the centuries, Russia has been invaded by the Mongols, the Moslems, the Turks, the Swedes, the Poles, the Austrians, the French, and the Germans. ... With this history, the Soviet Union has an understandable, deep-seated fear concerning unrest near its borders.

With this background, we must then remember that the USSR shares uneasy borders with three Moslem countries, Turkey, Iran and Afghanistan; that there is significant minority unrest within the Soviet Union; that twenty percent of the

Soviet population is Moslem; that a militant Moslem regime has come to power in Iran; and that the insurgents in Afghanistan are fighting to establish a similar regime there.

Seen in this light, the Soviet invasion of Afghanistan is analogous to our own reaction to unrest in Latin America. ... [It] is not some aberration committed by a nation bent on world domination; it is the inevitable consequence of the current mode of thinking found throughout the world. This thinking justifies military intervention, however brutal and dangerous, whenever a nation believes its national security might be diminished by unrest in another country. To avoid future Afghanistans, Czechoslavakias, Vietnams, and Nicaraguas we must lead the way to a new mode of thinking which recognizes that in the nuclear age military intervention is an obsolete mode of behavior. We must put both sides' past mistakes behind us and look to the future for new and better possibilities.

In the same way that I and my colleagues working on that Handbook were able to see the error of our nation's policies in Afghanistan in the 1980s, a forward-looking approach to our foreign relations today would have us question why we are now so intent on regime change in Syria, when it worked so poorly in Iraq and Libya. It would have us question why we insist that talks with North Korea must be about their unilaterally disarming—for that is what denuclearization of the Koran peninsula would be—when experts tell us that means no talks, which in turn means North Korea will improve and increase its nuclear arsenal.[122] But we shouldn't need experts to tell us that. As the North Korean case study showed, common sense would tell us the same thing.

DOROTHIE: If we had exercised that kind of foresight, diplomacy might even have prevented World War II, the most devastating war in human history. When Hitler invaded Poland in 1939, it was too late for diplomacy. We should have started twenty years earlier. That's when the Treaty of Versailles needlessly humiliated Germany and created fertile conditions for Hitler coming to power in 1933.

The value of resolving conflicts early in their formation process carries over to the personal level. We've talked about relationships having a kind of goodwill bank account. Now that our marriage's account has a large, positive balance, we tend to forgive slights, real or imagined. But years ago, when that balance was negative, Marty's slightest mistake would set me off, and vice versa. That, of course, made the balance even more negative, and we were probably headed for marriage bankruptcy. It took time for us to replenish that account. If you can start building goodwill earlier than we did, it will be easier to fall in love again.

MARTY: There's another way that "a stitch in time saves nine" works at the personal level. Almost all of the fights in our marriage had their roots much earlier than whatever set us off—sometimes going back to our childhoods. Trying to resolve such conflicts by dealing only with the immediate cause was an exercise in futility. We had to go deeper.

A men's weekend run by Creative Initiative brought the need for tackling conflicts early into sharp focus. One of the community's elders, Don Fitton, talked about how we all go through life with a frame of reference for filtering information. That's not a bad thing. We're bombarded by way too much information to let it all in, and most information can be acted on reflexively, without thinking. Every time I see a red light, I step on the brakes. I don't think, "Maybe they changed the rules and now red means go, while green means stop." Being that open would get me into big trouble.

But Don pointed out how a frame of reference also limits us. We can only see possibilities that fit within that framework. The frame of reference creates a set of blinders that keep us focused straight ahead. When I come up to a red light, acting reflexively is a good thing. But, Don went on, sometimes a disaster comes out of left field and blindsides us. Our blinders—our frame of reference—can keep us from seeing the warning signs in time.

He went on to note that, with men, the most frequent forms of being blindsided are, "Everything was going great at work, but then they fired me without any warning," and, "Everything was going great in my marriage, but then I came home to find my wife and kids and all the furniture gone." There were plenty of early warning signs, but they were outside the man's frame of reference, so he didn't see them.

To avoid being blindsided, we need to open up as early as possible to some seemingly crazy ideas—particularly those coming from our wives.

DOROTHIE: Of course, women also need to open up to some seemingly crazy ideas—especially those coming from our husbands. To return to the international theme, the same is true for nations. The Cuban Missile Crisis blindsided our nation because we looked at events solely from our own perspective—from within our frame of reference. If we had tried to see events through Soviet eyes, we would have recognized that they would be likely to do something to prevent our invasion hysteria from overthrowing their one ally in the Western Hemisphere. Doing that would have required us to practice the Golden Rule, the subject of the next section.

Hillel's Prescription for Holistic Thinking

The Talmud has a story about a smart aleck who went to the famous Jewish sage, Hillel, and demanded to be taught the Torah while he "stands on one foot." Given that Hillel had spent his whole life studying the Torah, asking him to condense it into a few words was an insult. But according to the story, the great sage met the challenge with aplomb by replying, "What is hateful to you, do not do unto others."

When Hillel's antagonist insists that the Torah is so long that there must be more, Hillel calls his summary "the essence" and states that, "all the rest is mere commentary." The smart aleck is shamed by the sage's insightful reply and goes off with a new appreciation for Hillel's wisdom and that of the Torah.

This story is highly relevant to our quest for holistic thinking and compassion because many of the recommendations we've offered for achieving that goal are instances of the Golden Rule cited by Hillel.

DOROTHIE: A personal example is the old fight Marty and I used to have in which each of us angrily accused the other of being angry. Both of us hated being treated that way, but each of us did it to the other. We needed to practice, "What is hateful to you, do not do unto others."

MARTY: An international example is the self-righteous indignation Americans feel whenever Russia tries to gain influence in Latin

America, while seeing Russia as needlessly meddling in other nations' affairs when it objects to the eastward expansion of NATO.

If something as simple as following the Golden Rule would solve most of the world's problems, why hasn't it already occurred worldwide? Because doing it is far from simple. It's often hard to see when we are not following the Golden Rule, and the Talmudic story about Hillel provides an excellent example. In the version of the story that started this section, I purposely left out two key points.[123]

First, the smart aleck is a Gentile, so the story is a Jewish put-down of Gentiles. Jews would be offended if the story were reversed, with a smart aleck Jew asking a Christian saint to teach him the Gospels while he stood on one foot, and then being made to look like a fool when the saint quoted the Golden Rule. (The Golden Rule is also the essence of what Jesus taught, so such a reversal of roles could easily be made.)

Second, in the full story, the Gentile first goes to Hillel's major competitor, a Jewish sage named Shammai. Shammai is understandably insulted by the man's rude question and angrily shoos him away. Only when the Gentile later visits Hillel is he shamed by an incisive answer. While the Talmud doesn't tell us, I am sure this story was created by followers of Hillel, not Shammai. This story therefore violates the Golden Rule a second time, because Hillel's followers would have been offended if Shammai's students had created its mirror image.

Even when trying to teach the Golden Rule, it is all too easy to violate it—not once, but twice. Constant vigilance and critical self-examination are needed.

DOROTHIE: And compassion.

MARTY: We need to carefully examine our thoughts and deeds—and our feelings (I beat Dorothie to the punch that time)—to ensure that we are seeing ourselves and the world as clearly as possible, so that we can be as consistent as possible with our stated ideals of holistic thinking and compassion. If we do that, we will have the greatest chance of averting personal and international catastrophes.

A Zealous Search for the Truth

Harry Rathbun and his wife, Emilia, founded Creative Initiative, the group that started us on this process for creating a new relationship map. Harry was also one of Stanford's most beloved professors of the mid-twentieth century. When a lecture series was created in his memory, former Supreme Court Justice Sandra Day O'Connor gave the first lecture, and she has credited him with being one of the most influential figures in her life.[124]

Harry was trained in both engineering and law, and he placed great faith in science. But he was more adventurous than most people with a scientific bent, and he extended the use of scientific methods to include solving interpersonal and global problems.

MARTY: Harry defined the scientific spirit as, "a zealous search for the truth, with a ruthless disregard for commonly held beliefs when contradicted by the observed data." I can still see a mischievous smile cross Harry's face when he came to "zealous" and "ruthless" in his definition—words not usually associated with science. Yet some of the greatest advances in science required precisely those qualities.

Einstein's discovery of the quantum or particle nature of light is a good example. For two hundred years, scientists had debated whether light was a particle or a wave. But in 1865, James Clerk Maxwell showed beyond a doubt that light behaved like a wave. It seemed like a closed case, with the wave team victorious over the particle team.

Thus, in 1900, when the famous physicist Max Planck had to assume that light behaved like a particle to explain a previously inexplicable phenomenon, he didn't take his own conclusion very seriously. Albert Einstein, a younger physicist with a more open mind, did. This "heresy" earned Einstein a Nobel Prize and laid the foundation for transistors, integrated circuits, personal computers, smartphones, and more.

Physicists now understand that the question, "Does light behave like a particle or a wave?" is the wrong question. Light sometimes behaves like one, and sometimes like the other. It's not an "either-or," but what Dorothie often calls "the big AND" when we're trying to figure out which of two possibilities is true in our personal interactions.

Both Planck and Einstein exhibited Harry's "zealous search for the truth," but only Einstein adhered to his "ruthless disregard for commonly held beliefs when contradicted by the observed data." Doing so was invaluable to his career and to the lives we now live.

DOROTHIE: Enough physics! Let's jump to how Harry's definition applies to interpersonal and international relations. What he called "a zealous search for the truth" describes the need for totality in this process—a requirement we've repeatedly illustrated. The old map will reject such total commitment as over-zealousness.

That's probably because totality led us to tear up that old map, and it preferred staying in one piece.

That same totality of commitment—that same zealous search for the truth—is integral to this whole process. Totality became a new identity for me. That's an essential aspect of the new map.

MARTY: Tearing up our old map required "a ruthless disregard for commonly held beliefs when contradicted by the observed data." Tearing something up is pretty ruthless, and the observed data was that our old maps—both interpersonal and international— were not working.

The excruciating pain we were in before we started this process should have been data enough on the interpersonal level, and eventually, it was. The number of needless wars we've gotten ourselves into and the millions of needless deaths they've caused should serve the same purpose in international relations.

But rather than a zealous search for the truth, most nations work hard at hiding from their past mistakes, which dooms them to repeat those errors. The section on Iraq shows that we failed to learn to "get curious, not furious" before going to war. We had made exactly the same error in Vietnam.

There's an even more startling example in which our nation *zealously hid* from the truth, rather than seeking it. On the first day of the Cuban Missile Crisis, October 16, 1962, when President Kennedy first learned of the Soviet missiles on Cuba, he was aghast that Khrushchev would be so reckless as to place nuclear-armed missiles so close to our shores. Forgetting that we had placed similar missiles in Turkey—a nation that shared a border with the USSR—Kennedy's secret taping mechanism caught him saying, "It's just as if we suddenly began to put a major number of

MRBMs [Medium Range Ballistic Missiles] in Turkey. Now that'd be goddamn dangerous."

Kennedy's National Security Adviser, McGeorge Bundy, was forced to remind him that we had done exactly that. Then, instead of seeing Khrushchev's move in a new light, Kennedy and his advisers zealously hid from the truth by using tortured logic to portray the Soviet's Cuban missile deployment as fundamentally different from ours in Turkey.[125]

Congress, the mainstream media, and the American population as a whole also refused to see the similarity between our Turkish and Khrushchev's Cuban missiles. We all zealously hid from that truth to protect our self-images.

Returning from the international to the interpersonal, logic should have been telling me that I needed to heed Harry's advice long before I met him but, paradoxically, I was misusing logic in a particularly perverse way that will be described in the next chapter. Although I claimed to be committed to the scientific spirit, I had not yet dedicated myself to "a zealous search for the truth." I had not yet learned to demand enough of myself.

Be Very Demanding

Being very demanding is contrary to the conventional wisdom that marriage requires compromise, and yet it was crucial to our success. Creating a truly loving relationship required us to demand a lot from ourselves and each other in order to find solutions that met both of our needs, no matter how impossible that might have seemed at first.

We also need to be very demanding at the international level, but with less emphasis on the actions of our adversaries and more on correcting our own nation's mistakes.

DOROTHIE: Some years ago, my hairdresser asked me for advice on the secret to a good marriage. The words that spontaneously came tumbling out of my mouth surprised me: "Be very demanding!"

That didn't make sense to me. At that point, I still thought that marriage was an exercise in compromise. While I didn't understand my own advice, it had come out with such certitude and power that I took time to figure out what it meant. After some thought, it made perfect sense.

The trick is not to demand what I think I want, but to demand what is right for both of us—and to spend as much time as it takes for us to figure out what that is. Resolving our disagreement over my twenty-fifth anniversary ring took about a month and, at first, neither of us could see a solution that worked for both of us. Twenty-three years later, our disagreement about the new car took less than a minute. And as both those stories show, the holistic solution was better for each of us than what either of us wanted going into the process.

Being very demanding works, but only if I'm using the new map.

MARTY: Being "the Princess and the Pea of relationship conflict," Dorothie has been very demanding in terms of how she needed our relationship to grow. As you've seen in a number of earlier stories, I often thought that she was being too demanding—that she wanted something unattainable—until we made it to the other side. At that point, I could see that the vision she was following was much more than a mirage—it was a little bit of heaven brought down to Earth, for which I became extremely grateful.

DOROTHIE: Being very demanding is an opportunity to make your relationship the best it possibly can be. In fact, it's the only way.

MARTY: Dorothie has demanded a lot of me, but she was careful to tell me that anything she asked of me, I had the absolute right to ask of her. That's part of how I came to see value in her demanding that I had to love her *because* she was angry. I, too, could demand to be loved as I was, instead of trying to pretend that I wasn't mad.

Moving from double standards made a huge difference in our relationship, and it would do the same in international relations. Our foreign policy would be far better if we demanded of ourselves the same kind of international behavior we want Russia and our other adversaries to follow.

There's a whole book, *The Record of the Paper*, showing how the supposedly liberal *New York Times* routinely criticizes our adversaries' violations of international law while overlooking our own, such as the invasion of Iraq in 2003.

DOROTHIE: "Be very demanding" has a much different meaning in the new map. In the old map it was a "me, me, me" demand. Now, I demand at least as much of myself as I do of Marty.

The same is true internationally. As a patriotic American, I want my nation to be very demanding of itself and to live up to the high ideals we hold as a nation. Only after we measure up to those standards do we have any hope of expecting others to pay attention to our demands that they behave better.

MARTY: In the old map, a nation that admits its mistakes is seen as weak, and citizens who demand more from their own nations are seen as unpatriotic. As we noted earlier, during the lead-up to the 2003 Iraq War, TV personality Bill O'Reilly said: "I will call those who publicly criticize their country in a time of military crisis, which this is, bad Americans." The horrendous results of that invasion, including for our own national security, show how badly the old map can lead us astray.

Those of us who try to correct our nation's errors by "being very demanding" also need to ask the same of ourselves. We need to offer our corrections from love for our nation, not from anger. Unrestrained anger, which has led our nation to commit horrendous mistakes, is the problem, not the solution.

There is a tension between "be very demanding" and "resist not evil," a concept discussed earlier in this book. But they are far from incompatible. Both are important paths on the new map we pieced together. In resolving that seeming tension, it's important to remember that the primary focus of our demands has been on ourselves. If the other party is open to change, as is true in our marriage, then demanding change on both parts can have a positive outcome. If the other party is not committed to this process, then the demands we make have to be focused even more heavily on our own behavior. That doesn't mean that we ignore our own needs or that the other person might not surprise us by changing in a very positive way.

The story about Marty's three-month long conflict with his father is a good example. His father, who was far from committed to this process and who could be quite difficult, made a shift that neither of us ever would have predicted. But until his father came around, Marty had to be demanding almost entirely of himself—to respond to his father's anger with compassion, not in kind. After three months, compassion won. Marty's father's love for him was great enough to overcome eighty-seven years of following a dangerously outmoded map. Love really can conquer all.

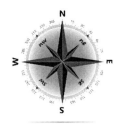

Chapter 8

How Logical Is Nuclear Deterrence?

In an earlier section, "A Stitch in Time Saves Nine," we noted how critically important it is to defuse conflicts, both personal and international, long before they explode. That is particularly true of the need to avoid a nuclear war. Afterward is too late. There is an urgent need for us to re-examine the logical foundation of our nuclear posture and correct any errors.

A concept known as nuclear deterrence is the first place to look, as can be seen from Secretary of State John Kerry's 2013 statement that, "a strong nuclear deterrent remains the cornerstone of US national security."[126] To enhance nuclear deterrence, large sums are being spent on revamping our nuclear forces—usually referred to as "modernization"—and there is strong resistance to any reductions in our 7,000-warhead nuclear arsenal[127] by large parts of the population, including Congress.

Somewhat illogically, nuclear deterrence is so rarely talked about these days that many people don't even know what the term means, although we are all betting our lives on that strategy working perfectly, forever.

In its simplest form, sometimes called Mutually Assured Destruction or MAD, nuclear deterrence threatens to destroy any adversary foolish enough to attack us with its own nuclear weapons. It seeks to *deter* such an attack by threatening to respond in kind, even though a full-scale nuclear war would destroy civilization. But as this chapter will show, that is a dangerous over-simplification that masks much more dangerous, illogical behavior.

Illogical Logic

Nuclear deterrence has been wrapped in a seductive layer of logic. The first section of this chapter therefore examines how people who claim to adhere to a strictly logical framework can behave highly illogically. As befits this book, it starts with a personal story in which Marty confesses to having made that mistake.

MARTY: As I've already noted, when I was a small boy, my emotions got me in a lot of trouble. If I was sad, I cried, and I was ridiculed as a cry baby. If I was afraid, I shrank back, and the other boys, smelling fear, would pounce on me.

But as I approached adolescence, the rational part of my brain developed and gave me a new tool for protecting myself. It could overpower and hide my emotions. However, in hiding my feelings from others, they also became hidden from Dorothie and me.

Early in our marriage, when I'd return from a business trip,

Dorothie would often ask me if I had missed her. Not having the good sense to admit that I didn't know how I felt, I would tell her I was too busy to notice. My response made her feel unappreciated and unloved. While I'm still not as in touch with my feelings as Dorothie, I now know how lost I would be without her.

Earlier in our relationship, I tried running the family based on logic. This was not a smart move in general, and it was worse because I was the only male in the house. (We have two daughters.) Trying to "logic" everything out kept failing but, illogically, I kept repeating that same experiment—until I found the courage to tear up my old map and try something new.

One of the most illogical things I ever said to Dorothie—though of course, I didn't see it that way at the time—was when she was feeling some way I didn't like. I told her, "You can't feel that way. It doesn't make any sense." Now I can see how illogical my comment was. Feelings don't make sense. They just are.

DOROTHIE: Years into this process, after things had gotten much better on all fronts, including Marty's overuse of logic, we were going through old pictures and other mementos. We came across an essay Marty had written in 1964, when he was nineteen and applying for admission to Tau Beta Pi, the Engineering Honor Society. In the excerpt below, he describes something I experienced repeatedly in our early relationship that hurt me deeply: his use of logic as a weapon to win arguments. Asked to describe his faults, he stated:

This leads to another of my faults—that of trying to argue an emotional issue on rational grounds. I will present rational arguments to support my side when they will do no good, since

245

*both parties' minds have been decided by non-rational means.
However, I sometimes enjoy these discussions, as the other
person or persons usually strike back with emotional pleas, and
in this world rationality is held to be more important.*

When we came across this essay, I was dumbstruck. Not only
had Marty tortured me this way—a habit which was, by then,
fortunately in the past—but the essay made it look like torturing
me had been a conscious decision.

MARTY: I can see how it looked that way, but my misuse of
logic as a weapon to win arguments had become an unconscious
reflex. That doesn't mean it was any less painful to Dorothie or
any less excusable. Thank God I came to see the limits of that kind
of "illogical logic."

It's ironic that, in my second year of graduate studies—so in
our first year of marriage—I learned something in an advanced
math class that should have stopped me cold in my tracks from
living in the "Kingdom of Logic." The class explored some deep,
seemingly paradoxical mathematical results, including Gödel's
Incompleteness Theorem. Proved by the brilliant Austrian (and
later naturalized American) mathematician Kurt Gödel, this
theorem proved that logic can't prove everything that's true. And
it did so very logically.

I was in shock. I came home and told Dorothie that I felt like I
was having a mental breakdown. I'd based my whole life on logic,
and here logic was telling me that it was not enough. It was literally
incomplete, as the name of Gödel's theorem clearly states.

Previously, my life built on logic had seemed like a sturdy brick
fortress. Now Gödel's Incompleteness Theorem was telling me that

my brick fortress was built on a foundation of sand and could be knocked over by the least disturbance. What could I do?

What I should have done is what I did years later: Stop basing my whole life on logic. Logic has its place, but it's just one component of our intelligence, not the whole thing. You can see that in the earlier story about moving beyond fear, in which my intuition warned me that I was about to step on a marital land mine before I was consciously aware of the danger. Only by paying attention to my fear—a non-rational emotion—could I steer the conversation in a safer direction in time to prevent Dorothie's exploding.

Using logic as a weapon had become an unconscious reflex because it had worked so well for so many years. It had rescued me from horrible situations into which my unchecked emotions previously would have thrown me.

What I failed to see was that my environment had changed. Dorothie was not out to get me, as the other kids had been. In fact, even those kids are now adults, and they're no longer out to beat me up. The experiment of using logic to protect me that had worked so well for so long was now producing constant, negative results in my marriage. But because I was afraid to tear up my old map based purely on logic, I illogically kept following it—even though I kept driving off cliffs.

Civilization has not yet driven off the nuclear cliff, but we cannot wait for that direct evidence to tear up our old map based on the logic of nuclear deterrence. We need to engage in a zealous search for the truth that ruthlessly disregards our current beliefs, no matter how deeply held, if they are contradicted by the observed data.

First data point: Nuclear logic places great emphasis on the credibility of deterrence. But how credible is it to threaten an action that will result in our own destruction? That illogical logic was captured in top-secret hearings before the Senate Foreign Relations Committee on September 16, 1980, in the following exchange between Senator John Glenn and Secretary of Defense Harold Brown, after a long argument about whether a new strategy made nuclear deterrence more credible:

> **Senator Glenn:** *I get lost in what is credible and not credible. This whole thing gets so incredible when you consider wiping out whole nations, it is difficult to establish credibility.*
>
> **Secretary Brown:** *That is why we sound a little crazy when we talk about it.*
>
> **Senator Glenn:** *That is the best statement of the day.*

Unfortunately, the conundrum of 1980 remains with us since, as we saw with Secretary Kerry's statement, nuclear deterrence is still regarded as the cornerstone of our national security.

Second data point: For nuclear deterrence to work, our adversaries must be rational enough for our threats to deter them, but we must be irrational enough for their comparable threats not to deter us. This need for irrationality on our part is usually swept under the rug, but the previously cited 1995 US Strategic Command report "Essentials of Post-Cold War Deterrence" was unusually candid on that point (emphasis added):

> *The fact that some elements [in the American nuclear command] may appear to be potentially "out of control" can be beneficial to creating and reinforcing fears and doubts within the minds of an adversary's decision makers. This essential sense of fear is the working force of deterrence.* ***That the US***

may become irrational and vindictive if its vital interests are attacked should be part of the national persona we project to all adversaries.

DOROTHIE: Whoever came up with the term *nuclear deterrence* was a marketing genius since it implies that it works—that it will, in fact, deter our adversaries. But nuclear deterrence can morph far too easily into nuclear chicken. Imagine the outcry if Secretary Kerry had said that nuclear chicken is the cornerstone of US national security. Yet in a sense, that's what he was saying.

MARTY: A third data point indicating that our deeply held belief in the power of nuclear deterrence might be wrong is the fact that we haven't carefully defined what the term means. Does it mean that we have nuclear weapons solely for the purpose of deterring a nuclear attack on us or our allies? That's the impression given by many statements from our government. But if that's the case, why have we used nuclear threats when the stakes were far lower? During the 1962 Cuban Missile Crisis, no vital national security interest made it worth risking destruction of our homeland. As President Kennedy observed in private, "it doesn't make any difference if you get blown up by an ICBM flying from the Soviet Union or one from ninety miles away. Geography doesn't mean that much."[128]

A more recent example in which nuclear threats are being used when our national existence is not at stake is our threat to attack Iran with nuclear weapons. This threat is contained in the Obama administration's 2010 Nuclear Posture Review (NPR). Of course, the NPR does not say that directly, but all the major media (including in Iran) put together two of its statements to reach that conclusion.

The document states that, "the United States will not use or threaten to use nuclear weapons against non-nuclear weapons states that are … in compliance with their nuclear non-proliferation obligations."

But that seemingly positive statement carries an implicit threat to attack Iran with nuclear weapons because earlier the NPR stated that, "North Korea and Iran have violated non-proliferation obligations."[129]

While the NPR states as a fact that Iran has violated its non-proliferation obligations, it should be noted that whether they are in violation is a matter of debate and interpretation. It also is noteworthy that a number of nations have accused us of being in violation of our own non-proliferation obligations. The Non-Proliferation Treaty (NPT) requires us, along with the other four recognized nuclear weapons states, "to pursue negotiations in good faith on … nuclear disarmament."

The NPT has been in force since 1970, and some nations question whether we have pursued the required negotiations, especially in light of statements by Secretary Kerry and others indicating that we have no intention of abandoning our reliance on nuclear weapons.

A fourth data point that raises questions about the logic of nuclear deterrence is the fact that world leaders have the power to start a nuclear war even when they are so incapacitated that they could not legally drive a car:

- Russian President Boris Yeltsin was frequently disoriented due to alcoholism.
- President Nixon had a serious drinking problem. For example, on October 11, 1973, British Prime Minister Edward Heath

requested a phone conversation with Nixon during the crisis produced by the Yom Kippur War. A formerly secret telephone conversation shows Nixon's National Security Advisor, Henry Kissinger, telling his assistant, "Can we tell them no? When I talked to the president, he was loaded."[130]

- In his memoirs, Tony Blair admits that while he was Prime Minister of Great Britain, his daily alcohol consumption was "definitely at the outer limit. Stiff whiskey or G&T before dinner, couple of glasses of wine or even half a bottle with it."[131]

Given that a failure of nuclear deterrence could destroy civilization, it is illogical that someone who could not legally drive a car has the power to start a nuclear war.

A fifth data point indicative of nuclear illogic is the fact that no one knows how risky it is to depend on nuclear deterrence—and that is the subject of the next section.

How Risky Is Nuclear Deterrence?

Throughout this book, we've talked about nuclear war as being a much more significant risk than society seems to think. This section explains why our perspective is in such marked contrast to society's complacency. First, let's look at the risk from a common sense perspective.

Imagine that a man wearing a TNT vest were to come into the room and, before you could escape, managed to tell you that he wasn't a suicide bomber so there was nothing to worry about. He didn't have the button to set off the explosives. Rather, there were two buttons in very safe hands. One detonator was in Washington, under the control of our president, and the other was in Moscow with the Russian president. You'd still get out of that room as fast as you could.

Returning to the real world, just because we can't see the nuclear weapons controlled by those buttons, why do we believe it is safe to stay here in a world with thousands of nuclear weapons? We should be plotting an escape route but society sits here complacently assuming that, just because the Earth's explosive vest has not yet gone off, it never will.

The risk is even greater because that story should have additional buttons in London, Paris, Beijing, Jerusalem, New Delhi, Islamabad, and Pyongyang—and terrorists are trying to get one of their own.

That intuitive explanation is reinforced by a more substantive examination of the risk.

MARTY: Society's acceptance of nuclear weapons stems largely from the fact that they came into being in 1945 and there hasn't been a world war since. In contrast, only twenty-one years elapsed between the First and Second World Wars, leading some to describe nuclear arms as "weapons of peace."

While nuclear weapons probably have lengthened the time between world wars, the real question is "by how much?" Even if they increased the expected time to 500 years—a time frame that most people see as highly optimistic—that would be equivalent to playing Russian roulette with the life of a child born today, because the risk of being killed in Russian roulette is one-in-six, and 500 years is roughly six times that newborn's expected lifetime. Of even greater concern, if the nuclear time horizon is more like 100 years, that child born today would have worse than even odds of living out his or her natural life.

But how does one estimate the risk of a catastrophe that has never occurred, much less reduce that risk? It may seem impossible, but it isn't. An engineering discipline known as quantitative risk analysis (QRA) was developed to estimate and reduce the risk of catastrophic accidents *before* they occur.

Applying QRA to a potential failure of nuclear deterrence might seem like a no-brainer. But in spite of almost ten years of my lobbying our government to do so, and in spite of a statement of support signed by several national security experts—one of whom served as the Director of NSA and the Deputy Director of the CIA—almost nothing has been done.

The old map which says nuclear deterrence "ain't broke, so don't fix it" is that powerful. An individual who held a high position within our nuclear command and control structure told me in a private conversation that he does not want the American public to learn how risky nuclear deterrence is. He fears that the public would react irrationally to that information, creating new national security policies that he believes would be even more dangerous than nuclear deterrence. I have less faith than he does in nuclear deterrence and more faith in the collective wisdom of the American people. That is why I hope that enough individuals will wake up and demand that our government assess the risk of our nuclear deterrence strategy failing. Only then will society begin to explore less risky alternatives.

QRA accomplishes the seemingly impossible by breaking down a catastrophic failure into *accident chains*—sequences of smaller steps that could ultimately result in the catastrophe. While we currently have no data on how frequently the catastrophe will occur, we often have lots of information on partial failures—excursions down the various accident chains that could lead to the catastrophe. By studying how frequently these excursions occur and how close they come to the catastrophic outcome, we can make a better estimate of the level of risk we face. That process also often highlights surprising ways to reduce the risk.

The July 2000 crash of the Concorde supersonic transport, which killed all 109 people on board, provides a good example. Prior to that crash, the Concorde had absolutely no fatalities in decades of use—as is now the case with nuclear deterrence. After the crash, the Concorde's fatality rate jumped from zero to being thousands of percent higher than the rest of the jetliner fleet. The small number of Concordes—only twenty were ever built—masked the danger until after the fatal crash, but greater attention to accident chains would have shown that there was a problem.

The accident chain for the fatal Concorde crash started with runway debris striking a tire. The tire blew out, causing a fuel tank to rupture. The leaking fuel caught fire, leading to the fatal crash.

Prior to this crash, it was known that the Concorde had tire failures 6,000 percent more frequently than the rest of the jetliner fleet, and that more than 10 percent of those tire failures resulted in fuel leaks. If more attention had been paid to these early warning signs, the fatal crash probably could have been averted.[132]

So what is the nuclear equivalent of the Concorde's exploding tires? To avert a nuclear catastrophe, we need to pay attention to events with the potential to escalate into a nuclear catastrophe before that happens—a version of "a stitch in time saves nine." Because a full-scale nuclear war would destroy civilization as we know it, even one nuclear near-miss over the last seventy years should wake us up. Yet, as we saw in the section on Cuba, 1962's crisis alone produced several near-misses: the near use of a Soviet nuclear torpedo, the near invasion of Cuba that would have been repelled by battlefield nuclear weapons, and Castro's pleas to Khrushchev to launch the missiles preemptively.

Let's skip over a few decades, during which a number of other excursions down nuclear accident chains occurred, and look at current times. Within the past eight years, there have been at least three significant nuclear close calls that have largely been ignored.

Most people know about the Georgian War of 2008 and the ongoing war in Ukraine, although the nuclear dimension to their risk is rarely mentioned. But even most scholars are unaware of the third close call that I refer to as "the July 2008 Cuban Bomber Minicrisis." QRA tells us that, just because it never became a full-blown crisis, that is no reason to overlook this incident. On the contrary, QRA sees it as valuable data.

At the time of the minicrisis, President Bush was moving forward with his Eastern European missile defense system, including placing American missiles in Poland. Although we saw these missiles as defensive in nature, Russia saw them as an offensive attempt to negate their nuclear deterrent. For more than a year before the minicrisis occurred, I had been warning[133] that these Polish missiles bore a dangerous resemblance to the ones we placed in Turkey in the Spring of 1962. Those missiles had put the idea in Khrushchev's mind to base similar, Soviet missiles on Cuba.

I wasn't sure what, if anything, Russia would do on Cuba to remind us how it feels to have hostile weapons close to your borders, but the risk seemed too high, given the possible consequences.

The first tremor occurred in October 2007, when Putin likened our missile defense system to 1962's Cuban Missile Crisis.[134] A more significant event occurred nine months later, in July 2008, when *Izvestia*, a Russian newspaper often used for semi-official governmental leaks, reported that, if we proceeded with the system, strategic Russian bombers would be deployed to Cuba.[135]

When asked about this in his Senate confirmation hearings as Air Force Chief of Staff, General Norton Schwartz responded that "we should stand strong and indicate that is something that crosses a threshold, crosses a red line."

While the Russian Foreign Ministry later discounted *Izvestia*'s report,[136] hawkish elements within Russia are clearly worried about our putting missiles close to their border in Eastern Europe. Khrushchev's similar concern about our 1962 Turkish missile deployment led him to place his own missiles on Cuba. If Russia's hawkish elements had prevailed in 2008, the minicrisis would have become a full-blown crisis, possibly rivaling 1962's.

The risk surrounding missile defense increased in May 2016 with the activation of a NATO system in Romania that Russia called "a direct threat" to its security.[137] The risk of a nuclear crisis in Eastern Europe was also increased by the Obama administration's decision to quadruple its budget for basing heavy weapons, armored vehicles, and American soldiers in that region, close to Russia's borders.[138]

Cuba provides the one bright spot on the nuclear risk front. On December 17, 2014, President Obama initiated a process to normalize relations with that nation—a move with the potential to defuse one of the nuclear tinderboxes of the world. Better relations with Cuba will reduce the risk of Russian bombers or other weapons being based there and creating a crisis.

In spite of that hopeful sign with respect to Cuba, the risk of nuclear war remains far too high. It's time we took a long, hard look at the logic that put a nuclear doomsday machine in the hands of fallible human beings. We must start looking for ways to reduce the risk of a nuclear disaster.

Too Few Carrots, Too Many Sticks

The previous sections in this chapter have exposed the illogical logic of nuclear deterrence as it is now practiced. Since we could not immediately rid the world of its thousands of nuclear weapons, even if society decided to do that—it would take years to dismantle them and properly dispose of their nuclear fuel—a newer, safer nuclear strategy is needed, at least as an interim measure.

This section shows that the language of international relations is highly skewed toward "sticks"—threatened punishments—and lacks language for the corresponding "carrots"—positive incentives. It therefore should not be surprising that nations use threats far more frequently than is prudent. A more compassionate, holistic strategy that tries carrots before threatening sticks would be much safer in the nuclear age.

MARTY: Nuclear deterrence is often talked about and has been described earlier. It seeks to *deter* unwanted behavior with nuclear threats. Nuclear compellence is a less-used term, but one familiar to students of nuclear strategy. In that approach, we threaten to destroy an adversary unless he takes some action that we want him to take. We are trying to *compel* him to take the desired action. In the Cuban Missile Crisis, Khrushchev's missiles were intended to deter a second American invasion of Cuba, while Kennedy's threats were designed to compel Khrushchev to remove his missiles.

Both deterrence and compellence involve threats or "sticks." It is disturbing that there is no well-established term for the "carrot" side of the coin. What should we call positive incentives offered to encourage an adversarial nation to change its behavior? It says something about our worldview—our international map—that such a term is lacking. We assume that our adversaries will only respond to force, not to diplomacy.

Worse, there is an existing, but derogatory, term used by opponents of diplomatic carrots: appeasement. That term is code for the behavior of British Prime Minister Neville Chamberlain when, in 1938, he gave in to Hitler's demand for a slice of Czechoslovakia known as the Sudetenland. Having averted war with Germany, Chamberlain returned to England and proclaimed:

We regard the agreement signed last night ... as symbolic of the desire of our two peoples never to go to war with one another again. ... a British Prime Minister has returned from Germany bringing peace with honor. I believe it is "peace for our time." Go home and get a nice quiet sleep.

Hitler invaded Poland a year later, teaching Britain that his appetite was insatiable. He was unappeasable.

Fear of appeasement has been used repeatedly to argue for, and then to justify, our military interventions, no matter how ill-fated they turn out to be. Unlike Harry Rathbun's "zealous search for the truth," it has been automatically assumed that appeasement never averts war and always leads to an even worse conflict later on.

With that background, you can see why President Lyndon Johnson was determined not to be seen as appeasing the Communists over Vietnam. On February 25, 1964, a now-declassified phone conversation shows LBJ telling his Secretary of Defense Robert McNamara, "you can have more war or you can have more appeasement."

Although Johnson cautioned, "we don't want more of either," he chose more war by sending well over half a million American soldiers to Vietnam.[139] Johnson's and America's fear of appeasement cost 58,000 American lives and between one and three million Vietnamese lives. Even so, we lost the war. We did not appease. Instead, we were humiliated.

Fear of appeasement was used again in an August 2008 article in *Newsweek* magazine to argue that the United States should send troops to Georgia to help that nation in its war with Russia. The article was titled, "Appeasing Russia: The historical reasons why the West should intervene in Georgia," and started off:

> *Is that "appeasement" we see sidling shyly out of the closet of history? ... As those of a certain age will recall, "appeasement" encapsulated the determination of British governments of the 1930s to avoid war in Europe, even if it meant capitulating to the ever-increasing demands of Adolf Hitler. ... It is impossible to view the Russian onslaught against Georgia without these bloodstained memories rising to mind.[140]*

If the United States had followed through on the article's recommendation for us to intervene in Georgia, it would have created a highly incendiary situation, probably leading to nuclear threats. And when nuclear threats are made, nuclear use may follow.

Compounding the illogic of the *Newsweek* article, Swiss diplomat Heidi Tagliavini, who headed a European Union fact-finding commission on the causes of the Georgian war, wrote (emphasis added): "Like most catastrophic events, the war of August 2008 had several causes. ***The proximate cause was the shelling by Georgian forces*** of the capital of the secessionist province of South Ossetia, Tskhinvali, on Aug. 7, 2008, which was followed by a disproportionate response of Russia."[141]

In other words, the EU fact-finding commission concluded that Georgia fired the first shots and must share blame for the war with Russia. It is illogical logic to criticize the United States as an appeaser for not fighting on the side of the nation that started the shooting. To me, not becoming involved in 2008's Georgian War sounds more like good, common sense, especially considering that Russia has thousands of nuclear weapons. Unfortunately and dangerously, biased media coverage continues to give most Americans the impression that Russia is solely to blame for that war.

The association of Russia with Nazi Germany continues unabated. In March 2014, after Putin annexed Crimea, Hillary Clinton stated, "Now if this sounds familiar, it's what Hitler did back in the '30s."[142]

But does appeasement deserve such a bad rap? In a 2010 paper, Yale History Professor Paul Kennedy argues that it does not. Professor Kennedy notes that appeasement's bad reputation is based on a single data point—Munich in 1938—and overlooks a large number of successes.[143]

He starts by noting that the first definition the dictionary gives for *appease* is "to bring peace, calm; to soothe." There's nothing negative about that.

He describes how Great Britain repeatedly appeased the United States in the latter half of the nineteenth century. His first example involves a border between British Guiana and Venezuela. Then he describes how the British cabinet overruled its own Admiralty and gave up its rights under the 1850 Clayton-Bulwer Treaty to equal control of the Panama Canal—a major appeasement. His last example is British capitulation over the border between Canada and Alaska, an action that outraged Canadians.

Professor Kennedy highlights the value of Britain's appeasement by citing how the United States came into World War I on Britain's side:

> *Kaiser Wilhelm II, who so eagerly reckoned to benefit from an Anglo-American war that distracted his European rival, was bewildered that the British kept giving way—kept appeasing ... In this case, appeasement worked, and arguably played a massive role in helping to bring the United States to an official pro-British stance as the two great wars of the twentieth century approached. Curiously, I have never seen any of our current American neocons and nationalists declare it was a bad thing that Britain [repeatedly appeased America.]*

Professor Kennedy then argues that even appeasing Hitler at Munich may have served a useful purpose by encouraging Britain to fight until he was deposed. Contrary to popular opinion today, Hitler's Munich demand was not that unreasonable, even though hindsight bias makes it appear that way.

In 1919, when the Sudetenland was given to Czechoslovakia during the breakup of the Austro-Hungarian Empire, many had argued that it should be part of Germany or Austria, since most of its population was German-speaking. But pressure from the new nation of Czechoslovakia won out over self-determination. It is ironic, since the principle of self-determination is what gave birth to Czechoslovakia.

Thus, many people in 1938 saw Hitler's demand for the Sudetenland as reasonable. Only after he swallowed the rest of Czechoslovakia and invaded Poland was it clear that he could not be appeased.

If Britain had gone to war over the Sudetenland in 1938, before Hitler's mania was clear, popular support for the war probably would have waned before Hitler was deposed. He would not have been seen as the unappeasable monster he really was. Thus, even if Britain had been able to win a hypothetical, less-bloody 1938 war, Hitler probably would have been left in power and World War II would merely have been delayed, not avoided.

With deterrence being such a major part of our old map and appeasement being so unnecessarily tarnished in that worldview, we need a new term to denote the carrot side of resolving international conflicts. Several have been proposed, but none has caught on adequately—some examples include strategic engagement, cooperative security, enlightened self-interest, and experimental cooperation. But more important than finding a new term is to start behaving differently—to start offering more carrots to countries with which we are in conflict, and threatening to hit them with fewer sticks.

Whenever we feel threatened by another nation, the old map directs us to behave aggressively and threaten it with ruin if it does not back down. That map sees diplomacy as weak and giving in to blackmail, thereby emboldening our adversaries to make greater demands in the future. Paradoxically, we expect other nations to give in when we never would. That illogical assumption needs to be reexamined and corrected before two nuclear-armed nations stumble into another crisis comparable to Cuba in 1962.

Of course, you—by yourself—cannot bring about such changes. But if enough of us experience the magic that compassion and holistic thinking can work in our personal relationships, our personal successes will form a foundation for societal change at the international level. Plus, we'll be happier.

Marty's Allegory of the Jungle

Years ago, Marty came up with the following allegory that helps explain why society is so resistant to tearing up its old map for national security and piecing together a new one compatible with the realities of the nuclear age.

Imagine you're a medical doctor who goes deep into the jungle, searching for natural remedies. You find a tribe with no knowledge of the modern world, but which knows of many herbal remedies, some even better than our modern medicines.

A tribe member comes down with excruciating abdominal pain that does not succumb to a first treatment of the usual herb for a stomach ache. The medicine man orders a second dose, at which point you examine the patient and realize this is appendicitis.

You tell the man he must leave the jungle and come with you to a hospital, where you will perform surgery and cure him.

263

The man asks, "What is surgery?"

You explain that you will cut open his abdomen and remove a small piece of his body that is causing the pain and will kill him if it is not removed. Then you will sew him up, and after a few days, you'll return him to his tribe a cured man.

Of course, the man refuses. He knows that the herb works most of the time, and that cutting open his stomach will surely kill him. His old map depicts the path that leads to life as certain death, and vice versa.

Modern men and women like to think that we wouldn't be so ignorant as to refuse life-saving surgery, but that's exactly what we're doing by continuing to follow our old map for national security in the nuclear age.

Conclusion

Conclusion

Moving from True Love at Home
to Peace on the Planet

As you've seen in Part 1 of this book, creating true love in our home took many years of hard work. But we did make it, and so can you. That proves the possibility of the first part of our subtitle, "creating true love at home."

But what about the second part: "creating peace on the planet"? How does individual change grow into societal change? How could your tearing up your personal relationship map and developing a new, more holistic one possibly carry over to world leaders doing the same on the international stage?

Of course, world leaders rarely, if ever, tear up their own maps. They are too invested in holding on to power to lead in such a courageous manner. They tend to wait until enough of us have gone through the difficult process of piecing together our own new maps, and only then—when it becomes necessary for them to do so in order to maintain power—do they adopt our new mindsets as their own.

That aspect of the process is illustrated by a statement attributed to Alexandre Ledru-Rollin, a French politician of the mid-nineteenth century. As a mob swept through Paris during the revolution of 1848, he is reported to have exclaimed: "There go the people. I must follow them, for I am their leader."

Even though that statement is probably apocryphal, it makes an important point: Societal change is always driven by individual change. Society cannot change until the individuals who compose it do, and once they change, societal thinking—and the actions of world leaders—follow automatically.

Think back to the presidential election of 1840 when anti-slavery candidate James Birney garnered only 0.3 percent of the vote. How did Abraham Lincoln win the presidency twenty years later, and the 13th Amendment abolish slavery just five years after that? How did an idea that was deemed radical and naïve, and that contradicted millennia of deeply held societal beliefs, become part of our social fabric in such a short time? One by one, enough Americans questioned the previous conventional wisdom until a tipping point was reached and a new consensus emerged.

History tells us about the role that the 1852 novel *Uncle Tom's Cabin* played in leading to the abolition of slavery. But Harriet Beecher Stowe's publishing her book didn't produce the required public reaction all by itself. People had to read it and think about it. If they liked what they read, they recommended *Uncle Tom's Cabin* to others, and they started talking about slavery in a new way. Each of those small actions built on one another until a tipping point was reached and slavery was abolished.

If that major societal change could occur so rapidly before radio, TV, and the Internet, imagine how quickly compassion and holistic thinking could spread today if enough of us will rise to the challenge.

We'd love it if you and enough other people made this book the *Uncle Tom's Cabin* for creating true love in more homes and greater peace on the planet. But, even if this book makes just a small contribution to raising global consciousness, we'll have succeeded—because, fortunately, we're not alone. There are many efforts underway, working in different ways, all trying to move society in the direction of peace and long-term sustainability. If each of those efforts moves society a little bit, all together we can move it a lot. And there is evidence for hope.

Growth in holistic thinking can be seen in the evolution of human societies to ever larger entities. Thousands of years ago, our primary allegiance was to our tribe or clan. Over time, that allegiance evolved to a larger entity, the city-state, and today it is to the nation state. It seems reasonable to hope, or even expect, that that evolutionary process will continue until we feel enough allegiance to the planet as a whole that wars between nations will seem as primitive as tribal warfare now does.

There is other evidence that compassion and holistic thinking are growing. Civilian deaths in war are now decried instead of being celebrated, whereas, during World War II, the firebombing of Hamburg, Dresden, and Tokyo were applauded by most Americans. And the number of nuclear weapons in the world, as well as the annual deaths due to war, are now roughly one-quarter of what they were at the height of the Cold War.

The environmental front also shows that compassion and holistic thinking are growing, and again one book—Rachel Carson's *Silent Spring*—is often cited as starting the process. As with *Uncle Tom's Cabin*, the book by itself would not have had any impact if it weren't for the actions of the individuals who read it and took its message to heart. Published in 1962, *Silent Spring* produced concrete results within a decade.

In 1970, President Richard Nixon, a name not usually associated with environmentalism, established the Environmental Protection Agency (EPA) and charged it with viewing "the environment as a whole." He insisted that the EPA treat "air pollution, water pollution and solid wastes as different forms of a single problem"—which was clearly a holistic perspective.[144] Three years later, the Endangered Species Act of 1973 was signed into law, also by President Nixon.

Depletion of the Earth's protective ozone layer through the release of man-made CFCs—originally used as a propellant in hair sprays and a refrigerant in air conditioners—was such a serious threat just a few decades ago that a 1992 *TIME* magazine cover story devoted to it warned: "This unprecedented assault on the planet's life-support system could have horrendous long-term effects on human health, animal life, the plants that support the food chain and just about every other strand that makes up the delicate web of nature."[145]

When the harmful effect of CFC's on the ozone layer was first brought to light, many questioned the science, just as is happening today with human-induced global warming. In spite of substantial opposition, the 1987 Montreal Protocol to cut CFC production in half was signed by 197 parties, including every member of the UN.

Three years later, that was changed to a total ban on CFCs by the year 2000. In consequence, the depletion of the Earth's ozone layer has been reversed and is on track to be fully healed in about fifty years.[146] This effort was so successful that many younger people are not even aware of this major environmental victory against what initially seemed like insurmountable odds.

Ronald Reagan, the American president who signed the Montreal Protocol, generally detested government regulation. But when enough individuals demand change—when a tipping point is reached—change does occur, even in a seemingly hostile political environment.

The fight against global warming also is showing progress. Data from the California state government shows that, from 2001 to 2014, electricity generated within the state from coal dropped more than 75 percent; nuclear dropped almost by half; and virtually all of that coal-fired and nuclear energy was replaced by solar and wind power.[147] When power imported from other states is considered, coal and nuclear assume a slightly greater role.[148] But it looks as if the better angels of our nature are not only winning the war on war, but also have a chance of winning the war on global warming, especially if they get an adrenalin shot from greater public interest. And greater public interest starts with each us—individuals becoming concerned and demanding change.

A Call to Action

MARTY: This section is an important one, and we ran into a problem that turned out to be a blessing. I wrote a draft that didn't seem inspiring enough to Dorothie. When I had difficulty seeing how much it needed to change, she even called it "boring" to get my attention—which it did. But what she wrote seemed ungrounded to me.

We wrestled with these different opinions for several days before what should have been obvious became clear. We are very different people who think very differently. In fact, and as you've seen repeatedly, Dorothie is more into feelings than thoughts, so my logical approach didn't "ring her chimes."

Recognizing that some of our readers will be more like me and some more like Dorothie, we've included both calls to action. We've put mine (edited to be less boring) first, and ended with Dorothie's (edited to be more grounded) because we expect more readers to be like her and wanted to end on that note.

Years ago, such differing opinions would have led to a fight about who was right. But now, with both of us committed to doing what's right to make this book as good as possible, our disagreement became an opportunity to illustrate one more time how a compassionate, holistic approach can work to the advantage of all concerned. With that preamble, here's my call to action:

What can you do to help accelerate the process of society becoming more compassionate and acting more holistically? Most critically, you can make those qualities central to your personal life. Doing so will make several, important contributions.

First, you will see an immediate payoff as your relationships flower. The small impact that each of us can have on changing the world does not feel concrete enough to most people, but seeing progress in your personal relationships is very concrete. And if you come to see previously inconceivable, positive changes in your own life, you will be a much more convincing advocate for similar changes at the societal level.

Second, you will become a model for what is needed globally.

The third way that your personal quest can help bring about societal change is to integrate compassionate, holistic thinking at both the personal and global levels. Becoming consistent in this way will make you an advocate for more effective national policies.

Talk with your friends about what you have discovered by reading this book and how it is changing your outlook. Use email, Facebook, and other social media to further your reach. Consider writing an online review of this book. Even just talking with friends helps to change the social climate.

If you feel that our nation needs to use a more compassionate, holistic approach to an issue, contact your Congressional Representative and Senators and tell them that. A major arms control treaty was ratified partly—and maybe even largely—because just 600 people called a Senator over three days in an organized effort.[149] As our program develops, we'll explore ways to make more things like that happen, so be sure to sign up on our website at anewmap.com.

Especially during the early years of our piecing together a new map for our relationship, Dorothie and I found it extremely helpful to have the support of others who were on the same journey. When you join our website, you'll become a participant in a virtual community of like-minded individuals who both give and receive support. We will keep you informed of new ideas and pose questions to help you delve more deeply into the material; and if you come up with a good idea, feed it back to us via the website's contact page so we can integrate it into the program.

Develop a local community to work on these ideas. If you belong to a church that already has a peace and justice group, see if it might find some of this book's ideas useful. Civic groups have the same potential.

If you're already part of a group working actively on the environment, peace, or similar issues, ask others if they are interested in exploring ways this book might help the group achieve its goals.

This part of our new map is necessarily incomplete. We haven't yet fully pieced it together, and we need your help in discovering how to best do that. It's a grand challenge, but one well worth taking on.

DOROTHIE: Okay, now I get to add my call to action. I fully agree that the most important thing people can do is to integrate compassion and holistic thinking into their personal lives. But I want to emphasize that the fundamental challenge we face today is for people to imagine a world where they can both love and be loved unconditionally.

What does a loving world look like to you? Do you feel scared, excited, or both? We can achieve this vision together, resulting in loving relationships, stronger families, and a safer world. We invite you to join us at anewmap.com, where you will find a community of people who have committed to tear up their old maps and piece together new ones.

We need you as a leader online and offline. We offer resources to empower you to draw up a new map and strengthen your leadership within your new community:

First, our website offers ongoing content, exercises, and videos, so you can strengthen your holistic communication and leadership skills. While you can learn from our posts, we also want you to share your own stories and lessons as emerging local and global leaders.

Second, we are developing programs for this community of social innovators to meet regularly in their local neighborhoods to discuss personal and global issues and to provide mentorship around those topics. Research shows that people are more likely to accomplish goals in groups, so this community is your team, working alongside you to improve your relationships at home and across the world. Become a leader in this community by organizing "Dinners for Six" or "Coffees for Eight" or whatever suits your creative spirit. Invite people from your own neighborhood or network, or join an existing group. Visit our website to start or join a gathering near you.

Third, help us draw up the new map for our community. Send us a note on the initiatives you are currently working on or aspire to work on and let us know how we can unite forces to amplify local leadership for global change.

The Vision

Many years ago, we undertook an awe-inspiring, but grueling, weeklong backpack trip through the back country of Yosemite National Park. The most exhausting leg of the trip was climbing Red Peak Pass—at over 11,000 feet, it's the highest trail in the park.

The climb felt interminable, especially in that thin air. We were exhausted. The trail kept looking as if it were about to top out, but then we'd round a bend and be disappointed to face yet another steep climb. We felt like we couldn't go on, but we had to. You can't hail a cab in the back country. The only way out was up.

Finally, we rounded a boulder-strewn bend and there was the pass. The vista[150] that opened up before us made all of that hard work worthwhile. Overcome by the beauty, we forgot our sore legs and blistered feet. We were elated.

That experience of climbing Red Peak Pass is like the process that we worked to move from fighting interminably to never being angry with one another again. At times, it was so difficult that we thought we couldn't go on. Fortunately, as with the hike up Red Peak Pass, there were some gorgeous stops along the way to feed our souls. But nothing compared to the feeling of making it to the top: heaven on earth.

We know at our deepest level that we are best friends forever. We can say anything, make any mistake, and not have to worry that things will fall apart. Each of us knows that we are loved unconditionally. This loving space we've created where each of us can be who we are, without pretense or masks, was worth all that hard work and pain.

That doesn't mean we didn't change—far from it. That safe, loving space created the potential for our true, inner selves to surface. Like a caterpillar shedding its protective cocoon, we emerged far better from this process—loved unconditionally, and loving unconditionally. It's a blessing that we wish for everyone in the world, which is why we've written this book.

If enough individuals will take on that climb up Red Peak Pass, we can solve the nuclear threat, global warming, and all the other challenges we face. That's also why we've written this book.

What's needed is the same at both the personal and the global levels—moving from anger, hate, and fear to compassion; moving from a "me-centered" world to holistic thinking. Moving from pain to joy.

If you haven't already done so, please join us.

Acknowledgments

We are extremely grateful to a number of Marty's colleagues with specialized expertise who reviewed the international case studies and provided feedback to make them as objective and accurate as possible.

Ambassador Karl Eikenberry and Dr. Yama Torabi independently reviewed the section on Afghanistan. Prior to serving as our ambassador to that nation from 2009 to 2011, Karl was a Lieutenant General in the US Army who served as Commander of the Coalition forces in Afghanistan from 2005 to 2007. He currently is Director of the US-Asia Security Initiative at Stanford University. Yama is Chairman of the Joint Independent Anti-Corruption Monitoring and Evaluation Committee in Afghanistan, and earlier was Executive Director of Integrity Watch Afghanistan.

Prof. Barton Bernstein reviewed the sections on Cuba and Vietnam. Bart is Professor of History at Stanford University.

Dr. Abbas Emami-Naeini reviewed the section on Iran. Although Abbas' academic training is in Electrical Engineering,

Marty has found him to be an invaluable and highly objective source of information on Iran.

Prof. Joel Beinin reviewed the section on Iraq. Joel is the Donald J. McLachlan Professor of History and Professor of Middle East History at Stanford University.

Prof. Bruce Cumings reviewed the section on North Korea. Bruce is the Gustavus F. and Ann M. Swift Distinguished Service Professor in History at the University of Chicago.

Prof. Norman Naimark reviewed the section on Russia. Norman is the Robert and Florence McDonnell Professor in East European Studies at Stanford University.

The fact that the above individuals reviewed particular sections should not be taken as their endorsement of everything said in that section or of this book as a whole.

A number of our friends provided helpful feedback on earlier drafts of this book, with special thanks going to Carol Baxter, Richard Duda, Don and Virginia Fitton, Julie Freestone and Rudi Raab, Barbara Kyser, Karen Matison, and Marisa Messina.

Our involvement with the Creative Initiative Foundation and the Beyond War Foundation in the 1980s was key to getting us started on this process and helping us see the connection between interpersonal and international relations. We thank the many individuals in those movements, too numerous to name here, who played important roles in that part of our lives.

Our journey was aided by a number of therapists, particularly Joanne LeMaistre, Susan Mark, Sheldon Starr, and David Willingham.

We also wish to thank Dr. Reed Kaplan for helping Dorothie regain a semblance of normalcy in a life that had been disabled by frequent, severe migraines. Without his help, she never would have been able to coauthor this book.

Ghislain Viau of Creative Publishing Book Design has our heartfelt thanks for going above and beyond the call of duty in shepherding us through the book design process.

We also want to thank Samantha Stein for her dedication in publicizing this book and her help in starting to build the new map community.

Lastly, we are grateful for the time and place in which we live, where it is possible to question such deeply held societal beliefs.

Notes

MARTY: We faced something of a dilemma about how to deal with references. On the one hand, we wanted this book to be as readable as possible, with what Dorothie calls "a low fog index." On the other hand, whenever we present information that is contrary to the conventional wisdom, it is essential to back it up with references that are as solid as possible.

We therefore opted for these end notes, which are less intrusive than footnotes, and made them easy to connect with their associated text by using sequential numbers. When the referenced material is long, I often indicate where in the document to find it, and in some cases I even provide key excerpts, so only readers who want to trace back to the original source need leave this book.

Most of these references are online, which is indicated by saying "*accessible online*" in the reference. While it would be nice to make those words serve as clickable links, that is obviously impossible in a printed book, and—because links become stale—it is also of questionable value even in an e-book. I have therefore created an online version of these notes, in which the words *accessible online* do, in fact, serve as clickable links. But I can update those links as I learn that they have become stale. You can help by reporting stale links to me via the Contact form on our website (anewmap.com) and, if possible, including a new link. If a document becomes unavailable online, I will change the note in the online version to read *not accessible online* or similar. You can find the online version of these notes at anewmap.com/notes.

1   Dimitri K. Simes, "The Realist: Reawakening an Empire," *The National Interest*, July/August 2014, pp. 5-15. The quoted text appears on the top of page 6. Accessible online.

2   The New York Times Editorial Board, "Vladimir Putin Can Stop This War," *New York Times*, July 18, 2014, page A22. Accessible online.

3   Carl Jung, *Man and His Symbols*, Doubleday, Garden City, NY, 1964, page 85.

4   That the Johnson Administration depicted the attack on the Maddox as "unprovoked" can be seen in the following excerpt from *US State Department, Protest to Hanoi, August 3, 1964*; "The United States Government takes an extremely serious view of the unprovoked attack made by Communist North Vietnamese torpedo boats on an American naval vessel, the USS *Maddox*, operating on the high seas in the Gulf of Tonkin on August 2." Accessible online. An audio clip of the key part of Johnson's now-declassified conversation of August 3, 1964, can be heard on Marty's blog post, "Avoiding Needless Wars, Part 1: The First Gulf of Tonkin Incident," which is accessible online.

5   Leo Tolstoy, *A Confession, The Gospels in Brief, and What I Believe*, translated by Aylmer Maude, Oxford University Press, 1971, pp 316-317. Here's the key excerpt:
   The passage which served me as key to the whole was Matthew, v. 38, 39: "Ye have heard that it was said, An eye for an eye and a tooth

for a tooth: But I say unto you, Resist not him that is evil" ... These words suddenly appeared to me as something quite new, as if I had never read them before. Previously when reading that passage I had always, by some strange blindness, omitted the words, "But I say unto you, Resist not him that is evil," just as if those words had not been there, or as if they had no definite meaning. Subsequently, in my talks with many and many Christians familiar with the Gospels, I often had occasion to note the same blindness as to those words. No one remembered them, and often when speaking about that passage Christians referred to the Gospels to verify the fact that the words were really there.

6 Charles Lane, "The Professor Who Lit the Spark," *Stanford* (Stanford University's Alumni magazine), Accessible online.

7 Jay Thorwaldson, "Emelia Rathbun, founder of Global Community, dies," *Palo Alto Weekly*, October 13, 2004. Accessible online.

8 The Robert Wilson quote starts at 33:27 on the DVD version of *The Day After Trinity*.

9 Anriban Nag and James McGeever, "Foreign exchange, the world's biggest market, is shrinking," *Reuters*, February 11, 2016. Accessible online.

10 Strobe Talbott, "Russia Has Nothing to Fear," *New York Times*, February 18, 1997, page A25. Accessible online.

11 Mark Landler and Helene Cooper, "U.S. Fortifying Europe's East to Deter Putin," *New York Times*, February 2, 2016, page A6. Accessible online.

12 Strobe Talbott, *The Russia Hand: Memoirs of a Presidential Diplomat*, Random House Paperback, New York, 2003, page 74.

13 Marty asked several people to review this section for accuracy because human memory, his included, is subject to error, and because he previously had strong emotions connected to the patent fight with RSA and his battle with NSA. Jim Bidzos pointed out several errors that now have been corrected. Adm. Inman found the description

of his conversations with Marty to be accurate. Lew Morris died in 2005, so Dr. Jim Omura, who cofounded Cylink with Lew, reviewed this from Cylink's perspective and found no errors.

14   Henry Corrigan-Gibbs, "Keeping Secrets," *Stanford*, November/ December 2014, pp. 58-64. Accessible online.

15   Martin Hellman, "Defusing the Nuclear Threat: A Necessary First Step," accessible online.

16   "Syria: Hillary Clinton calls Russia and China 'despicable' for opposing UN resolution," *The Telegraph*, February 25, 2012. Accessible online.

17   "Medvedev: Libya has influenced our position on Syria," *RT*, July 30, 2012. Accessible online.

18   George Ball, "COMMENTARY; AND NOW, THE REAGANEV DOCTRINE," *Boston Globe*, October 30, 1983. Accessible online through the *Boston Globe*'s archives.

19   Joshua Goldstein, "Syria War Reverses Trend in Battle Deaths," *International Relations blog*, July 4, 2013. Accessible online.

20   Anatoly A. Gromyko and Martin E. Hellman editors, *Breakthrough: Emerging New Thinking*, Walker and Co., New York, 1988, page 211. Accessible online.

21   Marina Krakovsky, "The Effort Effect," *Stanford*, March/April 2007. Accessible online.

22   Carol S. Dweck, *Self Theories: Their Role in Motivation, Personality and Development*, Psychology Press (Taylor & Francis Group), Philadelphia, PA, 2000, pp. 24-26.

23   Carol S. Dweck, 2011 Award for Distinguished Scientific Contributions, "Mindsets and Human Nature: Promoting Change in the Middle East, the Schoolyard, the Racial Divide, and Willpower," *American Psychologist*, November 2012, pp. 614-622. Accessible online. See also Eran Halperin, Alexandra G. Russell, Kali H. Trzesniewski, James J. Gross, Carol S. Dweck, "Promoting the Middle East Peace Process by Changing Beliefs About Group Malleability," Science, vol. 333, September 2011, pp. 1767-1769. Accessible online.

24 Plato, *The Republic*, Book VII. Accessible online.

25 Bill Kays confirmed Marty's recollection of this event and gave permission to be quoted.

26 Marty's "Stanford Engineering Hero" lecture is accessible online.

27 James Frieden, "Alice Paul and the Struggle for the 19th Amendment: What Really Happened." Accessible online. The key excerpt is: "[In 1912, just seven years before the 19th Amendment was adopted,] NAWSA leaders believed that passage of a national suffrage amendment was impossible." NAWSA stands for the National American Woman Suffrage Association, founded in 1890.

28 "WIN/Gallup International's annual global End of Year survey shows a brighter outlook for 2014." Accessible online.

29 The audio for an opening of "The Shadow" is accessible online.

30 Seumas Milne, "The demonisation of Russia risks paving the way for war," *The Guardian*, March 4, 2015. Accessible online.

31 Bob Woodward, *Bush at War*, Simon & Schuster, New York, 2002, pp. 339-340.

32 Carl Jung, *Man and His Symbols*, Doubleday, Garden City, NY, 1964, page 85.

33 "Transcript: Sir David Frost interviews Tony Blair," December 11, 2006. Accessible online.

34 "H.R.4655 Iraq Liberation Act of 1998." Accessible online.

35 A copy of the aide's handwritten notes is accessible online. He uses abbreviations, with "Hit SH @ same time – not only UBL," meaning "Hit Saddam Hussein at the same time – not only Usama Bin Laden." He says "Go massive. Sweep it all up, things related and not," near the bottom of that page. For more information, see Julian Borger, "Blogger bares Rumsfeld's post 9/11 orders," *The Guardian*, February 24, 2006. Accessible online.

36 Linda Feldmann, "The impact of Bush linking 9/11 and Iraq," *Christian Science Monitor*, March 14, 2003. Accessible online.

37 *The Washington Post*, "President Bush Holds a News Conference (Transcript)," August 21, 2006. Accessible online.

38 Colonel Wilkerson's quote starts at 1:25:30 on the DVD version of *Taxi to the Dark Side*.

39 David Brancaccio interview with Lawrence Wilkerson, February 3, 2006, for PBS's NOW program. The transcript is accessible online.

40 Phil Donahue's quote starts at 52:23 on the DVD of *Buying the War*.

41 Pew Research Center, Religion & Public Life, "The World's Muslims: Unity and Diversity; Chapter 1: Religious Affiliation," lists Iraq's population as being 42 percent Sunni and 51 percent Shia. Accessible online.

42 Mark MacKinnon, "Globe in Iraq: Desperate exodus in search of safe ground," *The Globe and Mail*, June 26, 2014. Accessible online.

43 George Washington University's National Security Archive, "Vietnam, Episode 11, Interview with Robert McNamara." Accessible online.

44 An August 3, 1964 "Telegram From the Department of State to the Embassy in Vietnam," which was then forwarded to the North Vietnamese refers to "the unprovoked attack" on the *Maddox* and to "the grave consequences which would inevitably result from any further unprovoked offensive military action against United States forces." Accessible online.

45 Michael R. Beschloss, *Taking Charge: The Johnson White House Tapes, 1963-64*, Simon & Schuster, New York, 1997, pp. 493-494, has the Johnson quote with some minor, inconsequential variations in the transcription (e.g., what I heard as "fire," he transcribed as "fired"). An audio clip of the key part of Johnson's conversation of August 3, 1964, can be heard on my blog post, "Avoiding Needless Wars, Part 1: The First Gulf of Tonkin Incident," which is accessible online.

46 Robert J. Hanyok, "Skunks, Bogies, Silent Hounds, and the Flying Fish: The Gulf of Tonkin Mystery, 2-4 August 1964," *Cryptologic Quarterly*, Winter 2000/Spring 2001 Edition, Vol. 19, No. 4 / Vol. 20, No. 1. Accessible online. The relevant excerpt is on page 3 (emphasis added):

Two startling findings emerged from the new research. First, it is not simply that there is a different story as to what happened; it is that **no attack happened that night**. Through a compound of analytic errors and an unwillingness to consider contrary evidence, American SIGINT elements in the region and at NSA HQs reported Hanoi's plans to attack the two ships of the Desoto patrol. Further analytic errors and an obscuring of other information led to publication of more "evidence." ***In truth, Hanoi's navy was engaged in nothing that night but the salvage of two of the boats damaged on 2 August.***

47 "Sea Action: 'This Is No Drill'," *Newsweek*, August 17, 1964, pp. 19-20.

48 Captain Herrick's cautionary cable is on page 49 of NSA's, "The Gulf of Tonkin Incident: The DESOTO Patrols and OPLAN 34A," which is accessible online. It also can be found in *The Pentagon Papers*, available in hard copy from major booksellers and accessible online by searching.

49 Robert J. Hanyok, "Skunks, Bogies, Silent Hounds, and the Flying Fish: The Gulf of Tonkin Mystery, 2-4 August 1964." Accessible online. The relevant excerpt is on page 3:

> Beginning with the period of the crisis in early August, into the days of the immediate aftermath, and continuing into October 1964, SIGINT information was presented in such a manner as to preclude responsible decision makers in the Johnson administration from having the complete and objective narrative of events of 4 August 1964. Instead, only SIGINT that supported the claim that the communists had attacked the two destroyers was given to administration officials.

50 Telegram From the Embassy in Vietnam to the Department of State, June 5, 1964, marked "Literally eyes only for Rusk and McNamara from Lodge." Accessible online.

51 Barry Goldwater's 1960 book, *The Conscience of a Conservative*, states at Kindle locations 964-967: "it is clear that we cannot hope to match

the Communist world man for man, nor are we capable of furnishing the guns and tanks necessary to defend thirty nations scattered over the face of the globe. The long-overdue answer, as we will see later on, lies in the development of a nuclear capacity for limited wars."

See also Nina Tannenwald, "Nuclear Weapons and the Vietnam War," *The Journal of Strategic Studies*, Vol. 29, No. 4, August 2006, pp. 675-722, which states: "Senator Barry Goldwater, campaigning for the Republican presidential nomination in May 1964, suggested in a speech that tactical nuclear weapons should be treated more like conventional weapons, and that they should be used in Vietnam." Accessible online.

52 "Dirksen and Halleck Say G.O.P. Must Make Vietnam an Issue," *New York Times*, July 3, 1964, page 7. Accessible online.

53 Charles Mohr, "Senator Arrives on Coast," *New York Times*, July 10, 1964, page 1. Accessible online.

54 The transcript of President Johnson's August 4, 1964 television address is accessible online.

55 "Vietnam: A Television History; Interview with McGeorge Bundy." Accessible online. In it, Bundy says, "there were two episodes toward the end of 1964 where I think he [President Johnson] decided not to uh, take action for essentially uh, uh special reasons. One of them was an attack uh, that occurred just before the election, and an action taken right on the eve of election might have magnified [the] effect one way or another that made it an inappropriate moment for serious choice. ... The [October 31] Bien Hoa attack brought strong recommendations from the field that there should be a uh, some kind of reply. That attack occurred uh, just [three days] before the election [on November 3], and although I don't recall hearing the president explain his decision not to act in terms of the election, I feel quite confident that uh, he uh, would have thought that taking an action uh, as large as this and in terms of its public impact on the eve of the election would be a mistake."

56 George McT. Kahin and John W. Lewis, "The United States in Vietnam," *Bulletin of the Atomic Scientists*, Volume XXI, Number 6, June 1965, pp 28-40, states: "there was one crucially important, though temporary and in a sense artificial, advantage which the U.S. enjoyed. This derived from the unequivocal provision in the Geneva Accords that elections would be held in July 1956, under international supervision, to unify the country under one government. In anticipation of these elections (and also because of its preoccupation with the economic rehabilitation of the North), the Vietminh initially honored a central provision of the Accords and abstained from militant tactics in the South. ... It was obviously a much surprised Vietminh that came to realize during 1955–56 that ... elections were not going to be held. When on July 16, 1955, the Diem government announced, with American backing, that it would defy the provision calling for national elections, it violated a central condition which had made the Geneva Accords acceptable to the Vietminh."

57 Hans M. Kristensen and Robert S. Norris, "Worldwide deployments of nuclear weapons, 2014," *Bulletin of the Atomic Scientists*, September 1, 2014. See Table 1. Accessible online.

58 Karen Robes Meeks, "Listen to Hillary Clinton compare Russian President Vladimir Putin to Hitler," *Los Angeles Daily News*, March 5, 2014. Accessible online.

59 Rick Atkinson, "The Road to D-Day: Behind the Battle That Won the War," *Foreign Affairs*, July/August 2013. Accessible online.

60 Col. David M. Glantz (US Army, Retired), "The Soviet-German War 1941-1945: Myths and Realities: A Survey Essay," presented at the 20th Anniversary Distinguished Lecture at the Strom Thurmond Institute of Government and Public Affairs, Clemson University, October 11, 2001. The table on page 14 shows that 80 percent of the German permanent losses were on the Eastern Front. Accessible online.

61 US Department of State, Office of the Historian, "Milestones: 1937-1945. U.S.-Soviet Alliance, 1941-1945." Accessible online.

62 Vladimir Putin, "Life Is Such a Simple, Yet Cruel Thing," *Russia Insider*, May 9, 2015. This English translation is accessible online. The original Russian language article is also accessible online.

63 Turner Catledge, "Our Policy Stated," *New York Times*, June 24, 1941, page 1 (continued on page 7).

64 Facsimiles of the 38 pages of *Operation Unthinkable* are accessible online.

65 Paul Boyer, *When Time Shall Be No More: Prophecy Belief in Modern American Culture*, Harvard University Press, Cambridge, MA, 1992, page 142: "*The Late Great Planet Earth* strengthened Reagan's prophecy belief, and at a 1971 political dinner in Sacramento shortly after a leftist coup in Libya (a nation mentioned in Ezekiel as one of Israel's invaders), Reagan observed somberly: 'That's a sign that the day of Armageddon isn't far off ... Everything is falling into place. It can't be long now. Ezekiel says that fire and brimstone will be rained upon the enemies of God's people. That must mean they'll be destroyed by nuclear weapons.'"

66 President Reagan seemed to be both attracted to and repelled by nuclear weapons, and came close to agreeing to abolish them at the 1986 Reykjavik summit with Gorbachev. Even so, his belief in the Biblical prophesies may have produced a dangerous, unconscious attraction to nuclear war as bringing about the Second Coming of Christ.

67 Fyodor Lukyanov, "What Russia Learned From the Iraq War," *AL Monitor*, March 18, 2013, Accessible online.

68 Radio Free Europe/Radio Liberty, "Ukraine's Tymoshenko Finally Appears, But Next Move Unclear," February 11, 2010. Accessible online.

69 Martin Hellman, "Ukraine: Why We Need to Stop and Think," March 6, 2014. Accessible online.

70 Steve Stecklow and Oleksandor Akymenko, "Special Report: Flaws found in Ukraine's probe of Maidan massacre," *Reuters* dispatch, October 10, 2014. Accessible online.

71 Radio Free Europe/Radio Liberty, "Kyiv Violence Steps Up Pressure To Reject Ultranationalists," September 1, 2015. Accessible online.

72 Ulrich Weisser, "No Digs at Moscow: The West has to stick to its promises," *The Atlantic Times*, March 2007 issue.

73 Benjamin Bidder, "Zhirinovsky's Follies: Nuclear Threats and Busty Ladies in the Race for Second-Place in Russia," *Spiegel Online International*, February 28, 2008. Accessible online.

74 Siegfried Hecker "Denuclearizing North Korea," *Bulletin of the Atomic Scientists*, May-June 2008, pp. 44-49, 61-62. Dr. Hecker states: "From 1994 to December 2002, International Atomic Energy Agency (IAEA) inspectors monitored the freeze of production facilities, while Yongbyon technical specialists were allowed to conduct periodic maintenance of the facilities. After the United States accused North Korea of operating a clandestine uranium enrichment program in October 2002, Pyongyang expelled the IAEA inspectors, withdrew from the Nuclear Non-Proliferation Treaty (NPT), and restarted its nuclear facilities." Accessible online.

75 The Federation of American Scientists, "Guide to Nuclear Facilities, DPRK Yongbyon web page," which is accessible online, says that the 50-MW(e) "reactor was expected to be completed in 1995." This reactor would have been ten times larger than the 5 MW(e) reactor that has produced all of their plutonium and made enough for approximately one bomb per year.

The Federation of American Scientists, "Guide to Nuclear Facilities, DPRK Taechon web page," which is accessible online, says: "North Korea's 200-MW(e) reactor was expected to be completed in 1996." This reactor would have been forty times larger than the 5 MW(e) research reactor.

In a private communication, Dr. Siegfried Hecker, former Director of Los Alamos, estimated that, before construction was stopped in 1994, the 50 MW(e) reactor was two to three years away from completion, and the 200 MW(e) reactor would have taken six years to complete. The wording I used in the text took into account the slight differences between Dr. Hecker's and the FAS's estimates of completion times.

76 Siegfried S. Hecker, "Lessons learned from the North Korean nuclear crisis," *Daedelus*, Winter 2010, pp. 1-13, says: "With the capabilities it already had or was soon to complete by the early 1990s, Pyongyang today could have an arsenal of a hundred or more nuclear weapons. Instead [because of the negotiated 1994 Agreed Framework], it has enough plutonium for four to eight weapons and currently is not producing more." A prepublication version is accessible online.

77 Hans M. Kristensen and Robert S. Norris, "Worldwide deployments of nuclear weapons, 2014," *Bulletin of the Atomic Scientists*, 2-14. Accessible online. Table 1 lists North Korea's arsenal as of that date as being "<10."

78 Siegfried S. Hecker, "Return Trip to North Korea's Yongbyon Nuclear Complex," November 20, 2010, states: "The 50 MWe reactor, which was near completion in the mid-1990s but abandoned during the Agreed Framework was being dismantled with large cranes." Accessible online.

79 James Dao, "Bush Administration Halts Payments to Send Oil to North Korea," *New York Times*, November 14, 2002, states: "The Bush administration said today that it would stop financing monthly shipments of fuel oil to North Korea, which are required under a 1994 arms control agreement, to punish North Korea for pursuing a covert nuclear weapons program." Accessible online.

80 Glenn Kessler, "South Korea Offers To Supply Energy if North Gives Up Arms," *The Washington Post*, July 13, 2005. Accessible online.

81 "The National Security Strategy of the United States of America," September 2002, says: "To forestall or prevent such hostile acts by our adversaries, the United States will, if necessary, act preemptively." Accessible online.

82 The full text of the 1994 "Agreed Framework Between The United States of America And The Democratic People's Republic of Korea," is accessible online.

83 Siegfried S. Hecker, "Lessons learned from the North Korean nuclear crisis," *Daedelus*, Winter 2010, pp. 1-13. A prepublication version is accessible online.

84 President Bush's December 19, 2003 speech welcoming Libya back into the family of nations said in part: "Today in Tripoli, the leader of Libya, Colonel Moammar al-Ghadafi, publicly confirmed his commitment to disclose and dismantle all weapons of mass destruction programs in his country. ... And another message should be equally clear: leaders who abandon the pursuit of chemical, biological and nuclear weapons, and the means to deliver them, will find an open path to better relations with the United States and other free nations. ... As the Libyan government takes these essential steps and demonstrates its seriousness, its good faith will be returned. Libya can regain a secure and respected place among the nations, and over time, achieve far better relations with the United States. ... old hostilities do not need to go on forever. And I hope that other leaders will find an example in Libya's announcement today." The full speech is accessible online.

85 Korean Central News Agency, "DPRK Foreign Ministry Spokesman Denounces U.S. Military Attack on Libya," March 22, 2011. Initially this was online, but has disappeared. The relevant excerpt reads:

The present Libyan crisis teaches the international community a serious lesson.

It was fully exposed before the world that "Libya's nuclear dismantlement" much touted by the U.S. in the past turned out to be a mode of aggression whereby the latter coaxed the former with such sweet words as "guarantee of security" and "improvement of relations" to disarm itself and then swallowed it up by force.

It proved once again the truth of history that peace can be preserved only when one builds up one's own strength as long as high-handed and arbitrary practices go on in the world.

The DPRK was quite just when it took the path of Songun ["Military First"] and the military capacity for self-defence built up in this course serves as a very valuable deterrent for averting a war and defending peace and stability on the Korean Peninsula.

86 Choe Sang-Hun, "South Korea Disputes North's Dismissal of Armistice," *New York Times*, March 13, 2013, page A6, mentions North Korea canceling the armistice, threatening the U.S. with nuclear attack, and evacuating citizens to tunnels. Accessible online.

BBC News, "North Korea cuts military hotline with South," March 27, 2013, mentions North Korea cutting the hotline to South Korea and warning that "war may break out at any moment." Accessible online.

87 The full report, "Essentials of Post-Cold War Deterrence," 1995, is accessible online. The quoted text is on the next to last page, in a bullet point that reads: "Because of the value that comes from the ambiguity of what the US may do to an adversary if the acts we seek to deter are carried out, it hurts to portray ourselves as too fully rational and cool-headed. The fact that some elements may appear to be potentially 'out of control' can be beneficial to creating and reinforcing fears and doubts within the minds of an adversary's decision makers. This essential sense of fear is the working force of deterrence. That the US may become irrational and vindictive if its vital interests are attacked should be part of the national persona we project to all adversaries."

88 Choe Sang-Hun, "North Korea Offers U.S. Deal to Halt Nuclear Test," *New York Times*, January 11, 2015, page A7, is accessible online and states:

Until now, the United States has dismissed North Korea's routine demand for an end to its joint military exercises with South Korea.

The North has called them a rehearsal for an invasion while the United States and South Korea have insisted that their annual war games are defensive in nature.

But the North's latest proposal included a new incentive for Washington, offering to temporarily suspend nuclear tests in return for a suspension of the joint military exercises this year.

89 "Department of Defense Operations During the Cuban Crisis" is accessible online and states: "To mask widespread preparations for the actions proposed, Admiral Dennison suggested that we announce that our forces were preparing for an exercise. PHIBRIGLEX 62, a large-scale amphibious assault exercise, previously scheduled for the period October 15-20, provided a cover for our Caribbean preparations."

While the "actions proposed" are not spelled out in that paragraph, elsewhere the document talks about "a blockade of Cuba," "if necessary, the removal of the Castro regime to assure the permanent removal of these weapons," and the possible need "to take the missile bases out of Cuba by ground action."

90 Choe Sang-Hun, "North Korea Offers U.S. Deal to Halt Nuclear Test," *New York Times*, January 11, 2015, page A7. Accessible online.

91 Malcolm Byrne, "The Secret CIA History of the Iran Coup, 1953," November 29, 2000, *National Security Archive Electronic Briefing Book No. 28*. Accessible online. Document V at the end of the article, "Mounting Pressure Against the Shah," has most of the quoted material on page 37. The remainder is in Appendix B, also accessible at the end of the article, "London Draft of the TPAJAX as Cabled from Nicosia to Headquarters on 1 June 1953," page 23, point (5).

92 Kennett Love, "Royalists Oust Mossadegh; Army Seizes Helm," *New York Times*, August 20, 1953. Accessible online.

93 United States District Court, Southern District of Florida, V. Case No. 93-241-CR-Highsmith, Affidavit of Howard Teicher, January 31, 1995. Accessible online.

94 Joyce Battle, "Shaking Hands with Saddam Hussein: The U.S. Tilts toward Iraq, 1980-1984," *National Security Archive Electronic Briefing Book No. 82*, February 25, 2003. Accessible online. Search on "don't ask" to find the relevant part.

95 Shane Harris and Matthew M. Aid, "Exclusive: CIA Files Prove America Helped Saddam as He Gassed Iran," *Foreign Policy*, August 26, 2013. Accessible online.

96 A positive view of the agreement is expressed in Richard Nephew, "Based on breakout timelines, the world is better off with the Iran nuclear deal than without it," Brookings Institution, July 17, 2015. Accessible online.

   For a negative view, see Olli Heinonen, "Iran's Nuclear Breakout Time: A Fact Sheet," The Washington Institute, March 28, 2015. Accessible online.

97 John R. Bolton, "To Stop Iran's Bomb, Bomb Iran," *New York Times*, March 26, 2015, page A23. Accessible online.

98 Theodore C. Sorensen, *Kennedy*, Harper and Row, New York, 1965, page 705.

99 Fedor Burlatsky, *Khrushchev and The First Russian Spring: The Era of Khrushchev Though The Eyes Of His Adviser*, Scribners, New York, 1988, page 169.

100 Minutes of Meeting of the Special Group (Augmented) on Operation MONGOOSE, 4 October 1962. Accessible online.

101 United States Senate, Select Committee to Study Governmental Operations, "Alleged Assassination Plots Involving Foreign Leaders: An Interim Report," November 20, 1975, pages 71-73. Accessible online.

102 The Joint Chiefs of Staff, "Memorandum for the Secretary of Defense: Justification for US Military Intervention in Cuba," March 13, 1962. Accessible online.

103 Robert F. Kennedy statement recorded on presidential tapes, October 16, 1962. See page 452 of the transcript in Timothy Naftali

and Philip Zelikow (Editors), *The Presidential Recordings: John F. Kennedy: The Great Crises, Volume 2*, Norton, New York, 2001.

104 *TIME*, September 21, 1962, page 21, second column.

105 Fedor Burlatsky, *Khrushchev and The First Russian Spring: The Era of Khrushchev Though The Eyes Of His Adviser*, Scribners, New York, 1988, page 171.

106 The National Security Archive, "Last Nuclear Weapons Left Cuba in December 1962," December 11, 2013. Accessible online.

107 Svetlana V. Savranskaya, "New Sources on the Role of Soviet Submarines in the Cuban Missile Crisis," *Journal of Strategic Studies*, Vol. 28, No.2, 2005, pp. 233-259. See especially pages 246-247. Accessible online.

108 Barton J. Bernstein, "Reconsidering the Perilous Cuban Missile Crisis 50 Years Later," *Arms Control Today*, October 2, 2012. Accessible online.

109 Jerold L. Schecter, translator and editor, with Vyacheslav V. Luchkov, *Khrushchev Remembers: The Glasnost Tapes*, Little, Brown, Boston, 1990, pp. 176-177.

See also Barton J. Bernstein, "Reconsidering the Missile Crisis: Dealing with the Problems of the American Jupiters in Turkey" in James Nathan (Editor), *The Cuban Missile Crisis Revisited*, St. Martin's Press, New York, 1992, page 124, notes 179 and 180. These add the proviso (missing from Khrushchev's memoirs) that the missiles should be fired preemptively *if* the US invaded Cuba and intended to occupy it. Bernstein notes that the second proviso has little effect since it's hard to tell if an invasion will be followed by an occupation. And, since Castro was convinced that an American invasion was imminent, at least in his mind, he was arguing for preemptive use of the missiles. Thus Khrushchev's memoirs, while leaving out the provisos, still appear to convey what Castro was thinking.

110 Scott D. Sagan, *The Limits of Safety: Organizations, Accidents, and Nuclear Weapons*, Princeton University Press, Princeton, NJ, 1993, pp. 136-137.

111   Given the urgency of ending the crisis, the agreement between Kennedy and Khrushchev was worked out hastily and subject to interpretation that caused the risk of nuclear war to continue well after the iconic "thirteen days" that are usually said to comprise the crisis. For example, when Castro refused to allow on-site inspections that Kennedy and Khrushchev had included in their agreement, the Soviets left tarps off the missiles as they were being transported from Cuba by ship so American reconnaissance planes could verify their removal. Even so, Kennedy questioned whether our non-invasion pledge still held, and American preparations for an invasion continued into November. See David G. Coleman, "The Missiles of November, December, January, February: The Problem of Acceptable Risk in the Cuban Missile Crisis Settlement," *Journal of Cold War Studies*, Vol. 9, No. 3, Summer 2007, pp. 5-48. Accessible online with appropriate access.

112   Laurence Chang and Peter Kornbluh (Editors), *The Cuban Missile Crisis, 1962*, The New Press, New York, 1998, page 392, first column.

113   Jim Hershberg, "Anatomy of a Controversy: Anatoly Dobrynin's Meeting With Robert F. Kennedy, 27 October 1962, *The Cold War International History Project Bulletin*, Issue 5, Spring 1995. Accessible online. In it, Kennedy's speechwriter and confidante Theodore Sorensen is quoted as saying:

"Ambassador Dobrynin felt that Robert Kennedy's book did not adequately express that the 'deal' on the Turkish missiles was part of the resolution of the crisis. And here I have a confession to make to my colleagues on the American side, as well as to others who are present. I was the editor of Robert Kennedy's book. It was, in fact, a diary of those thirteen days. And his diary was very explicit that this was part of the deal; but at that time it was still a secret even on the American side, except for the six of us who had been present at that meeting. So I took it upon myself to edit that out of his diaries, and that is why the Ambassador is somewhat justified in saying that the diaries are not as explicit as his conversation."

114 Rodric Braithwaite, "The Soviet Withdrawal from Afghanistan Didn't Sort Out the Country—Will Ours?", *History News Network*, June 11, 2011. Accessible online.

115 Steve Coll, *Ghost Wars: The Secret History of the CIA, Afghanistan, and Bin Laden, from the Soviet Invasion to September 10, 2001*, Penguin, New York, 2004, page 90.

116 Ronald Reagan, "Message on the Observance of Afghanistan Day," March 21, 1983. Accessible online.

117 Steven R. Weisman, "Afghans Mix 'Sovietization' and Free Market," *New York Times*, May 15, 1987, page A6. Accessible online.

118 Carol Grisanti, Robert Windrem, Jim Poplin and Janullah Zada, "Afghan warlord urges revolt against U.S., Karzai: Audiotape obtained by NBC News calls for death of American commander," *NBC News*, May 31, 2006. Accessible online.

119 Joanna Paraszczuk, "Afghanistan's Hekmatyar Announces Support For IS In Fight Against Taliban," *Radio Free Europe/Radio Liberty*, July 7, 2015. Accessible online.

120 Christian F. Ostermann and Mircea Munteanu, "Towards an International History of the War in Afghanistan," 1979-1980, The Wilson Center, July 12, 2011. Accessible online. The Brzezinski quote is in Volume 1 (clickable from that page) and can be found by searching on "reassure Pakistan" and going to its second occurrence.

121 Eliot A. Cohen, "War Without Pity, War Without End," *The Wall Street Journal*, August 2, 2013. Accessible online. This is a book review of Sheila Miyoshi Jager, *Brothers at War*, Norton, New York, 2013. The review notes:

"The story of American statesmanship in Korea isn't particularly inspiring. It includes the decision, Ms. Jager writes, 'to rely on incumbent Japanese officials to carry out the essential functions of governance' during the initial post-World War II occupation—to which 'the Koreans reacted with outrage.'"

122 Stephen Bosworth and Robert L. Gallucci, "Reasons to Talk to North Korea," *International New York Times*, October 28, 2016. Accessible online. Bosworth was responsible for negotiations with North Korea during the first Obama administration, and Gallucci served the same role during Bill Clinton's presidency.

123 "The Torah on One Foot." Accessible online.

124 Charles Lane, "The Professor Who Lit the Spark," *Stanford* (Stanford University's Alumni magazine). Accessible online.

125 Sheldon M. Stern, *The Week the World Stood Still: Inside the Secret Cuban Missile Crisis*, Stanford University Press, Stanford, CA, 2005, p. 50. This covers both JFK's "goddamn dangerous" comment and how we zealously hid from it.

126 John Kerry, "Remarks at Ploughshares Fund Gala," October 28, 2013. Accessible online.

127 Hans M. Kristensen, "US Nuclear Stockpile Numbers Published Enroute To Hiroshima," Federation of American Scientists, May 26, 2016. Accessible online.

     See also the Department of Defense's "Stockpile Numbers, End of Fiscal Years 1962-2015," accessible online.

     The latter document makes clear that the 2,300 weapons awaiting dismantlement are not included in the 4,571 weapons listed for 2015.

128 Timothy Naftali and Philip Zelikow (Editors), *The Presidential Recordings: John F. Kennedy: The Great Crises*, Volume 2, Norton, New York, 2001, page 441.

129 Department of Defense, *Nuclear Posture Review Report*, April 2010. Accessible online.

130 Michael Dobbs, "Haig Said Nixon Joked of Nuking Hill," *The Washington Post*, May 27, 2004, page A29. Accessible online.

131 Tony Blair, *A Journey: My Political Life*, Knopf, New York, 2010, page 613.

132 Le Bureau d'Enquêtes et d'Analyses (BEA) pour la Sécurité de l'Aviation civile, "Accident on 25 July 2000 at La Patte d'Oie in Gonesse (95) to the Concorde registered F-BTSC operated by Air France: Report translation f-sc000725a." Accessible online, but it is a large download (12.5 MB).

The most relevant material is on pages 93, 94, and 146, with page146 stating:

"As of 25 July 2000, it appears that the rate of tyre deflation/ destruction on Concorde was on average one occurrence per 1,500 cycles (or 4,000 flying hours). This rate fell over time and the proportion was no more than one occurrence per 3,000 cycles (or 8,000 flying hours) between 1995 and 2000. By way of comparison, on long-haul aircraft, such as the Airbus A340, this rate is of the order of one occurrence per 100,000 cycles."

On average, the Concorde therefore experienced tire failures $100,000/1,500 = 6,700$ percent more frequently than other long-haul aircraft. Our claim that "more than 10 percent of those tire failures resulted in fuel leaks" comes from page 93's saying: "there are fifty-seven cases of tyre bursts/deflations ... Twelve of these events had structural consequences on the wings and/or the tanks, of which six led to penetration of the tanks."

133 This note provides the basis for my claim that, "For over a year before the minicrisis occurred, I had been warning that these Polish missiles bore a dangerous resemblance to the ones we placed in Turkey in the Spring of 1962."

My paper, "Risk Analysis of Nuclear Deterrence," appeared in the Spring 2008 issue of *The Bent of Tau Beta Pi*—the magazine of the Engineering Honor Society. On page 17, I state:

"And, today, we are in the process of deploying a missile defense in Russia's backyard (Poland and the Czech Republic) over strenuous Russian objections. A possible Russian response would be to threaten deployment of a similar missile defense in Cuba, much as our Jupiter missile deployment in Turkey was the stimulus for Khrushchev deploying his Cuban missiles."

This paper reached readers in March 2008, four months before the July 2008 Cuban Bomber Minicrisis and is accessible online. While not publicly accessible, an earlier October 2007 draft in my possession (and possibly the editor's as well) shows that my concern predated the minicrisis by at least nine months. Extending from "at least nine months" to "over a year" depends on my memory and therefore is not as certain. I remember warning of the danger that 2008's Polish missiles might have a similar effect as 1962's Turkish missiles for months before that.

134 Vladimir Putin, "Press Statement and Answers to Questions following the 20th Russia-European Union Summit, Marfa, Portugal," October 26, 2007. Accessible online.

On being asked "if Russia is ready to respond positively to President Bush's latest initiative for cooperation in missile defense in Europe?" Putin replies: "I recall how things went in a similar situation in the mid-1960s. Similar actions by the Soviet Union, when it put rockets in Cuba, precipitated the Cuban Missile Crisis. For us the technological aspects of the situation are very similar."

135 Peter Finn, "Russian Bombers Could Be Deployed to Cuba," *The Washington Post*, July 22, 2008, page A10. Accessible online.

136 Alex Rodriguez, "Are Russians deploying a hoax?", *Chicago Tribune*, July 26, 2008. Accessible online. This contains both General Schwartz's "red line" statement and the Russian Foreign Minstry's denial of the original report.

137 Andrew E. Kramer, "Russia Calls New U.S. Missile Defense System a 'Direct Threat'," *New York Times*, May 13, 2016, page A6. Accessible online.

138 Mark Landler and Helene Cooper, "U.S. Fortifying Europe's East to Deter Putin," *New York Times*, February 2, 1016, page A6. Accessible online.

139 Bill Moyers, *The Bill Moyers Journal*, November 20, 2009. The transcript, which is accessible online, has the two Lyndon Johnson quotes.

140 John Barry, "Appeasing Russia: The historical reasons why the West should intervene in Georgia," *Newsweek*, August 11, 2008. Accessible online in slightly modified form.

141 Heidi Tagliavini, "Lessons of the Georgia Conflict," *International Herald Tribune*, October 1, 2009. Accessible online.

142 Karen Robes Meeks, "Listen to Hillary Clinton compare Russian President Vladimir Putin to Hitler," *LA Daily News*, March 5, 2014. Accessible online.

143 Paul Kennedy, "A Time to Appease," *The National Interest*, No. 108, July-August 2010, pp. 7-17. Accessible online.

144 Jack Lewis, "The Birth of the EPA," *EPA Journal*, November 1985. Accessible online.

145 Michael D. Lemonick, "The Ozone Vanishes and Not Just Over the South Pole," *TIME*, February 17, 1992. Accessible online. The cover is also accessible online.

146 US Environmental Protection Agency, "Ozone Layer Depletion," March 9, 2016, states: "the ozone layer is healing and should fully recover by about 2065." Accessible online.

147 California Energy Commission, "In-State Electric Generation by Fuel Type," May 6, 2016. Accessible online.

148 California Energy Commission, "Total Electricity System Power," September 10, 2015. Accessible online.

149 The New START Treaty, which reduced both American and Russian nuclear weapons, was ratified, but only after a key Senator, who had been undecided, changed his position and supported the Treaty. Phone calls by roughly 600 concerned constituents appear to have played a major role in making that happen. Here's what happened:

    The Treaty had been signed by President Obama in April 2010, but ran into opposition in the Senate, which had to ratify it before it came into force. Even though there had been extensive Senate debate by the Fall of 2010, some of the Senators opposed to the Treaty argued that a vote should be delayed until 2011, when some new Senators would have been elected and seated. Proponents argued that this was purely a political move, there had been adequate debate, and there should be an up or down vote so each Senator could state where he or she stood.

Delaying the vote might well have caused ratification to fail since that requires a two-thirds approval and the Republicans, who tended on average to oppose the Treaty, were expected to gain seats in the election. In fact, they ended up gaining six seats, their largest increase in sixteen years.

To bring New START to a vote, it first had to be voted out of the Senate Foreign Relations Committee, where it was bottled up in September 2010. Senator Johnny Isakson (R-GA) was a key vote and on the fence. A concerted effort by several NGOs got approximately 600 constituents to call his office during the three days prior to the committee vote. Isakson got off the fence and voted to bring the Treaty to a floor vote, though without saying how he would vote on the floor. In December, when that floor vote took place, the same kind of effort was mounted again, and Isakson did vote for the Treaty. While 600 phone calls in three days make a major impression on a senator, 600 people are only 0.006 percent of Georgia's population.

I am personally aware of this process because I supported it financially. I am not a citizen of Georgia, so I could not participate directly.

150   A picture I took of our Girl Scout group at the top of Red Peak Pass in 1972 is accessible online, but does not convey the full majesty of the vista. Dorothie is visible in our photo, left of center, wearing a blue, flowered hat, unfortunately hiding most of her face. A photo taken by another hiking party at a different time (with them in the picture) shows the vista and is accessible online.

About the Authors

We married as polar opposites. Marty loves logic and taught electrical engineering at MIT and Stanford. Dorothie is intuitive and puts more stock in feelings.

Not understanding those differences nearly destroyed our marriage. By learning to honor each other's perspective, we were able to make anger a nightmare of the past and create a loving space in which we recaptured the true love we felt in our initial infatuation.

That also led us to fall in love with the world as a whole, and we found that the same principle that saved our marriage—compassionate holistic thinking—will save the Earth.

Martin Hellman

I am a world-class fool and proud of it. My research on encryption was originally seen as a fool's errand, but it recently won me and a colleague the ACM's million-dollar Turing Award—often regarded as the Nobel Prize in computing. Following Dorothie down an uncharted path that even she could not fully describe until we reclaimed the true love that we felt when we first met also seemed like a fool's errand, but it proved even more rewarding. Even a million dollars can't buy true love.

Thirty-five years ago, during the height of the Cold War and with Dorothie acting as a catalyst, I shifted my research from encryption to international security. What was the point in inventing fantastic, new encryption schemes if no one might be around to use them in fifty to one hundred years?

That shift led me to co-edit a 1988 book with Moscow's Prof. Anatoly Gromyko aimed at discovering the equations of survival needed for the nuclear age. *Breakthrough: Emerging New Thinking* received critical acclaim from individuals ranging from Soviet President Mikhail Gorbachev to former CIA Director William Colby.

As a professor at Stanford University, I am affiliated with its Center for International Security and Cooperation, where I work on bringing a risk-informed approach to our nation's nuclear strategy. To do that, I have intensively researched international conflicts that could escalate to nuclear threats and even use. Seven of those conflicts are included as case studies in the book.

Dorothie Hellman

After spending several decades following a relationship map that had me repeatedly driving off cliffs, I found the courage to tear it up and piece together a new map that allowed me to reach the place of love, acceptance, and peace where I'd always wanted to dwell. To get there, I have spent more than half my life studying anger, fear, and grief, as well as joy, love, and compassion. Practicing compassion was particularly important in my journey and is the centerpiece of my part of this book.

I was trained as a CPA and worked at Touche Ross—now Deloitte. I left that career to become a full-time volunteer at the Beyond War Foundation, where I served as Vice President for Financial Support in the 1980s.

Marty and I have been together for fifty years and, as you'll learn from this book, we had to navigate some very rocky patches and fall in love with our planet to recover true love in our home.

anewmap.com

CPSIA information can be obtained at www.ICGtesting.com
Printed in the USA
BVOW02*1702061016

463878BV00001B/1/P